MYSTERIES
Encounters with the Unexplained

John Blashford-Snell

MYSTERIES

Encounters with the Unexplained

THE BODLEY HEAD
LONDON   SYDNEY
TORONTO

British Library Cataloguing
in Publication Data
Blashford-Snell, John
Mysteries: encounters with the unexplained.
1. Curiosities and wonders
I. Title
001.9'4   AG243
ISBN 0-370-30479-9

Printed in Great Britain for
The Bodley Head Ltd
9 Bow Street, London WC2E 7AL
by Redwood Burn Ltd, Trowbridge
Set in Linoterm Plantin
by Keyset Composition, Colchester
First published 1983

CONTENTS

To Gwen,
Betty and Judith,
whose encouragement
and inspiration have
driven me on.

LIST OF ILLUSTRATIONS

Grateful acknowledgements are due to the following for permission to reproduce photographs, as follows:

To the author for nos. 1, 2, 3, 6, 10, 26 and 29; to *The Daily Telegraph* for nos. 13 through 20; to Operation Drake for nos. 5, 23, 24, 25 and 30; to Alison Hines for no. 4; to the Scientific Exploration Society for no. 7; to Ray Pringle-Scott for nos. 8 and 9; to *After the Battle* Magazine for nos. 11 and 12; to Col. J. W. Harris for no. 21; to Dr. Andrew Penny for no. 22; to Sgt. Thompson, Army P.R. staff, for no. 27; to Capt. David Kirby RE for no. 28; to the Kenya Wildlife Management and Conservation Dept. for no. 31; and to Ian Redmond for no. 32.

MAPS

The maps were redrawn and lettered by Linda Page.

ACKNOWLEDGEMENTS

Everyone loves a mystery, and many of the expeditions which we have undertaken have been aimed at sorting one out. Indeed, modern scientific exploration is very often launched to solve a puzzle.

In this book I have put together a collection of experiences involving my friends in many lands. Some events I've been closely associated with, and in other cases, my knowledge has been gleaned from colleagues who were intimately involved with the incident. I owe a great deal to those mentioned here and much to many whose names do not appear. If any credit is due, it is to them. I repeat what I have said in previous works: that I count myself fortunate to have such an understanding and helpful circle of friends, and privileged to have led some of the finest people—servicemen and civilians—in the world.

I am again most grateful to Mr H. M. Stephen, Managing Director of the *Daily Telegraph*, for his continued advice and encouragement, and to John Anstey, Editor of the *Telegraph Sunday Magazine*, for his kind permission to publish the photographs taken on the Blue Nile Expedition. I am also deeply grateful to Ian Redmond for the use of his splendid cover photograph of the salt-mining elephants of Mount Elgon. Ian, an energetic young scientist who accompanied us on Operation Drake, has already established a reputation for himself as a conservationist and field researcher with a nose for unusual animal stories. His extraordinary underground photo of 'Loxodonta africana' was made after extremely careful preparations and with no little risk to himself. He is writing his own book about this unique phenomenon and his research at Mount Elgon. I also appreciate the great help of my old friend Christopher Sainsbury with the maps and photographs. My appreciative thanks go to June Hall, who did so much to encourage me to write this at a time when I needed at least thirty hours in each day!

I am also deeply indebted to Sally Harris, my grossly overworked PA, and my long-suffering wife, Judith, who have done so much of the typing and proof-reading.

ACKNOWLEDGEMENTS

Many friends have contributed to the book: Michael Gambier, who was with us in Zaire and Papua New Guinea, and Richard Snailham, who has accompanied me on almost all the major expeditions. I am most grateful to Michael Cable and Andrew Mitchell, whose help with the material on Operation Drake was invaluable. My thanks also go to the author and leading authority on the Loch Ness Monster, Tim Dinsdale, for his many briefings on that fascinating subject and for giving me his excellent books on that intriguing mystery. My quotation from his *Loch Ness Monster* is reproduced by kind permission of Messrs Routledge & Kegan Paul. I've a feeling Nessie will be with us for a long time yet, but the dedication of Adrian Shine to this fascinating search deserves special mention and I am most grateful to him for all his hospitality and advice.

The unique magazine *After the Battle* has been a fund of information and interest and I am indebted to Winston Ramsey for his kind assistance.

My most sincere gratitude goes to the British Army and in particular, to my Regiment, the Royal Engineers, who have always given so much encouragement and support to one of their madder sappers!

J. B.-S.

AUTHOR'S FOREWORD

Even in the short span of my life the progress of science is mind-boggling, and in a very few years we shall be living in the 21st century, by which time much that we now take for granted will be obsolete, overtaken by new knowledge. Under such an expansion of technology, it is not surprising that many intelligent people find it difficult to see that there is anything mysterious remaining to be discovered and that few mysteries will remain unsolved for much longer. I don't believe this. It seems that the more we discover, the more there remains to be explained. The greater our scientific knowledge and the better our technology, the more it can be used to penetrate the puzzles of the past and perhaps even overturn long-held assumptions.

Only a few years ago, it was popular to scoff at the Loch Ness phenomenon, but with the introduction of sophisticated underwater detection equipment, many *bone fide* scientists are saying 'There must be something there'. If we believe that an enigma is a fact that cannot be explained in any usual manner, then perhaps a new approach is needed to unravel it. This does not necessarily call for a person of high intelligence, but quite simply for one with an inquiring mind and determination—someone who is driven by insatiable curiosity. It is curiosity that drives most modern explorers on.

I have no particular desire to conquer a peak or an ocean nor to be the first man to achieve some particular feat, though, I must confess, even if the challenge is not of primary importance, I still derive satisfaction in striving 'to seek, to find' without yielding. But it is the quest for the unknown that is paramount. Therefore, I believe that I am justified in using every possible human and technical aid to achieve the aim and solve the problem.

The expeditions with which I have been involved in the last quarter of a century are noted for their size, logistical back-up and the number of scientists. I know it has been said that with the huge amount of equipment, manpower and technical expertise, it is hardly surprising that our teams have got through where others have

11

failed. In reply, I point out that I do not explore to find out something about myself, nor to compete with others, therefore I do not feel compelled to obey any self-imposed rules for physical challenges.

Some will say why not leave mysteries alone? I wonder what Drake and Raleigh would have replied to such a question when they set out to overcome their enemies, the elements and the unknown, in their separate quests four hundred years ago. It's not in the nature of an adventurous human to ignore puzzles, indeed, were we to do so, many of our great break-throughs in science would never have happened.

The unexplored lands on maps of old were labelled 'Terra incognita' and even 'Here be dragons'. Today, the unmapped and little-known areas are shown as 'Relief Data Incomplete' and, although they may have been overflown, or even tramped across by armies, these are often the regions of greatest interest to the modern scientific explorer. Perhaps he is really a man who reduces fantasy to reality.

As the world's population expands, food and energy grow scarcer. Coal, gas and oil fields are still being discovered, as are stocks of nuclear fuel. But, whereas years ago it was largely the profit motive that prompted the search, today it is a desperate need to maintain our standards of living and the quality of life. Apart from this, there are important aspects of medical research, the possibilities of new drugs being discovered, and the endless battle against disease. We still have much to learn of nature and of life, both above and below the sea. Only in recent history have we been able to penetrate the watery depths effectively, and I believe that in the next century our attention will turn more and more to the ocean floor—if only to recover all the gold dropped by our ancestors!

But most important of all to me is my belief in youth. As I write, there are over 458,000 unemployed youngsters, eighteen and under, in Britain. Elsewhere in the world there are many more. My experience on Operation Drake and my job as Commander of the Army's Youth Adventure Training Scheme at Fort George have kept me very much in touch with the young and given me the opportunity to hear about their hopes and aspirations. If we are to have an eye to the future, I believe we must look to our young people. It is quite clear that there are just as many, indeed, probably more, with the same spirit of adventure that Stanley and Livingstone possessed.

The youth of today want to be stretched and challenged. In the past, National Service went some way to do this and more recently, other outdoor activities have been offered. There are, however, many young people who do not regard the latter as true challenges with a real sense of purpose behind them. Prince Charles summed it up in a phrase when he said that the youth of today wanted 'some of the challenges of war in a peacetime situation'. None of us wants war, but expeditions do offer unrivalled opportunities of this type. However, travel is costly and you often have to produce a return ticket even to get a visa. Frontiers are becoming increasingly difficult to cross and the world's hostile tribes have exchanged their poisoned arrows for surface-to-air missiles! It's not always easy for the young to find a legal, exciting challenge that they can afford. As many of the stories in this book will show, we've always taken youngsters on our large-scale expeditions, and in the future I hope to take even more. There's no doubt that they profit through this experience and help international understanding, and that the work they carry out can be of real benefit to mankind.

However, of all the tasks they ever tackle, there's no doubt that the most popular is an intriguing mystery. Thankfully, there'll never be any shortage of those to explore!

JOHN BLASHFORD-SNELL
31st JANUARY 1983

1

Underwater Quests

===

One huge malevolent eye stared unblinking at me.

'I promise you—it is real. There is a very big gun lying just beneath the sea—you must come and see it,' implored the Greek police officer, as we sat sipping a glass of cold Keo on the waterfront of the sleepy little port in southwest Cyprus.

This was an intriguing mystery. Many of the older people at Paphos had told me a tale of a great cannon believed to have disappeared in the 16th century. When the Turks had ruled Cyprus, they had stationed a garrison in the square fort on the harbour wall of Paphos. It was said that on top of the battlements they placed a huge cannon. Reportedly this artillery piece was able to hurl a ball to any part of the town and thus the Greek Cypriot inhabitants lived under constant threat. Eventually there was a revolution and the Greeks managed to capture the castle and butcher the Turkish garrison. Like so many before it, this revolt eventually failed, but when the Turks returned to Paphos, they found the great gun had gone. With customary efficiency and ruthlessness, they took numerous prisoners and in an effort to discover the whereabouts of the cannon, burned and tortured them to death, but they never discovered where it was hidden. Its disappearance remained a mystery.

Naturally, everyone thought that the gun had simply been lowered over the battlements into the water and on previous expeditions, we had made exhaustive searches of the sea bed beneath the wall of the fort. We found a few cannon balls, but no gun. To throw a shot into the town, it must be a sizeable piece and would probably weigh several tons, not an easy thing to move overland. If the cannon was not in the immediate area of the fort, the Greeks had probably dragged it away into the town, but then it was most likely that the Turkish inquisitors would have found it. Where on earth could it be hidden? Everyone in the port had their own theory. One thing was sure: the great gun had vanished without a trace; perhaps the legend, like so many others, had no basis in fact.

Thus, when the powerful figure of Corporal Wickens had brought two police officers, who claimed to know the whereabouts of this legendary gun, I was pretty sceptical. However, it was a warm night, Greek music echoed from the bar and overhead the cloudless sky glittered with twinkling stars, and I was in a benign mood. 'Have a beer,' I invited, pulling over an extra couple of chairs for the visitors. They sat down, the barman brought ice-cold Keo and we toasted each other. After a long pause, the larger of the officers said slowly, 'You know the legend of the great gun?' I nodded, passing him the dish of salted nuts. 'I have seen it,' said the younger officer, looking very solemn.

'Where?' I enquired, still sceptical.

'It is near here, on the other side of the headland, very close to the shore,' he gestured. 'I can show you the place, sir.'

'All right,' I said. 'We'll have a look at your spot tomorrow; when can you accompany us?'

'I am off duty tomorrow afternoon,' replied my informant. 'I'll come to the jetty then.'

That night I wrote in my log, 'Is this another wild-goose chase— or are we about to solve the mystery?'

It was four o'clock in the afternoon and the worst heat of the day had gone when the reconnaissance party boarded the tug and we set out on yet another quest for the long-lost cannon. Frankly I was not very hopeful, but the sea on the Moulia reef was too rough for diving and it seemed a useful way of keeping my team in training. Rounding the headland, we followed the constable's directions and headed in to the sheltered beach. 'Getting pretty shallow,' cautioned the helmsman. Fifty yards ahead the waves rolled over a reef. 'We can't go in much closer,' I said over my shoulder to the policeman. 'Where do you reckon it is now?'

'There,' he said, 'just beyond the rocks.' His finger pointed at the line of black shadows. The tug rolled in the gentle swell.

'That'll do,' I said. 'Drop anchor, we'll swim in from here.' With a splash, half a dozen divers equipped with only masks, breathing tubes and flippers, jumped in and, fanning out in an extended line, twenty feet between each man, they began to flipper slowly towards the shore. For about ten minutes we searched. There was nothing but bare rock and sand. Suddenly Corporal Jones's excited voice rang out above the sound of the waves. 'It's here, it's here,' he yelled, 'a damned great gun.' And there indeed it was—so it really did exist! At first, all we could see was the breach sticking up about eight inches above the sand. It was lying in four feet of water and within a few minutes, we had uncovered two feet of it. It was certainly pretty big. Although I could only see the breech, it was almost two feet in diameter. It had been protected by the sand in which it lay and the heavy black metal bore no growth or encrustations. I was surprised to see it was so plain and seizing the boss, pulled myself down for closer examination. My eyes searched for some embellishment or mark, but there was none. However, I could see it was obviously an iron cannon—and so large that it was unlikely to be a ship's gun.

'What a monster,' said the public relations officer, who had come to see the fun. 'How are you going to lift it?' That was the problem. The cannon was buried in deep sand at an angle of 45 degrees. To landward and seaward, there were low reefs. The problem was that it must weigh at least two tons, it was going to need some pretty good lifting tackle to move it. To get our 100-foot landing craft, Z 11, above it was out of the question.

Walking onto the beach and standing in the warm white sand, I looked around. Just inland rose the massive natural rock slabs in which were carved the 'Tombs of the Kings' and running down from them was a narrow track. This track was obviously very old and made a relatively smooth path through the rock formations. 'Did the Greeks drag the gun down this path?' I wondered, 'and then somehow push or float it out to its hiding-place?'

Takis, the museum curator, suddenly appeared, running down the path. 'Is it true?' he shouted. 'Your radio operator tells me that you have found it.'

'Well, we've certainly located a big gun,' I replied, 'but until I can get it out, it's difficult to say if it is the one in question.'

'How will you do that?' asked the excited archaeologist.

'We'll blast a channel through the inshore reef. Meanwhile we'll bring the recovery vehicle ashore from Z 11 and try to get it over the headland to this point. Then we'll run out the winch cable for divers

to fix to the gun, then heave ho and it should be like pulling a tooth,'
I explained.

'Wonderful, wonderful! I must go and telephone the Director in
Nicosia—and the newspapers,' said Takis, rushing off again
towards the town.

So it was, at dawn next day, that our divers laid the charges they
had spent the previous evening preparing. The wind had gone about
and a heavy swell made the work difficult. Several sappers had to be
treated for lacerations after being swept against the reef. On shore
REME fitters had driven the massive Scammell recovery vehicle to
the site and were already running out their heavy steel cables. *Z 11*
lay two hundred yards out, providing communications and refresh-
ments. By 8 a.m. we were ready to fire the first set of charges; the
police cleared the area and the fuse was ignited. Suddenly, low
overhead, came an Army Auster aircraft containing several senior
officers who had flown down to witness the operation. It banked
sharply over *Z 11* and came straight over the beach. Frantically I
waved it away as the spluttering fuse burned down. With a dull roar,
the charges exploded, sending a column of spray straight upward at
the Auster, which, none the worse for a drenching, flew straight on!
One more bang, then the cable was fixed and the winch took up the
strain. The demolitions had done the job and in a few minutes the
crowd of onlookers could see the great black, iron cannon in the surf.
Inch by inch it was dragged like a stricken whale to the beach. 'Can't
find any sign of a carriage,' said Corporal Jones, emerging from the
surf as I took a closer look at the gun. 'How many poor devils were
torn apart or roasted alive to preserve this secret?' I wondered. Eight
feet long and weighing over two tons, our prize was carried by the
Scammell in triumph to Paphos port. That night Cyprus Radio
credited us with solving the mystery. I knew, however, that to leave
the metal exposed to the air would ruin it in no time, so we lowered it
into the harbour to await the construction of a special preservative
bath.

Eight years afterwards Judith my wife and I went back and walked
amongst the ruins on the headland. Some spectacular finds had been
made on land since our expeditions and to our amazement, we found
that we had been camping only inches above a wonderful mosaic
floor of a villa. I discovered that although Paphos had gained much

in its knowledge of the past, the present situation had greatly
deteriorated. Now Turks and Greeks lived behind barricades, and
the houses bore the signs of the civil war. Takis, the museum
curator, found us in the Crusader Castle overlooking the harbour.
'Welcome, welcome,' he said, embracing me. 'Have you seen your
great gun? It is in a place of honour on the quay.' We strolled into the
little port and at once saw the cannon, mounted on a carriage in front
of the local Cyprus Navy Headquarters. I raised my camera. A
sentry rushed over. 'It is forbidden to photograph military
weapons,' he explained politely. 'Things have changed,' apologised
Takis. But it had been another mystery that had brought me to
Paphos in the first place.

It had all started when I was a young officer serving with the Royal
Engineers in Cyprus and had been invited to meet the local Chief
Civilian Administrator. 'I expect you are wondering why I asked you
here this evening,' said the Commissioner, raising his gin and tonic.

'You said you were interested in discussing an underwater
project,' I remarked.

'Yes, that's quite right.' His eyes twinkled, and without pausing
he said, 'Have you ever heard the legend of the Port of Paphos?'

As the warm evening darkened and the crickets began their
nightly overture in the garden of the Residence, I listened intently to
Ivor Williams, Commissioner of Limassol, outlining with Welsh
fervour his theory about an extensive port that had once existed at
Paphos in the south-east corner of Cyprus.

It seemed that the great harbour owed its origin to the important
temple of the Goddess of Love, Aphrodite, situated a few miles away
at the village of Kouklia. Every year, my earnest host told me,
thousands of beautiful girls came to Cyprus to worship there. Ivor
had done some calculations and deduced that hundreds of ships
would have been needed to transport them. 'There must have been a
port to shelter such a fleet,' he said, lowering his voice as he did so.
'Where else would they have sheltered?'

'Has anything been reported?' I asked.

'Well, there are rumours, and some interesting aerial photographs,' replied the Commissioner. He drew a battered brown file
from the desk behind him and passed it to me. The charts within had

been sketched over with a possible outline of a harbour some 4500 yards by 1000.

'But this is vast,' I commented. 'How on earth could it disappear?' 'Earthquake, I reckon,' said Ivor. 'I think an earthquake caused it to sink, probably with a great many ships.'

His servant came and went, soundlessly refilling our glasses, and it was late when he said, 'Well, there it is, my boy, a great mystery, do you think you could solve it?'

'I can have a jolly good try,' I replied with genuine enthusiasm.

The Army thought it a good idea to launch an expedition to help the Antiquities Department and promote Anglo-Cypriot relations. Solving the mystery of the disappearance of the 'Eighth Wonder of the World' might even attract some recruits for the Army! So it was that in August, 1959, I stood with a group of National Service soldiers in the Paphos museum, whilst Takis, the assistant curator, told us the history of this famous area. The soldiers shuffled, sniffed, coughed and scratched; archaeology was not a subject close to their hearts. 'So you see, each year many, many ships came from all over the Mediterranean bearing young maidens.' The men raised their eyebrows. 'He's on about skirt,' whispered a lad from Leeds, waking his nodding neighbour with a prod in the ribs. 'Ough!' grunted Sapper Robins, taking an instant interest in the lecture.

'The young women were unmarried,' explained the curator, 'and it was necessary that they should be virgins.' Even Rampling, the medic, was awake now. 'They left their ships at anchor in the port and walked up through a place we call the beautiful gardens, where they worshipped and made offerings with terracotta figurines. At Kouklia there was a great temple, in the centre of which was a fifteen-foot phallic symbol. This is a model of the original,' said the curator as he tapped a black monolith on which he was leaning. Then, with a wry smile, he added, 'it is said that so many maidens came to be initiated that some had to wait here until the winter.'

'Bet there weren't no shortage for t'ordination in them days,' muttered Rampling.

Our mission sounded simple. The underwater section of 33rd Independent Field Squadron, Royal Engineers, would explore the sea bed off Paphos with a view to establishing possible evidence of a large port or harbour. Complete with a hundred-ton flat-bottomed and open-decked Royal Engineer 'Z' craft, thirty-five soldiers, piles of underwater diving equipment, plus an eager Army public relations officer, the expedition arrived at Paphos. The introduction of a spot of ancient sex into the task was a splendid catalyst, and the team set about its work with considerable enthusiasm. Thus, for several weeks during four summers, we surveyed the sea bed and brought up tons of pottery, marble, glass and metal.

One of our earlier finds was the wreckage of a man-o'-war, whose cannon lay scattered like giant sea slugs on the Moulia Reef a mile off shore. It was whilst working on the reef that we came across a slightly different mystery. The corned beef was getting hot in the sun as we munched our lunch a mile out to sea when the Cypriot fishing boat came alongside. 'We've got visitors,' grunted my skipper. 'Local chap called Christos wants to see you, sir.'

The swarthy fisherman sat down heavily and accepted the mug of warm lemonade. 'Bad place,' he said, pointing a finger at the waves breaking on the reef.

'Yes,' I admitted, thinking he was referring to the dangerous currents, but he wasn't. He told a strange tale of a terrible sea monster that destroyed the fishermen's nets and even threatened boats. 'What's it like?' I asked, and received a description of something like a huge shark or a whale, but the Med. isn't noted for sharks, so what could it be?

'If you can kill it,' said Christos, 'we'll buy every one of you a beer.'

I'd never seen anything bigger than a large, harmless grouper at Paphos and that night I sat in the moonlight on deck, wondering what on earth it could be. However, I was certain Christos and his friends were telling the truth. During the night I dreamt about sea monsters!

Next day we had just raised the last of five large cannon, the wind was freshening from the south-west and I decided to have a final look round in case we had missed anything. Flipping along over the rocky bed, I came to a ravine and peered down. There, momentarily revealed by the waving sea weed, was something smooth, grey and round, like a metallic cylinder lying at right-angles across the sandy floor of the cleft. I turned around slowly. 'Whatever is that?' I thought and jack-knifing my body, I slid down into the rock.

The undersea gorge was larger than appeared from the surface; towards one end it opened up and I found myself swimming into a low cave. The cleft was simply a large crack in the roof. The grey cylinder now looked about twelve inches in diameter and got thicker as it disappeared into the gloom of the cavern. Grasping the rock, I pulled myself down and under the ledge. For a few moments all seemed black, then as my eyes grew accustomed to the dark, I perceived a movement. A small cloud of sand billowed up. To my left the cylinder moved or I should say, 'twitched' and at the same time, the floor slid forward several feet. Still puzzled, I stared in and it was another few moments before I realised I was hovering between the roof of the cave and the back of a giant sting ray. An arm's length in front, I could make out the gentle mound of its head, one huge malevolent eye stared unblinking at me, behind stretched the huge tail that had first attracted my attention. It was very large and I could only hazard a guess that its wings were ten feet from tip to tip. If the creature were to panic, it would smash me against the roof of the cave or lash me with its whiplike tail. Being above the beast, I reckoned that the bayonet-sharp, venomous spine located beneath the tail was my least worry.

My fear was overcome by curiosity. Why did it stay so still? Perhaps it had been stunned by our underwater blasting. Hardly daring to breathe for fear that the rattle of my valve would disturb the creature, I inched backwards from the black hole. Once my tanks scraped the roof and the huge animal twitched and flexed its wings, but at last I was back in the light and speeding up to the surface. 'What's that in the crack?' shouted Lance Corporal Jones, who had been watching my ascent. Tearing out my mouth piece, I yelled back, 'the monster of the Moulia Rocks—it's a bloody great sting ray. Prepare a five-pound charge of plastic explosive,' I ordered, 'and tell Christos to come and see the monster, we'll need his evidence if we're to get that beer!' Christos the boatman had been fishing nearby and now he swam over and, donning face-mask, kicked his way down to the monster's lair. He shot back ashen and convinced. Five minutes later the sea erupted in a towering white plume as the demolition charge detonated inside the cave. Thus ended the monster, but we never got our beer. 'It's far too big to be killed by you,' laughed the fishermen, in spite of Christos's assurances.

In August 1960 I returned to England and got married to a tall, cheerful brunette. My new partner, Judith, was an excellent swimmer and became the general manager to the underwater expeditions, which now went on almost continuously. Solving the mystery of Paphos became an obsession that almost cost me my life on at least one occasion. We searched and searched—at night I continued our quest in my dreams—and then towards the end of one particularly gruelling day, I made a discovery that sent the adrenalin racing through my bloodstream and almost led to disaster as I was struggling to bring up a heavy marble slab.

The needle on the pressure gauge was well inside the red danger zone. After a few more deep breaths the air supply would stop abruptly and the aqua-lung had no reserve. I cursed my stupid stubbornness for causing me to neglect one of the basic safety rules of diving that would now probably cost me my life.

Letting go the inscribed marble slab, I fought to control my breathing and watched the precious artefact twirling down into the tangled seaweed. For ten minutes I had struggled, using up far too much air, to bring the slab to the surface from its watery grave amongst the waving sea grass forty feet below. I had found it jammed between rocks near the infamous Moulia reef and felt certain that the inscription would provide a valuable clue to the riddle of the origins of the great port of Paphos.

Above me the late afternoon sun glittered on the waves, and as I rose quickly to the surface, still the air held out, although the needle was now right against the stop and I hardly dared to glance at the gauge.

I'd ditched my fourteen-pound weight belt on the sea bed, so I tried to control the ascent with my breathing. 'Too fast, too fast,' I kept saying as I rose in the cloud of bubbles. I felt a twinge in my leg, but thankfully, I had not been down long enough to risk the dreaded bends.

As I broke the surface the valve went clunk, signifying the end of the precious air supply. Tearing the mouth-piece out, I sucked in air and sea water. The dipping sun was blinding and the strong wind blew the short waves into my face. Looking under water, I noticed with interest that the sea bed was sliding past. Two more mouthfuls of water left me feeling horribly sick and an awful rattling noise came from my chest. A red film was clouding my vision.

'In an emergency, don't panic. Think,' I repeated the advice I had so often given my divers, but I felt terribly tired and even thought was an effort. To get a good mouthful of air, I turned over on my back and, at the same time, tried to release the useless aqua-lung. One shoulder strap came off at once, but the other was sticking. Now I was drifting with the current straight towards the foaming outline of the reef. How ironical that the rocks, whose earlier victims I had been investigating, should claim me as well.

Suddenly the strap came undone and the tanks dropped away, leaving me free to swim with what strength I had left. Rolling over I noticed that the sea bed was now only twelve feet below. I still had a chance, and in the far distance the bridge of *Z 11* was rising and falling in the swell. My instinctive cry for help only wasted valuable energy. I tried to swim but, despite the fins I wore, my leaden legs could not even hold me against the current. The waves breaking on the jagged rocks of the reef were clearly audible. Each second their boom grew louder.

Two hundred yards, I thought. Five minutes if I'm lucky. What a damned silly thing to do, leave the other divers and go off alone after some antique tombstone.

Again I tried to swim, but my legs refused to answer the command. 'Conserve your energy for the reef. There's still a chance of clinging onto a rock, if you can get through the outer breakers,' said optimism. 'Some hope! You've seen the dragon's teeth, they even slice you open if you touch them in calm conditions,' replied pessimism and realism together.

'You're a bit off course,' said another voice and I turned my head to see one of the expedition's boats about thirty yards away. Kneeling in the bows was the young Army public relations officer, who had come out to cover the story.

Drowning men are supposed to relive their past in the last few seconds, but I must confess that I had been too busy trying to survive to consider my short life-history. However, had I done so, I feel I could have looked back on twenty full and exciting years. It would be rather like being caught in the slips after hitting a couple of fours and a good six in one's first game for the school cricket XI.

Our work at Paphos had produced conflicting conclusions. We

found tons of artefacts, one or two carved marble pillars and other stones that had quite clearly been quarried. There were 'causeways' of great square slabs with an eerie, unnatural appearance, and there were cups and saucers 'Made in England'.

Although there was a general pattern to these discoveries indicating they might have sunk within a great harbour, the wall of which could have stretched from Paphos to the Moulia rocks, there was no real evidence of the wall or mole itself. The question remained—were the 'causeways' natural and had the artefacts gone down with sinking ships? One Cyprus newspaper claimed we had discovered 'the Eighth Wonder of the World', but archaeologists, including the famous Sir Mortimer Wheeler, who came to examine the huge pile of artefacts, could come to no firm conclusion and left us to scratch our heads. Frankly I was not convinced that we had proved beyond reasonable doubt that the great harbour had ever existed. We suspected that the causeways were natural beachrock which often has an extraordinary man-made appearance. But the real problem was that in those days none of the archaeologists could dive and therefore everything had to be brought to the surface for their examination.

I was due to return to Britain in December 1961, and therefore I decided to have one last really thorough look at the area to see if we could unravel the mystery. The sea bed was littered with the rubbish of the centuries. The museum was overflowing with our discoveries, but alas, due to lack of any conservation expertise, the splendid cannon we had raised from the Moulia reef in 1960 was now a rusting relic.

However, in July 1961 we launched the most ambitious expedition to date, titled 'Operation Aphrodite II'; it consisted of a task force of boats, vehicles, light aircraft and the faithful Z 11, plus almost a hundred soldiers and civilians. The Royal Navy made some preliminary echo soundings for us and the RAF flew special sorties with infra-red cameras.

The people of this quiet corner of Cyprus were awestruck by the incredible effort the British, who had now given them independence, were putting into solving some ancient legend. The press was also interested and the expedition needed a special Public Relations section to deal with the growing number of enquiries.

I felt very conscious of the need to show some success for all this effort. It was rather like being on a mountaineering expedition. To satisfy sponsors completely, one must reach the summit. But in this case, I did not know where the summit was, what it looked like—nor even if it existed!

On one trip to England I had spent days in London trying to find an expert who could dive, but without success. Eventually I had contacted a well-known archaeological establishment who promised to find someone for us.

I was most surprised when a very beautiful lady arrived at Paphos and announced that she was an archaeologist. To the soldiers, longing to see their wives and girl friends, the sight of this stunning creature, clad only in a tiny yellow bikini, was almost unbearable, and the divers' output doubled overnight because, I suspected, it gave them more opportunities to discuss their finds with her. To be fair, our archaeologist kept her favours very much to herself, but it was not long before I discovered two of my team having a bitter quarrel over her. I realised this demanded action and the next evening, invited her to dine with me at the quayside café.

As the moist warm night descended, the wine flowed and this undoubtedly helped me to reach the point. When I told the lady of the problem, she laughed, 'But they're only boys'.

'I know, but they do find you devilishly attractive,' I replied.

'What do you want me to do about it?' asked the living Aphrodite with a smile. The bikini was part of the problem, so I suggested she might wear a one-piece bathing costume. She gave me a gorgeous smile and said, 'Certainly, John, which piece do you want me to wear?' That year we brought up a record collection of artefacts! However the puzzle of the lost harbour remained unsolved.

Ever since I'd dived in Cyprus I had been fascinated by the greatest underwater mystery of all—Atlantis. In *Timaeus and Critias* Plato wrote, '9000 years before Solon [who lived *c*. 600 BC] the Atlantic was navigable; and there was an island situated in front of the straits which are by you called the pillars of Heracles.' The philosopher goes on to describe Atlantis as being an island and '. . . was the way to other islands, and from there you might pass to the whole of the opposite continent which surrounds the true ocean.' Scholars have assumed that he is not referring to the Mediterranean, which he terms a harbour and not a 'real sea'.

I became fascinated by the subject and read more and more about it, always seeking a clue to the site of Atlantis.

Today Plato's date is regarded as suspect and many of his statements on Atlantis are questionable. Scholars seem divided in their opinions as to whether it was inside or outside the Mediterranean, however, most archaeologists think Plato was writing about the Minoan civilization of Crete which had been destroyed by volcanic eruption.

It is interesting that Marcellus, a Greek geographer writing in the first century, had said that Atlantis consisted of 'seven islands . . . and also three others of immense extent'. This was the first completely independent description since Plato, and Marcellus went on to say that the middle one of the larger islands was dedicated to Poseidon, god of the Atlanteans. He gives its size as 'a thousand stadia' and writes that the people 'preserved the remembrance of their ancestors on the Atlantic island that had existed there, and was truly prodigiously great; which for many periods had domination over the islands in the Atlantic Sea.' Some historians felt this pointed towards the Azores or the West Indies. Then, in 1933, Edgar Cayce, the renowned American psychic, predicted that a portion of the temple of Atlantis would be found near Bimini, in the Bahamas. He even indicated that his followers should expect the discovery in 1968 or 1969!

Well, that was enough to launch streams of explorers at the flat, featureless scrub and swamp island conveniently only a night's sailing east of Miami Beach. However, it was not until September 1968 that a Bimini fisherman enjoying the name of Bonefish Sam led Dr Manson Valentine, an archaeologist from Florida, to a strange line of rectangular stone slabs lying on the sandy sea bed in about twenty feet of water half a mile off the western side of the island.

Manson Valentine, a veteran explorer with considerable experience of searching for archaeological sites all over the world, was amazed by what Sam had shown him. He reported two lines of stones running roughly parallel for six hundred metres. They appeared to be laid as a pavement—regular, polygonal and flat. He considered them shaped and aligned in a pattern. Obviously they had been there for a considerable time. However, not everyone agreed with Dr Valentine and the question was, quite simply, are the stones natural or were they quarried, shaped and position by man?

Professor John Hall of Miami University Archaeology Department examined the causeway or road, as the formation was now being called, in 1970. Bearing in mind that almost similar natural formations exist nearby, John Hall considered the Bimini stones to be natural beachrock which had been eroded and cracked into their curious rectangular shapes. He found no evidence of quarrying or engineering by human hand.

However, there are other formations of fractured beachrock in the shallow sea off the Bimini coast and it is not beyond the realms of possibility that ancient man could have transported slabs from one site to form a megalithic construction at another. The story of the builders of Stonehenge is well known—the giant stones being brought from the Welsh Mountains 120 miles away, with the aid of rafts and rollers.

The real proof of the origin of the Bimini causeway would be the discovery of prehistoric artefacts in the structure and, although a few items of interest had been found, there was nothing conclusive. There were other underwater mysteries around Bimini—stories of granite blocks, complete with strange carved orifices, marble slabs, lintels and columns.

I talked to octogenarian Bill Egerton Sykes, then Chairman of the British Chapter of the Explorers Club, and himself an expert on Atlantis. Bill leaned back in the heavy leather chair of his London Club and holding his glass of vintage port in both hands, said firmly 'Well look here—I used to think that Bimini might be the site, but I'm not sure now; however, the only way to satisfy your curiosity is to go and look.' By now I'd already met Manson Valentine and seen some fantastic underwater mosaic photographs taken by the underwater explorer, Dimitri Rebikoff. I became so interested in the mystery that when I was asked to join the Board of the Institute of Underwater Archaeology, I readily accepted.

By the time the Ice Age had ended, round about 10,000 BC, the Atlantic sea level had risen and thus the low-lying areas near what are now the Caribbean and the southern coasts of the United States became one of the most interesting parts of the world for the study of underwater archaeology.

In 1978 an international group of explorers, scientists and underwater experts formed the Institute of Underwater Archaeology. Their aim is to engage in underwater archaeological research to promote scientific research that will aid in the study of the origins of civilisations and the manner in which man has existed with his oceanic environment.

The Institute was aware of the suggestion that 'if the great submerged plateaux of the Bahamas were dry land in the relatively recent past, as seems certain, then their shallow waters might well yield signs of occupancy by ancient man'. This theory was put forward by Manson Valentine, who suggested that an expedition might usefully study several sites in the region.

In 1981, as the dust of our last big expedition, Operation Drake, was beginning to settle, I was asked if I'd lead this reconnaissance. Back in our London dungeon, I was growing paler by the hour as we edited films, wrote reports and hacked through the mounds of paperwork. Ten days in the sun to seek Atlantis was not so unattractive.

The expedition's mission was to examine selected areas of the sea bed around Bimini to see if there was any evidence of man-made structures. David Pincus, the Executive Secretary of the Institute, offered to make all the arrangements in Miami, and Mary Jo Bell of Houston kindly secured a generous donation which made it all possible. We had roughly a week for the work and as I stepped down on the warm concrete at Miami Airport, the weather forecast was fine. It was early May and the sea was deep green and flat. Nevertheless, I took the precaution of getting a stock of seasickness pills including a new device—like a corn plaster that you stuck behind the ear to prevent the loss of balance which apparently causes most travel ills. Being a rotten sailor, I'll try anything.

At his home in Fort Lauderdale, David Pincus had his whole family mobilised to help and, joined by Mick Boxall, the swarthy Royal Signals Corporal recently back from hunting giant lizards on Operation Drake, and Alison Hines, our photographic assistant from London, we packed and loaded the vessels for the short sea trip to Bimini.

There were two boats: a 46-foot yacht *Fond Trait*, expertly handled by a rugged young sea dog, Clark Shimeall, and a 58-foot motor vessel *Lagniappe* under Captain Jim Turner and his wife. Both boats had kindly been lent by their owners as a donation to the Institute. We also had an underwater TV team from Aqua Vision International and they provided valuable photographic and video film support, which would enable us to film whatever we discovered. In addition we were joined by a stockily built master diver, Les Savage, who acted as Diving Officer and provided a mass of sophisticated underwater equipment from his own company and a most useful 19-foot Zodiac inflatable. There were even light aircraft for aerial reconnaissance purposes.

Seldom have I seen such a well-organised expedition and much to my delight, I'd had little to do to put it on the road!

Coming aboard the *Fond Trait* at midnight, I found David and Clark stowing the last of the T-bone steaks in the freezer, whilst a beautiful brunette with the greenest eyes I've ever seen, handed me a cool beer. She was not only good looking, but she was also an excellent cook!

'What can I do to help?' I asked. 'I guess you can check the rifles,' said Clark, indicating a mini arsenal of semi automatics in a locker and adding, 'Pirates and drug-runners are getting pretty bad in these waters—a man and woman got hit only last week.' The guns and ammo inspected and the crew briefed on their possible use, we slipped out of the dock between the towering condominiums of the Miami waterfront and sailed east towards the dark horizon.

Bob Marley's reggae droned from the yacht's hi-fi as the compass light reflected in the helmsman's incredibly green eyes—'just like a cat,' I thought as the gentle swell began to lift us and I checked the 'corn plaster' behind my ear. Apparently it was quite a choppy crossing, but I felt nothing and only woke at dawn as we crossed from the dark blue of the ocean into the emerald green of the Bahamas banks.

As we cruised towards the flat, scrub-covered island, I wondered what I expected to find. The submerged 'causeway' was clearly the centre of attraction, but until we tunnelled beneath the great stones with the water jet, we had no way of knowing if they were positioned by man. They certainly looked highly regular.

I suppose secretly I hoped to find some evidence on land, but it had already been put to me that the near-featureless Bahamas were frequently swept by hurricanes which would flatten and destroy anything. As for the slates, marble and other items we'd heard of, we'd simply have to wait.

'Well, John—there you are, Alice Town, Bimini,' said David. 'We've got you there, now it's over to you.' I must take David Pincus on more expeditions, I noted!

With the minimum of formalities, even for the arsenal, we tied up, watched the tourists pouring in aboard the Chalk Seaplanes from Miami and awaited *Lagniappe*. A fresh breeze wafted the smell of cooking from the shanty town, whilst our green-eyed cook produced mouth-watering eggs and bacon. In the clear water of the harbour, two large nurse sharks swam lazily to and fro beside our hull. 'Plenty more out there,' said Clark, pointing to the lagoon with his chin, 'they come in to breed.' I made a mental note that wading through the lagoon might be an interesting exercise.

When *Lagniappe* was in, we went straight into action and sailed to the Moselle Reef. It was said that a considerable quantity of quarried granite had been found on the reef, north-west of Bimini. Apparently some 35 years before, divers had raised many of these stones which barges had transported to Miami to construct a breakwater. One of our divers reported that on a previous visit to the Moselle Reef, he had seen a number of granite blocks and what appeared to be the remains of a ship. Our pilot produced photographs which clearly showed drillings that would have been used in quarrying the granite within the last hundred years.

As with most underwater searches, the first problem is to get the divers to the right place. So, whilst the boats anchored off the reef, we flew overhead to guide our underwater sledge team on to the approximate site of the granite. Underwater there was little to see. Clearly, most of it had been recovered and taken to Florida. However, there were signs of building materials—roof slates. Diving down against the strong current, I pulled myself into one of the many pot holes that dotted the reef and brushing aside the sand, revealed a conglomeration of slates, but they were packed like sandwiches—side by side. Then, amongst the slates, I found something else—a rusty cannon ball and then a heavy metal pin. 'A wreck

31

site,' I shouted to David as I surfaced. Further examination confirmed our opinion. The slates were probably ballast and I was certain they'd never been on a prehistoric roof.

Then a diver came up with a heavy metal bomb or shell fragment—rather modern, but an air reconnaissance gave us a clue. The 'pot holes' were probably bomb or shell craters. Certainly their pattern looked like that, and we were told the reef had been used as a target in the Second World War. So, at the end of the first day, one mystery was solved and we returned to Alice Town to sample the delights of Ernest Hemingway's old home—now a noisy pub.

Next we tackled the 'Camel's Eye' site. This extraordinary pattern, looking from the air like a camel's head and eye, is found in shallow water some five miles north of Bimini. Reports of marble columns, blocks and lintels on a small reef were investigated. We tried to get *Lagniappe* over the area, but heavy seas gave us a real pounding and at one moment I thought we'd be joining the statistics for wrecks at Bimini. Heading east into a rising sea, I was determined to find the reef. The *Lagniappe* stands high and it was only a short time before a huge wave came racing into us like an express train—catching us beam on and knocking us down with a shattering crash. Crockery and equipment went flying before we lurched upright and Jim Turner swung the wheel homeward. Finally our plane flew over and guided the expedition Zodiac to the site where a marker buoy was airdropped. A large shoal of barracuda prevented immediate investigation and bad weather curtailed further operations. However, our film team had visited the site previously and it seems from the fact that 'packing case' timber was discovered under the marble, that this is also the location of a wreck carrying building material.

Now we came to the research into the causeway. Our Cessna enabled me to have a good aerial view of the site before we began. Taking a short run along the big strip on South Bimini, we roared up over the low scrub; a welcome blast of cool air whipped in through the open window. As we swung out over the shallow sea, the pilot gestured at the water. 'Drug runners,' he yelled over the roar of the engine and then I saw it—a Dakota DC3 lying upside down on the reef, landing wheels skyward like the legs of some stricken bird. Bimini, I discovered later, is littered with the wrecks of aircraft that

1. Paphos. Divers prepare to haul out the great gun. In the background, the expedition ship, *Z 11*.

2. Paphos. The great gun first emerges from the sea.

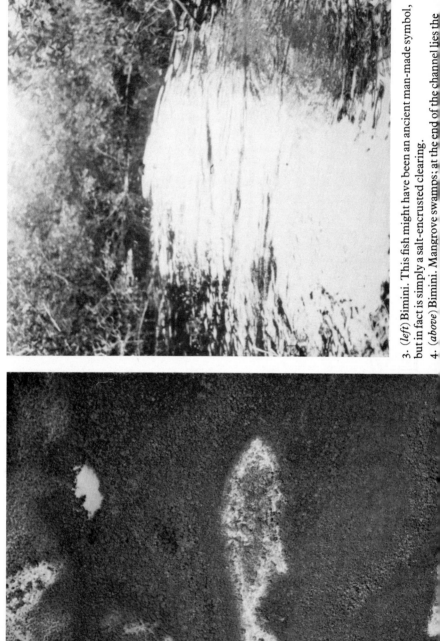

3. (*left*) Bimini. This fish might have been an ancient man-made symbol, but in fact is simply a salt-encrusted clearing.

4. (*above*) Bimini. Mangrove swamps: at the end of the channel lies the

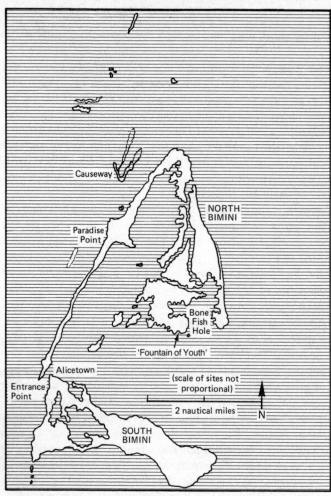

1. Bimini Atoll, and the submarine 'causeway'
under investigation.

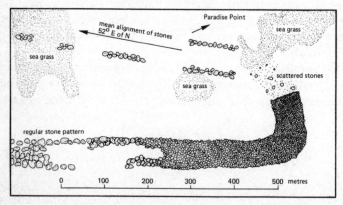

Paradise Point

mean alignment of stones
52° E of N

sea grass

sea grass

sea grass

scattered stones

regular stone pattern

0   100   200   300   400   500   metres

have disposed of their narcotic load and been conveniently written off.

Over Paradise Point we were at 1000 feet when I saw the symmetrical J shape of the Bimini causeway. It ran north-east with a hook at the southern point and stood out sharply against the sand and weed beds. 'Like a great grey walking-stick lying in a puddle,' I thought. We could see *Fond Trait* and *Lagniappe* standing off, two white blobs against the deep blue sea. It certainly looked unnatural and my curiosity heightened. 'Let's go back,' I said, 'I must get underwater.' As we turned away, the TV team was already lowering their equipment into the water.

If anything, the causeway looked less interesting when seen close up. For hours we surveyed it with divers and the video TV. The expedition was indeed fortunate to have the use of this equipment. It consisted of a studio-quality 3-tube prismatic colour video camera adapted for underwater use. It could be diver-controlled or submarine-mounted. It had already been tested to a depth of 2,500 feet, but this was its first sea trial. The control equipment was mounted in shockproof cases on *Lagniappe* and consisted of both black-and-white and colour monitors, video tape-recorders and a digital control unit and mini computer. This computer enabled the camera to be put to many uses, including recording on both video tape and discs and to pass information on to the diver's viewfinder. Thus, as a diver was towed along behind our craft, the underwater scene appeared extremely clearly on the monitor screens. It had very high definition and, being fitted with a 6 mm wide-angle lens, gave a depth of focus from lens contact to infinity and had ultra-low light-sensitivity. The fixed focus coupled with extreme wide angle enabled the camera to give better results at closer range than the human eye's perception in poor visibility. When our jet pumps stirred up clouds of sand, the camera could still penetrate, which was extremely useful. We also used a fascinating little machine: like a mobile rugby ball, the motorised Aqua Scooter could pull a skin diver around at a couple of knots just below the surface. It also scared the life out of a passing nurse shark!

We saw that the causeway consisted of a pavement of flat blocks of considerable size and weight (thickness of 50 to 100 cm and dimensions of up to 5 metres square) which were found in lines forming the J shape on the sea bed. In general the rows of stones ran parallel with the shoreline. Most had a rounded cushion-like cross section and at first sight did look like a man-made causeway. The corners were set at right-angles and many of the slabs have a distinctly square appearance. Close inspection shows that opposing blocks are of identical material.

We had been provided with several sketch maps of the 'Harbour' made up with the slabs and a first-class mosaic photograph beautifully produced by Dimitri Rebikoff. However, by slowly towing a diver with the video camera behind the boat, we obtained an excellent view of the 'causeway' and saw that the slabs were not continuous, as indicated in the sketch maps, although they do extend for at least 300 metres parallel with the shoreline. Nor were they as regular as has been supposed.

Using the jet pump, David Pincus excavated around and under some of the stones. However, contrary to popular rumour, no pedestal or supporting pillar rocks could be found. In fact the slabs appeared to be lying on a bed of sand. Samples indicated that they were made of a limestone beachrock and appeared to consist of shell fish. In fact, the causeways were similar to others I'd seen in the Mediterranean years before and I was convinced that this causeway was a natural formation, although I'll admit it did look very unnatural. In 1980, scientists Shinn and Tompkins obtained seventeen oriented cores and examined them with x-radiographs. In the magazine *Nature* (Vol 287 of 4 September 1980) Marshall McKusik and Eugene Shinn reported, 'Two areas of the formation were studied, and both show slope and uniform particle size, bedding planes and constant dip direction from one block to the next. If the stones had been quarried and relaid there is no reason to suppose bedding planes would carry stratigraphically from block to block. The sedimentary laminations clearly show that these were not randomly laid but a natural, relatively undisturbed formation.'

That night, as the hippies strolled the waterfront in Alice Town and 8 mm blue movies flickered on sails, our team re-ran its rather less spectacular video films—somewhat sadly, we agreed that it did not look as if Poseidon had been at Paradise Point.

★

Nevertheless, there was still a mystery to investigate. A spring of apparently fresh water, located in the mangrove near Bone Fish Hole, North Bimini, was, according to popular legend, a possible site of the 'Fountain of Youth' which the Spanish explorer, Juan Ponce de Leon, may have been seeking when he discovered Florida in 1513. It was believed that to bathe in the spring would ensure perpetual youth, and there was a rumour that the waters contained certain chemicals. I wondered if there might be a link between this legend and the story of Atlantis. So it was, on a relatively cool but thundery morning, that we piled equipment into Les Savage's Zodiac and set off across the shallow lagoon that is the centre of Bimini. As we edged over the bars, our propeller grinding through the sand, large black shadows glided away—the place was simply crawling with sharks.

Although the site was fairly well known and I'd seen it from the air, it took the ascent of a mangrove tree by Clark Shimeall finally to locate the spot. To reach the spring we had to push the boat into a narrow channel which ran for fifty metres through the mangrove swamp. The thunder rumbled and rain began to fall in heavy spots as we approached the 'Fountain of Youth'. Eager to be first there, I pushed ahead, wading in the shallow water and holding aloft my cine camera and the sterile specimen bottles we should need to sample the magical water. Suddenly, the channel opened out to reveal the spring—in fact, a deep pool, but before I could utter a word my feet sank deep into quick-sand and I plunged, cameras and all, up to my neck in the water. 'Oh well! Let's hope it is the Fountain,' said my colleague, and pulling on our face masks, we plunged into the spring. The well—if that is what it was—measured around 10 feet deep and was some 38 feet in diameter. Underwater it was as clear as crystal. Dark snake-like mangrove roots protruded from the sides, but the water was quite fresh to drink. The thought of several middle-aged men diving around in a supposed Fountain of Youth seemed faintly ridiculous.

It is rumoured that the water of this well contained lithium, so out came the specimen bottles and samples were taken from various depths. Lithium is used for treating various psychiatric disorders and may be something of a tranquillizer, so perhaps this was the reason for the legend. However, although we all felt tired after the visit and on return to *Fond Trait* I slept for almost two hours, this may have been due to sheer exhaustion.

Back in Britain, the Canon Company once again cleaned up my cine camera—'"Fountain of Youth" seems to have done it good!' they commented, and water samples were tested in Miami and Berlin, but, alas, there was no more lithium than you'd expect in any water nor indeed any unusual constituents.

Possible archaeological sites, including lines or grooves on land and in the sea, were overflown. However, such features are not unknown in limestone country and have been reported elsewhere in the Bahamas. Other shapes, one of which bore a striking resemblance to a fish, were seen on land, but these are also considered to be natural. We felt that the Bimini 'causeway' was a natural formation, caused by the development of beachrock along successive shore-lines. The expedition found no evidence of any ancient man-made structures in the sea around Bimini nor on land, although it is easy to understand how the interesting beachrock formations, relatively modern building materials, originating from wrecked vessels and fascinating shapes, possibly created in the shallow seas by strong currents and tides, may give the impression of 'lost civilisations'. Of course, those who have suggested such possibilities should not be ridiculed, for without detailed examination of the site it is impossible to make any accurate assessment of the probabilities. Maybe there is something at Bimini, maybe Edgar Cayce was right, but we didn't find it; but we did see how honest folk could be made to think there was something here—after all, it's in the Bermuda Triangle.

So, a very pleasant expedition came to an end—the first great success was my corn plaster seasick preventative, which was really put to the test on the trip back to Florida.

Our second success also happened as we sailed home. *Lagniappe* encountered an abandoned 22-foot motor boat named *Mister D*. No-one was aboard and Jim Turner sent over a boarding party. The boat was in seaworthy condition and a white flag was found tied to a paddle, possibly as a distress or surrender signal. The craft had towing lines attached fore and aft, but these had not been cut. There were no keys for the motor, but it was fuelled up and in good order. The boarding party discovered a bolt-action rifle, a large quantity of various types of small-arms ammunition and a flare pistol. A number of life jackets, camouflage uniforms and explosive were also aboard. The matter was reported to the US Coastguard, then the boat was taken in tow and handed over to US Customs on arrival in Fort Lauderdale.

'What happened to the crew of *Mister D*?' asked my host Dan Osman, when I got back to his apartment in Miami. 'Oh, that's a mystery,' I said.

2

Lost Colonies
and Lost Cities

===

He claimed to have found a great white city deep in the jungle.

As so often happens you reveal another tantalising mystery whilst pursuing the main aim of an expedition and thus it was that whilst hacking our way through the claustrophobic rain forest of the infamous Darien Gap in 1972 I heard of Caledonia Bay—'The Lost Colony of the Scots'.

In the Chronicle of Pedro Martin de Andleria, written in the early 16th century, the River Darien is mentioned as flowing into the Gulf of Uraba. Later the river changed its name to Aparto, but the area between Panama City and the Mountains of Colombia became known as Darien. At about the same time the Spaniards called it Castilia del Oro—Golden Castile. It was so named for very good reasons; it can blame its troubled history on the fact that its jungle-covered land was rich with gold. Since 1501, when Rodrigo Bastidas became the first known traveller to visit the Darien, men have battled for the soft yellow metal. In 1502 when Columbus arrived he saw 'greater evidence of gold on the first two days than in four years in Hispaniola.' The Indians even wore solid gold breastplates, which they were quite happy to exchange for small bells or trinkets costing almost nothing. Later came Nuñez de Balboa, who was to cross the isthmus and discover the Pacific.

It was to this area that William Paterson, an erratically brilliant Scot who helped to found the Bank of England, brought colonists from over the Atlantic. He called it 'this door of the seas, and the key of the Universe', and believed that he could make it a bridge between East and West. He proposed to build a port through which would pass some of the richest trade in the world. His concept was an

39

excellent idea but as events were to prove, the timing was wrong.

It was in July 1698 that five ships carrying 1200 people left Leith in Scotland and four months later dropped anchor in a beautiful natural harbour on the Darien coast which they named Caledonia Bay. It was sheltered from the ocean by a long, hilly peninsula. 'The land on the peninsula is extraordinarily good, and full of stately trees fit for all uses, and full of pleasant birds, as is also the opposite shore, and hath several small springs which we hope will hold in the driest season.' Soon after arriving, Paterson wrote: 'Our situation is in one of the best and most defensible harbours, perhaps in the world. The country is healthful to a wonder, in so much as our own sick, they were many when we arrived, are now generally cured. The country is exceedingly fertile and the weather temperate.'

The Indians, too, were friendly, and soon found that they had nothing to fear from the good Scots. After two months of internal wrangling, they got down to building a settlement, which they named New Edinburgh. The Scots expected attacks by the Spanish, and started to build a fort, but owing to lack of leadership it was never completed. The greatest danger, however, was from the English Governors of Jamaica, Barbados and New York, who forbade English ships to trade with the new Scottish colony. The reason is uncertain, but it was probably pure jealousy of the Scots. There was another problem. None of the five ships of the expedition could leave the harbour. They were unable to sail to windward and at certain times of the year the wind blew from the north-east, straight into the harbour mouth. Two ships did try to escape but one was captured by the Spaniards when she ran aground and the other took a month to cover one hundred and twenty miles, returning eventually to New Edinburgh. The result was that no provisions could be brought in. The outside world was as much use to the colonists as if they had been on the moon.

In April 1699 the rain started. Only then did Paterson realise why there were no white settlements between Portobello and Cartagena, for with the rain came the mosquito which, though he did not know it, carried yellow fever and malaria. After six months, a quarter of the colonists had died. 'Our men did not only continue daily to grow more weakly and sickly, but more without hope of recovery, because about the latter end of the month of April, we found several species of the little provisions we had left in a manner utterly spoiled and rotten.' In June Paterson himself fell ill, and was carried aboard the *Unicorn*. To the other survivors this was the signal to abandon the colony. Four ships with hardly enough healthy men to crew them left the Bay. The *Unicorn* and the *Caledonia* arrived at New York having lost 255 men. The *Endeavour* was abandoned at sea, while the *St. Andrew* was chased by the Spanish fleet and 137 men perished. She eventually reached Jamaica with an Army officer in command.

Of Paterson, when he reached New York, it was said 'he looks more like a skeleton than a man. God grant he may recover . . . the grief has broke Mr Paterson's heart and brain, and now he is a child.'

The story of the colony did not end there. More ships sailed from Scotland. Only some arrived at Caledonia Bay, and they were met by a few survivors of the first expedition who had returned from New York. Different problems confronted the newcomers. Rumours of Spanish attack were common. Squabbling was continual, and no overall leader emerged until Captain Alexander Campbell of Fonabs arrived. He immediately set out with two hundred men and with the help of friendly Indians located, attacked and defeated an approaching Spanish force in the jungle. On returning to Caledonia Bay he found it blockaded by the enemy fleet which then proceeded to disembark men on the flanks of the town. Campbell sent out scouts to check on their progress, but these were picked off by snipers in the thick forest. The rest withdrew hastily to the besieged settlement, where not only fever but also a fire took its toll. The siege lasted for just over a month. The defenders seemed to have absolutely no chance of survival, but when it was least expected, the Spanish General offered astonishingly generous terms of peace. The Scots would be allowed fourteen days to stock their ships, and to sail with the next favourable wind with all their guns and ammunition. Naturally enough the offer was accepted and on 12 April 1700 the last Scotsman left New Edinburgh. The Spaniards were left to reign supreme over the steaming isthmus. The colony was abandoned to Nature; it was only the matter of a few years before the jungle had overrun the whole place and nothing was left of human making but the earthworks.

So only three years after the Scots, in a wave of almost hysterical enthusiasm, had subscribed almost half their nation's capital to set up 'this noble undertaking' it had been crippled by the quarrelling of its leaders, deliberately opposed by the English, whose King and Parliament they had defied, and forced out by the Spanish. Nine ships of the company had been sunk or destroyed and over two thousand souls had perished on that fever-ridden coastline. It was a sad end to Scotland's last act of independence from the English crown.

In 1972, whilst wrestling with the problems of the British Trans-Americas Expedition, I flew along that coastline and, using a map in John Prebble's outstanding book, *Darien Disaster* (Secker and Warburg, 1968), we found an area which looked very like the lost colony. A storm was raging and there was nowhere to land, but nevertheless we were able to circle for fifteen minutes and take film and photographs of what I felt sure was the site of the ill-fated Scots colony of 1699. During my journey through that awful forest I had often heard intriguing rumours about a lost tribe said to be descended from the Scots. Hundreds, possibly thousands of accounts must have been written about the colony and yet today it has been swallowed up by the avaricious jungle. What had happened to all those Europeans who had lived and died on this lonely coast? The mystery intrigued me and I determined to return one day.

So, in 1976, I formed a Reconnaissance Expedition of three girls and seven men, with the backing of the Scientific Exploration Society and the Explorers Club. The members came from Britain, Panama and USA. They were to include Vince and Barbara Martinelli from New York, who had been with us in Nepal and now came as quartermaster and caterer. From Miami came my old friend Dr Dan Osman and an amusing nurse named Linda. A US Army NCO, Sgt. Mel Trafford, volunteered to be our diver, whilst the British contingent included a highly efficient PR executive, Ruth Mindel, who had joined our organisation in London and now acted as general manager and treasurer. Andrew Mitchell, a light-hearted 23-year-old zoologist from Jersey, became our chief scientist, whilst my ever-smiling aide, Chris Sainsbury, recently returned from a voyage on a square rigger, was in charge of sea movement, as well as all photography.

I wrote in advance to the Director of Panama's Patrimonio Historico and obtained an archaeologist who could also act as liaison officer. On the way to Panama I bumped into a colourful character named Tristan Jones in a New York City radio station. He was a Welsh seafarer of the old tradition; a lone sailor who has sailed on almost every stretch of water in the world and has now become a well-known author. Tristan had even navigated rivers rising in the high Andes of South America with a clumsy sailing boat. As we left the studio we swopped yarns and talked of the many places where we had almost met each other. 'I'm just off to somewhere I'm certain you haven't been to,' I said.

'Where the hell's that?' my salty friend replied.

'Oh, it's a little-known bay called Punta Escoces,' I replied.

As we got into the lift he turned and winked, 'Was there last month, old fruit,' he grinned. Of all the incredible coincidences I discovered that he had indeed only just come from Caledonia Bay. Furthermore, to our great interest, he told us that he had actually seen a tribe of primitive white people; rather short in stature, with red hair and blue eyes. 'Must be Scots, looked just as if they had come from Sauchiehall Street!' he joked. But he was quite serious about their existence. (In *The Incredible Voyage*, Bodley Head, 1978, he gives an account of his visit.)

Tristan Jones's words were still ringing in my ears when I reached Panama three days later. The horrors of a previous battle with the jungle were almost forgotten. Indeed, it really felt good to be going back to Darien and, thankfully, many old and valuable friends still remained from our last visit. In Panama, Chris and Andrew had already done most of the preparation.

I visited the all-important Guardia Nacional and saw Colonel Flores who had helped us previously. It was Easter and he regretted that all his men were on leave so none could accompany us. 'You know our jungle well enough anyway,' grinned the Colonel, indicating that he had no objection to my operating unescorted so close to the Colombian border. True to her word the Director of the Patrimonio Historico had maps and a young archaeologist ready. These, coupled with air photographs obtained by Andrew, were vital to our quest.

Meanwhile, Ruth had gathered in an impressive stock of liquor

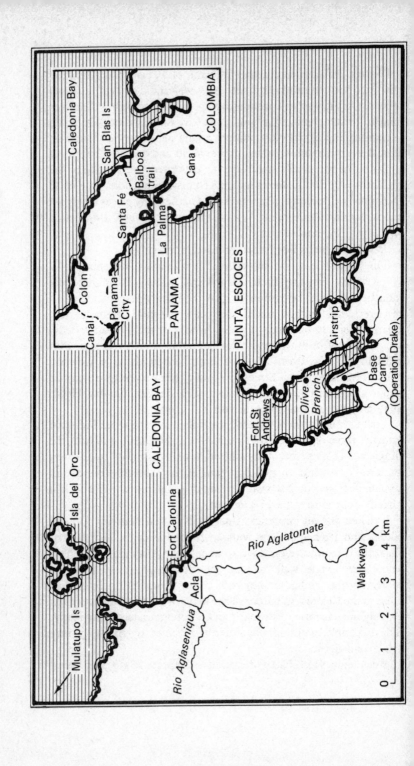

and arranged an airlift to a grass landing strip on an isolated islet about ten miles north of our target. The rest of our team arrived from New York and Miami and the hunt was on.

Winging away from the high-rise hotels of Panama City, we were soon over the dense forest of the Darien Gap. Memories flooded back of those desperate days in 1972 when our column had struggled through the green twilight world beneath the tree tops. I'll never forget the day I'd first entered that infamous jungle. We'd marched all day across the open plain, under the searing sun when we saw the forest. It didn't start slowly, but came at us just like a solid wall. I'd paused to look back at the sunlit savanna before entering this strange new world with its giant trees and buttress roots. Ahead of me was a tunnel of greenery, arched over by tangled growth and hung with trailing vines. The light was reduced to faint patches of yellow on the leaf-strewn floor, from which grew a garden of small plants. Ahead danced some large and beautiful butterflies with iridescent blue wings. Once in the tunnel, I began to meet the numerous small creeks and stream beds over which we struggled on the slippery rock slabs, or through the glutinous, oozing mud. Nor will I forget the horrific screams of howler monkeys nor the buzz of hornets and the sudden crash as some giant tree fell to the ground at the end of its life. There is always sound: even if only the drip of rain, the roll of distant thunder or just the rustle of leaves as a large hairy bird-eating spider makes his way warily across the forest floor.

It's a strange exotic land and yet to those early European settlers, whose homes we were seeking, it must have been a frightening, unfamiliar place. But now, four years later, the track we had hacked so laboriously was a two-way vehicle highway, with the greedy jungle cut back for fifty yards on either side. Four thousand feet beneath us, the familiar undulating green was slashed open by the dusty brown scar that disappeared into the purple foothills.

'Took us six weeks to reach that village in 1972,' I shouted to Barbara and Linda, sitting behind me. The girls nodded their acknowledgement and peered down at the placid vegetation that looked so innocuous. Now the ground was rising up as we approached the Caribbean coast and a few miles ahead I could see the shimmering blue sea and the emerald isles of Mulatudo, Tubuala and Tupak. The villages, tightly packed huts crowded on coral outcrops, lay inside this protective barrier of swampy islands. Mulatudo airstrip had been built on the longest stretch of dry land and the pilot aimed the plane at its eastern end. Brilliant white egrets rose in alarm from the mangrove as we roared in and then with a bump and a thump, we were down and taxiing towards Chris Sainsbury who, having arrived alone with the cargo three hours earlier, was somewhat relieved to see us.

'Welcome to Mulatudo,' he grinned, his fair skin already showing the effect of the glare. 'Actually, I thought for a time that I'd got the wrong island, but as I had all the liquor, I knew you'd find me!'

'Where are Andrew and Gricelio?' I asked.

'No sign,' shrugged Chris.

'Probably been eaten,' remarked Ruth, who was still feeling the effects of the 54 ticks she'd collected on a quick visit to a densely forested area two days before. They'd been devils to remove and had defeated lighted cigarettes, salt and insect repellent. Only vodka applied in an eye bath to the loathsome creatures had made them release their grip. Perhaps that is the origin of the saying, 'As tight as a tick!'

However it was strange that our advance party was not here to greet us. Only a handful of unsmiling Cuna Indians had appeared and without orders from us were already carrying all our worldly goods to the beach. Dan mentioned that because of the high Cuban population in Miami he had learned some Spanish so that he could treat with them. Thus he was quickly despatched in a narrow sailing dugout to the nearest village. 'Make sure my camera case stays dry,' yelled Chris. The doctor in his new role of interpreter looked decidedly uneasy and was already bailing the boat with a gourd. No sooner had he left than a motor boat appeared bearing our wild-eyed zoologist, Andrew. A shock of towsled black hair flowed from beneath his Army jungle hat, giving him the appearance of a Cuban revolutionary. 'Terribly sorry I'm late, spot of bother with the Chief,' he explained.

'But I thought we had a letter from the Government to him,' I replied.

'Yes, we did, but wrong Chief! However, it's alright, Gricelio had a spare sheet of official paper and we borrowed a typewriter, produced a new letter, forged a good signature and here it is,' he panted. 'Now we've told the Chief that you are our great leader and that the letter to him is only entrusted to you—so when you meet him you can hand this over.' So it was a little time later I confronted the Chief in the spacious 'village hall'. Surrounded by his people the wizened little man in a cowboy hat listened whilst the local schoolmaster read aloud the official document. I sat, still wearing my freshly whitened pith helmet, looking as resolute, dignified and self-confident as possible, for I knew the Cuna of old, and what they and I should expect of each other. When the reading was over I used the schoolmaster and Gricelio to explain in more detail what we were about. There were few questions and I sensed that we were not entirely welcome. However, the Chief provided boats and boatmen to accompany us for the expedition (at an inflated price), and we wasted no time in getting underway.

'Did you see the Albinos, John?' queried Dan, who had been examining two or three of the fair-skinned blond-haired Indians.

'Yes, they are reasonably common,' I replied.

'But there are so many and they don't seem as severely affected by the sun as Albinos usually are,' continued the doctor. 'Do you think they are lost Scots?' enquired Barbara, ever anxious about her ancestry. The conversation ended in laughter as Vince, taking up his quartermaster's duties, got us all loading the boats.

It was early afternoon as our flotilla of outboard-powered dugouts sped across the mirror-like waters between the islands, heading south-east to Punta Escoces, 'Scots Point'.

Canoes expertly paddled by stocky Cuna girls in brilliant scarlet and yellow dresses and shawls emerged from the coconut groves in the landscape that would rival any *National Geographical* spread. Gold nose-rings and chest-discs flashed in the sun as their dusky brown arms worked in unison. Occasionally the light breeze lifted a shawl to reveal dark flashing eyes and strangely Mongol features.

The dugouts leaked and as we came out of the shelter of Golden Isle into the gentle swell, a wave or two slopped over the bow. However this did not detract from the beauty of my first sea-level view of Punta Escoces or as the Scots called it, New Caledonia. The leaning palms and golden beaches, the coral gardens and running surf, bright green hills and the shadowy mangrove at the far end of the inlet all combined to make this place one of the most bewitching natural harbours I have ever seen.

Domitri, our leading boatman, suggested we base ourselves in some empty 'pueblos' of the Cuna village and we came ashore with a Panamanian flag flying. The huts were furnished with basic furniture, kitchenware and even a few 'hamacas' of the same type that had inspired Christopher Columbus's men to adopt this convenient sleeping arrangement. The history of the area is fascinating and intrigued me. In 1503 Columbus arrived off the coast seeking a way around the world and although he knew it not, he was only 40 miles from the Pacific; but it was four centuries later before the Panama Canal linked the oceans. Sir Francis Drake is also thought to have used this hidden bay as a secret raiding base and named it Port Pheasant. Perhaps his expert seamanship had enabled him to sail out against the contrary winds that had plagued the Scots' captains.

During the dry season a small family of Cuna lived in the village to harvest the coconuts. Domitri agreed with a local lady that we should rent two of the houses and we moved in. By dusk Barbara had the kitchen set up, Ruth was happily surprised to find avocado pears were free, Andrew was in hot pursuit of the swarming blue land crabs that scuttled amongst the palms and Mel had reconnoitred the underwater obstacles near the beach. Gricelio was questioning the locals about artefacts and Dan had spotted another Albino. The sun set in a blaze of orange behind the Darien hills and in the last rays, Chris filmed the Explorers Club flag that barely moved in the humid evening air.

After supper we spread out the maps and air photographs and, fortified with a glass of luke-warm J and B, planned the next day's exploration. Now we should know if all the research would pay off. John Prebble's book gives a good description of the town and our archaeologist was confident that we would locate evidence of foundations.

However our first task was to search the shores of Caledonia Bay to find the actual Scottish encampment, Fort St. Andrews. So leaving one party to examine the shoreline reefs, I took another through the coconut groves towards a promontory on which the old Scots maps showed the refuge. We found a stream of clear water running from the hills and I felt it should lead to our objective, but the vegetation grew thicker and the brook became a swamp, so moving inland again, I began to cut with my machete. Suddenly the ground dropped away steeply and I stumbled down into a shallow ravine. On either side the undergrowth fell back revealing a clean-cut channel in the coral. There was no doubt this was the moat of Fort St. Andrews.

Whilst Andrew and I measured up, Vince and Barbara followed the zig-zagging ditch. We were elated at our early success and spent the rest of the day searching the area.

The spoil from the moat had been used to build up ramparts and several bastion positions and a gateway were apparent. The vertical-sided moat was filled with sea water to a depth of approximately three feet for the first twenty yards at its seawards end. It was uniformly cut and approximately four yards wide at the water level. The gateway or gap in the rampart was also four yards wide. The ditch went right across the neck of the promontory with an entrance to the sea at one end and a mangrove swamp at the other. Searching the rampart, Barbara discovered glazed 16th-century potsherds; they were certainly European, but it was too early to say if they were Scots or Spanish. Nearby Vince found a small cannonball. Gricelio reckoned it was the type fired from a light cannon which was probably the heaviest weapon the besieging Spaniards could have dragged through the jungle. Inside the Fort there were depressions that might have been attempts at wells and on the seaward side a battery position for the guns commanded the harbour entrance. Broken pottery littered the ground everywhere.

Later Vince found evidence of the lookout post on the point, but there was no sign of the battery on the mainland side of the sea gate. Indeed, it looked as if successive landslides had widened the harbour entrance.

The Scots' first defences were said to be a 25-foot-high rampart across the neck of the isthmus on which the colony stood. In an attempt to discover this, Linda and I cut our way through the dense undergrowth and up the steep slippery ridge behind the village. Insects rose in swarms from the bushes whilst underfoot armies of leaf-cutter ants busied themselves with their perpetual tasks. At last we reached the crest, panting for breath and bathed in sweat.

'You're not an explorer,' gasped Linda, 'you're a masochist.'

Alas, there was no rampart and although we did find some brick-work in the supposed area, that was one of our failures. Nor did we find the cemetery of the Scots where the Spanish reported 400 graves. However, we did discover an overgrown airstrip, built years before by Dutch planters, which would not be too difficult to reopen and could well be useful for a future expedition.

After a hard day's work in the swamp, I grabbed towel and soap and made my way through the dense foliage to a clear stream behind the camp. Plunging into the wonderful cold water was blissful. I'm not sure how long I'd been bathing, but something bright caught my eye and I realised that I was being watched. A few yards away, partly hidden by a clump of bamboo, I saw a human leg—a white leg. Slowly I rose from the water and, wrapping the towel around me, walked up the bank as if I'd seen nothing.

As I drew level with the bamboo, I spun around and confronted the 'peeping Tom'—to my utter surprise, it was a woman—a stocky little lady with short blonde hair, white skin, blue eyes and a ruddy complexion. Her features and dress were typically Cuna Indian and I realised at once that she was an Albino. Although somewhat shy, she laughed and let me look closely at her face. There was no doubt that a seafarer could mistake such people for long-lost Scots. The only word she knew in English sounded like 'Robinson'—amazingly it appeared to be her name!

Underwater the real interest was to look for the wrecks of various ships reported to have sunk in the bay. One was the *Maurepas,* a French merchantman of 42 guns. In December 1698 this fine vessel had sought the protection of the Scots from the Spanish fleet and its captain, Duvivier Thomas, enjoyed the isolated colonists' hospital-ity as he told them the news of the outside world. Whilst the Frenchmen drank and feasted with their new-found friends, rumours circulated that the *Maurepas*'s hold was filled with treasure taken in a raid on the Spanish port of Cartagena.

However, the weather deteriorated and the bay was closed by strong winds blowing straight into the sea entrance. It was to be a tragic Christmas Eve. When Captain Thomas inexplicably set sail on the morning of 24 December, most of his crew was still the worse from the previous night's revelries. Great waves were pounding through the sea gate, but they weathered the storm and hit the hidden rocks. At first little damage was done and when Captain Pennecuik in the *St. Andrew* came to the rescue, he advised Thomas to drop anchors and wait for the calm. Sadly, whilst riding the fury of the seas, both chains broke and the *Maurepas* was swept back onto the rocks, this time causing a great tear in her hull. As she began to sink, Pennecuik took command, ensuring the safety of Captain Thomas and as many Frenchmen as could be rescued.

These angry survivors were housed on board the *St. Andrew* for many weeks, their ungrateful manner being caused by the loss of the 60,000 pieces of eight and the wealth of trading goods lost on the stricken *Maurepas*. The Scots, too, were obsessed by this unobtainable treasure!

Thus, following the maps in John Prebble's book, Ruth, Dan, Mel and I took air photographs, charts and compass, sailed out in Domitri's leaky dugout and quickly found the reef. The sea heaved gently under a cloudy sky, heavy with rain, as we took our bearings. Sitting in the bow I passed directions to Dan, who directed Domitri's steering. 'Left, left, bit more, steady, now.' Ruth dropped the marker. In fact the Scots might have approved as we were using inflatable whisky advertising bottles as buoys.

When we had completed the designation of the search area, Mel and I flopped into the warm water. Hoping to pick up a fish for supper, I carried a powerful harpoon gun and swam along the surface with only snorkel gear whilst Mel descended to the sea bed at the end of his safety line. Shimmering bubbles mushroomed upwards from the aqualung as the diver quartered the area. The spreading coral was alive with small, brightly coloured fish darting in and out. There was nothing unusual to see, but I guessed that the *Maurepas* would have gone down behind the reef. So, having checked the shallow water, we now concentrated our search in the depths beyond. Mel kicked his way down the cliff into the gloom; without a breathing-set I could only follow him to about five fathoms, but I could see he was now on a flat, sandy floor broken only by the occasional rock. Twenty feet beneath me, guided by his wrist compass, he moved slowly back and forth across the area, his gloved hands reaching up to check dark items on the sea bed.

'A few shapes that look as if they might be coral-encrusted cannon in the cliff,' said Mel as he surfaced. 'I've got a couple of pictures.' He handed the underwater camera to Ruth and I helped him aboard. It was getting too dark to see and as we had to conserve our limited air supply, I decided to call off the search until next day. As yet there was no definite information, so we secured our buoys against the freshening wind and returned to dinner of avocado hash.

Next day dawned with bright sunshine and a fairly calm sea. We were over the reef by 8 o'clock. The green and yellow plastic whisky bottles still bobbed about in the gentle swell as we dropped down into the grey world. Mel was soon on the sand and I noticed he had changed his search pattern. As I watched I could see he was probing something. Indeed there seemed to be a light-coloured shape, a mound stretching out of visibility. We discussed it on the surface. 'It's over a hundred feet long and about fifteen wide,' reported the diving sergeant. 'There are lumps sticking out of it and the sand in the mound is less dense; after I've broken through the surface I can push a harpoon in easily for its entire length.' Ruth and Dan listened intently as our voices began to show excitement. 'It certainly sounds just like a wreck, probably buried deep in the sand with encrusted spars projecting,' I said. 'Is it light enough for photographs?' asked Ruth, handing Mel the camera. He nodded, replaced his mouthpiece and sank onto our find.

The billowing mass of silvery air bubbles drifted up from the sea bed as fifty feet below my companion worked away at the irregular outline of the mound. The rattle of his demand valve was the only sound to disturb this silent world.

Suspended in the clear, warm water, I watched for the diver's signal. Then for no good reason, I turned round and an awful lump formed instantly in my throat. The shark, its great tail moving rhythmically from side to side, was approaching in slow motion. The pointed head, the beady unblinking eye, the narrow fins, all blended into one blue-green, streamlined shape. My harpoon gun came up instantly and as it did the denizen of the deep swung past; swimming effortlessly. I felt the wash of his wake but he was soon lost beyond the misty limit of the underwater visibility. The theme tune from *Jaws* was still echoing through my mind when somewhat thankfully I climbed aboard our boat.

We checked the position of what we hoped would be the *Maurepas*, but could not for the moment throw any more light on the wreck.

On our last day we rose early, breakfasted on our American Army rations and loaded the long piraguas. The used pots and pans, plus a pile of surplus rations we gave to the Cuna girls in whose huts we had stayed.

In the sea gate a large green turtle lay sentry-like and watched us leave. The palms waved in the breeze above the ruined fort and, looking back, I could easily imagine a lone piper playing a lament on the deserted headland. An hour or so later we landed at Mulatudo. Jose, another Albino, kindly let us stay in his two-storey, tin-roofed home and even found some beds and sheets for a few of us.

Next day, we hoped, the aircraft would arrive to take us home. Meanwhile we talked about our finds to the Indians and watched the young people dancing. Girls with pudding basin hairstyles and brightly coloured dresses shook their maraccas at dancing boys with pipes of Pan. 'You pay one dollar for every photo,' demanded a grim elder. As I was using a cine camera this would clearly be expensive so we gave him a dollar to cover everyone's pictures!

By the school we were shown a large cannon barrel, 170 cm long and 33 cm at the breech. 'Escoces,' grunted the schoolmaster, pointing at the gun, but it was too rusty to be sure. 'It come Punta Escoces, one white man bring, many years ago,' continued our guide. 'White man, son of Dr Paterson,' he continued.

'That's not possible,' said Dan, 'but how do they know about Paterson?'

'Oh, it's in the folklore, I suppose,' said Chris, and I remembered seeing children with wooden effigies of a man in a top hat and frock coat. Another mystery.

As darkness fell and little lamps with naked flames flickered in the tightly packed huts the humidity seemed to close in on us. From the assembly hall came an eerie chanting as women bent over their needlework responding to the exhortations of a priest, or was he a politician? The ceremony was beyond our understanding so we retired to the cantina to drink a reasonably cool beer and watch a small pet monkey chasing cockroaches.

As I went to bed I saw Jose by the glow of his cigarette sitting in a dark corner of his verandah. 'Any mosquitoes?' I enquired. 'No mosquitoes, Señor,' he replied and, thankful that I needn't unpack my net, I flopped on to the white sheet and the lumpy mattress. As I slipped into unconscious oblivion I felt something prick my toe. Assuming it was an insect I kicked out, then fell asleep.

The storm broke at 1.15 a.m. and the rain upon the tin roof would have woken the dead. Then I realised my bed was wet. 'Oh hell,' I thought, 'the rain's coming in.' As I rose to investigate I felt the call of nature and so, groping for my torch, I stumbled down the external staircase to the evil-smelling loo. The rain had ceased as I ascended again but my torch revealed something that made me freeze. The stairs were dripping with blood. In six bounds I was in my room and, supposing murder to have been committed, seized my harpoon gun in defence. As I did so something brushed my hair and raising my torch beam I saw a bat flitting around the room. Then the light caught the bed and to my dismay I saw it was drenched in blood which, even now, dripped steadily on to the floor forming bright red pools. My legs were scarlet from the knees down. 'Ruth,' I hissed through the cubicle wall. 'What is it?' came a sleepy reply. 'You'd better give me a hand, I think I've cut a vein or something,' I whispered. Ruth padded in. 'Mind where you tread,' I cautioned. 'What on earth . . . ?' She stood looking at me in horror.

Dan arrived next. 'Hell, John,' he said, 'what did you do?' I could remember nothing untoward happening, except the prick in my toe just before I'd fallen asleep. Having cleaned me up Dan looked puzzled. 'I've never seen anyone bleed so much from such a tiny cut!' exclaimed the doctor. 'It's about a quarter of an inch long on your toe.' Then he added, 'Say, is there any history of blood disease in your family?' and on being assured that there wasn't, he said, 'Have you cut yourself recently?'

'Yes,' I replied, 'yesterday on my knuckle.' There Dan found a perfect scab. So dosing me with antibiotics and plastering up the cut, he left me to sleep.

At dawn the room looked like a slaughter yard and, interestingly, the blood had still not congealed. 'John, I've made some enquiries,' said Dan at breakfast. 'I reckon that bat you saw was a vampire. Apparently the local people are often bitten; and because the creature injects you with a powerful anti-coagulant to make it easier for them to drink your blood, you will bleed profusely,' he explained.

Of course I should have remembered how our horses had suffered during the Darien crossing in 1972. 'There's only a four per cent chance of a bat carrying rabies,' Dan continued, 'but I suggest you start the shots the moment we get back to Panama City.'

Thus in the months that followed I was to undergo no less than three different series of anti-rabies injections, a total of thirty-two jabs in my stomach and backside. By comparison the bite was nothing, so I do hope the bat got alcohol poisoning from his cup of my blood!

Our plane arrived on time and as we flew back to Panama, the sky grew dark, waterspouts raced across the bay and the rains came, bringing the mosquitoes and the dreaded malaria that had decimated the early settlers.

In a very short time, our team had achieved an incredible amount and attracted world-wide interest. We had broken new ground: a detailed examination would follow. Thus the way was prepared for the forthcoming worldwide expedition—Operation Drake. But there were funds to be raised, a team to recruit and equipment to assemble before all the mysteries of Caledonia Bay could be explored. One thing, though, was certain; we all came back with the utmost respect for the brave Scots who died in those steaming jungles almost three hundred years before.

Three years later the dramatic story of the ill-fated Scottish colonists came vividly alive for the young explorers of Operation Drake, as they helped with the excavation of the site of Fort St. Andrews and unearthed a wealth of finds and features that very clearly illustrated the tragic enterprise and enabled them to visualise with great clarity what life in the settlement must have been like.

They worked under the inspired direction of 23-year-old Cambridge archaeologist, Mark Horton, who rapidly established a reputation as one of the great personalities of the massive round-the-world expedition. Although distantly related to that grand old man of archaeology, Sir Mortimer Wheeler, he actually reminded most people more of Magnus Pyke, as he waved his arms around and enthused wildly about some point of academic interest. His involvement in his subject was so total that virtually nothing could distract him. This was proved in typical and very amusing fashion when he was giving our chairman, General Sir John Mogg, and a party of visitors a guided tour of his excavations at Acla. A long, green snake suddenly slithered across the path right in front of the General. I reached for my revolver, but was beaten to the draw by a Guardia major who, armed with a shotgun, blasted it to oblivion. As the sound of gunfire died and the dust cleared and people almost literally began picking themselves up off the ground, Mark could be heard prattling on about his beloved artefacts as if nothing had happened at all.

Following the discoveries of our 1976 reconnaissance, Mark arrived to find the remains of Fort St. Andrews completely overgrown with a coconut plantation and thick impenetrable undergrowth up to ten feet high, so he and his teams of young helpers started by cutting a swathe four hundred yards long and ten to fifteen yards wide through the middle of the area, followed by a series of parallel swathes cut at right-angles to form a rectangular grid. Altogether about half the total interior area of the fort was cleared in this way, and then excavations were made in and around features of particular interest. These included a circular powder house, the well which is known to have been sunk during the siege after the main outside water source came under fire from the Spanish artillery, and a section of the ramparts and bastions where gun positions and the site of a guard room were clearly identifiable.

Vast numbers of artefacts were meticulously logged. Two storage houses near the main entrance to the fort yielded large quantities of green and yellow beads for use in trading with the Indians, bits of pottery were discovered all over the site, while excavations near the three-sided south bastion of the ramparts led to the discovery of a hoard of military relics, including musket balls, a flintlock mechanism, a pike end, knife blades, and a bronze sword hilt. Among some of the other more interesting items that turned up were a Spanish rowel spur, a selection of bronze shoe-buckles and a Scottish coin bearing the crown and thistle and the date 1695.

Also found were some long-stemmed clay pipes with the initials P and G imprinted on them, and these played a vital part in confirming a major triumph for the Joint Services diving team, as I shall now relate. Their project, in which young explorers were able to take part, started disappointingly when the mound which had excited us so much during the earlier reconnaissance turned out to be nothing more than a natural feature of the sea bed. Anthony Lonsdale, an ingenious electronics expert who uses a special metal-detection device called a proton magnetometer to locate wrecks buried under sand, continued to check every square yard of the bay, but got nothing except false alarms. One big register on the magnetometer seemed promising, but turned out to be a barge full of railway lines—a decidedly twentieth-century relic left behind by the same ill-fated Dutch plantation company that built the airstrip.

San Antonio Reef, which was considered to be the most likely location for the *Maurepas*, proved to be devoid of anything exciting, although some sections of worm-eaten oak were found in the area. More timbers were discovered at Pink Point, where the Scots had sited a battery of cannon to cover the entrance to the bay, but again there was no sign of a wreck. It began to look suspiciously as though the ship, along with her pieces of eight, had broken up completely or been salvaged by either the Spanish or the French after the colony had been abandoned. There is no doubt that both countries knew of the wreck and the lure of the fabled treasure would have been just as much of an incentive to them as it was to us.

At this point the search was switched to look for the *Olive Branch*—one of two resupply vessels sent out from Scotland, which, having arrived in Caledonia Bay, burned to the waterline and sank, after the ship's cooper accidentally dropped a lighted candle while tapping brandy from the barrels in the hold and caused an instant inferno. It was known from the diaries of the colonists that she had gone down almost intact and that the fire had not completely destroyed her. But this being so—where was she?

The team made good use of the special diver propulsion unit 'Sea Horse'—a one-man torpedo-like underwater tow which enabled them to cover large areas of the sea bed without expending excessive air supplies. They concentrated their attention on an area close in to the shore on the eastern side of the bay. This sheltered spot was thought to be where the colony would have had its anchorage. Here, sure enough, Tony Lonsdale soon got readings that indicated something fairly substantial spread over an area roughly thirty-five yards long by nine yards wide, and when the divers went down and probed in the mud they made contact with wood and coral concretion.

The site was on a steep mud slope that dropped off the edge of the coral reef. At the shallow end there was live coral at a depth of six feet, while at the other end one could go down twenty-five feet before sinking into thick ooze. Underwater visibility was bad at the best of times and became non-existent once this silt was stirred up. Not quite what one expects in the Caribbean!

The team often had to work in pitch-blackness, using water jets and an air-lift suction pump, as well as shovels and buckets to clear glutinous mud, sand and coral fragments. After some considerable time, a piece of timber was prised out and brought to the surface for close examination by a marine archaeologist, who was able to confirm that it definitely came from an old sailing ship, as it consisted of a sandwich of pine and oak with a layer of felt and tar in between. This method of protecting the hull from certain wood-boring parasites by adding a sacrificial outer casing of pine was a common feature of sixteenth- and seventeenth-century European vessels—particularly those bound for tropical waters.

The next sample provoked even more excitement. It was immediately identifiable as a piece of deck planking, and it was badly burned on the underside, while the nail holes were charred right the way through, thus indicating a fire down below of sufficient intensity to make the nails glow red hot. We soon realised that we had found a virtually complete ship and the evidence pointed to its being the *Olive Branch*—but it was another three weeks before final, indisputable proof was forthcoming. The breakthrough came when, after much careful probing, the divers uncovered a number of barrels, some of which were still intact. Down on the sea bed they sifted delicately through the silt that clogged the barrels in the hope of finding something of the original contents, while up above, on the *David Gestetner*—the giant inflatable that served as a diving-platform—the results of these painstaking labours were awaited with almost breathless anticipation.

The air of tension was further increased by a hair-raising incident that had taken place a few days earlier. One of the divers, Warrant Officer Marc Moody, was down on the bottom, filling a bucket with silt in zero visibility, when there was a tug on the rope and the heavy pail was snatched away. Marc assumed that it had been hauled in by those up top on the platform, but when he surfaced he was puzzled to find that this was not the case. Nobody knew anything about it and there was no sign of the bucket.

The disappearance remained a mystery until, shortly afterwards, the Guardia hauled in the fishing nets they had set nearby, and there, thrashing around in the mesh, was a number of sharks including two man-eaters—a five-foot Mako and a ten-foot Hammerhead. It did not take too much imagination to put two and two together and come up with a chilling possibility as to who or what might have stolen the bucket.

Marc and his colleagues were understandably a little twitchy after that and every time something brushed unexpectedly against them down in the gloomy, pea-soup depths, they nearly jumped out of their wet-suits. Even the excitement caused by the discovery of the barrels could not entirely take their minds off the spine-tingling thought of what might be nosing around them as they worked.

Meanwhile the contents of several barrels were panned out like gold dust and passed up for examination. The first cask yielded a pronged fork and a few slivers of bone which suggested that it might have been part of a consignment of salt pork or beef; the next two were empty, and the fourth was full of nails. It was the fifth that provided the vital clue in the distinctive shape of three clay pipes that were identical to those found at Fort St. Andrews—they even carried the same P and G initials, which, it was irreverently suggested, might stand for Porridge Gobbler. It was known that the cargo of the *Olive Branch* included a batch of such pipes, since this was listed on the manifest—which is still in existence—along with Scots bonnets, Bibles, buttons, beads, glass drinking-cups, hunting-horns, mattocks, looking-glasses and pewter jugs.

Great were the celebrations that followed this positive identification. The only disappointment was that lack of time meant that it was impossible to undertake a full excavation. It was estimated that this would require a further six months and so will have to wait for a follow-up expedition in the future.

However, before the team finally packed up and left, it located the ship's rudder, which was fully intact with the shaft and pintles still attached. This discovery made it possible to plot the orientation of the wreck and piece together the sequence of events leading up to her sad end.

The team's underwater photographer, Flight Sergeant Ray Pringle-Scott, told the probable story in his report of the project. 'Everything became clear. When the *Olive Branch* caught fire, she was evidently anchored with her bows into the wind. The blaze started in the afterhold and roared downwind to engulf the stern first. As the inferno inched forward against the wind, the ship would have started to settle by the stern, causing all the loose gear and cannon to tumble aft. This would explain the two large magnetic readings—one at each end of the site. The bow section would probably still contain the spare anchors and forward cannon, securely lashed down, while the main deck guns, with their breechings burned through, would most likely have rolled aft as she settled. The picture was complete.'

It remained only to photograph all the finds and plot them on the master plan, and then to rebury the exposed timbers to conserve them. This very nearly produced a last-minute disaster, when several tons of silt suddenly slid into the main area of excavation and almost engulfed two of the team.

Back on land, the total success of the historical and archaeological projects was nicely rounded off when Mark Horton and his team of youngsters unearthed evidence which enabled us to prove beyond a reasonable doubt that the Lost City of Acla had been rediscovered. Acla was only the second European township to be established anywhere on the American mainland. It was from there that Balboa, the first European ever to gaze upon the Pacific Ocean, later set out across the isthmus, taking with him the dismantled parts of four ships which were to be reassembled on the other side. It was also the place where Balboa met an unjust end, when political conspiracy resulted in his being publicly executed in the main plaza. Thereafter, Acla was never quite the same again, and although it lingered on for some years as a gold-mining and trading community, it seems to have been finally abandoned around 1560.

Over the years, historians have often speculated about the exact location of the site, but although several went and poked about in the general area, no one managed to pinpoint it with any certainty.

In 1976 I had been taken to see a wall purporting to be all that remained of Acla, but it proved to be something of a red herring, though I was not the first to be diverted by it. It was examined in 1953 during the expedition of King Leopold of the Belgians by Dr. J. M. Cruxent, who was, however, unable to come to any definite conclusion about either its date of origin or its purpose.

After clearing the area all around the wall and digging a trial trench across the centre of it, Mark Horton decided that it seemed most likely that it was part of the Spanish fort San Fernando de Carolina, which is known to have existed in the area between 1785–93. The only artefact discovered nearby—the base of a glass wine bottle of an 18th-century type—was evidence to support this theory.

It was at a spot several hundred yards further inland on the same headland that Mark eventually found the more conclusive evidence he was looking for—pieces of decorated Spanish pottery of a kind known as Isabela Polychrome, which was common in the early part of the 16th century, but which has never turned up on any site founded after 1540. This discovery came at the very last moment, only days before the archaeological team was due to pack up and leave, when Jacinto Alemendra, a young archaeologist of the Panamanian Patrimonio Historico happened to walk into an area of dense bush and spotted a small heap of pottery lying on the ground. Mark immediately concentrated his entire effort on excavating this particular location, which had been ignored up until that moment.

The Isabela Polychrome fragments taken together with other topographical, geographical and historical evidence left little doubt in Mark's mind that the site of Acla had indeed been found and when he presented his case to experts in Panama and Britain, they confirmed this. It was a major archaeological coup, which the head of Panama's National Institute of Archaeology hailed as an extremely exciting discovery that provided a vital clue to the European settlement of America.

Another mystery had been solved.

The success of Operation Drake led HRH The Prince of Wales to encourage us to stage a repeat and by 1981, I was looking for fresh exploration tasks. The possibilities are enormous and in no time, numerous offers were pouring in. We'd decided to name the new venture Operation Raleigh, and commemorate the founding of English-speaking America by Sir Walter Raleigh's colonists in 1584. As Raleigh himself had visited Latin America, it seemed a good place to start our search. I didn't have to look far. Frank Dawson, enthusiastic member of the Explorers Club, knew the area well and was a keen amateur archaeologist. He was quickly telling me that for centuries, persistent legends of a fabled lost city had survived among those who live along the wilderness coast of Eastern Honduras. It was believed that in pre-Columbian times the region had been the home of a great civilisation with large areas of cultivation, traversed by roads and canals. The agriculture would have fed the population gathered for defence, culture and worship in the impressive stone-built cities that today still peer out of the ever-encroaching forest.

For almost four hundred years the Indians of this area have been telling of Ciudad Blanca. These reports have been endorsed by early explorers, who claimed they came across a massive white, walled city of ancient temples and palaces, in the little-known region behind the coast. It is supposed to stand upon a jungle-covered limestone ridge and modern government maps show it as being between the rivers Platano and Wampu. However, the cartographers have added a question mark.

None of the sightings has been confirmed, but in 1856, rumours were so rife that an imaginative engraving, depicting the ruins of Ciudad Blanca, was published in Honduras.

Frank, a rugged Texan, spoke fluent Spanish and had been on two expeditions in the area. One had used helicopters to investigate a series of high, white cliffs that were held in awe by the local Indians. From a distance these cliffs, rising up above a jungle-fringed river, did look a little like buildings, for there were plentiful 'doors and windows'. However, these were found to be natural holes in the limestone and the only inhabitants were some especially ferocious jaguars.

In recent times, Honduran bush pilots have reported sighting glimpses of tall white walls in the untracked jungle. Snake and jaguar hunters have returned to the coastal villages with yarns of a mysterious ruined city. Somewhere, in the 16,000 unmapped square miles of wilderness, men swear there exists the last great lost city of the Americas—and, like Tutankhamen, there is even said to be a curse upon those who venture there!

One eyewitness was a German flyer who, some thirty years or so ago, had crash-landed his single-engined aircraft through the canopy of the rain forest. By a miracle, he'd lived and, knowing his survival drill, had tracked through the green hell following first a stream, then a river, to the sea. When he was rescued, several small gold statues were clutched to his breast. He claimed to have found a great white city deep in the jungle where he'd dug up the treasures.

The authorities flew him back and forth over the trees, but he couldn't (or wouldn't) find it again. However he always planned to return and launch an expedition, but died and with him went the secret.

That's how I became involved in this intriguing project. The question is—does Ciudad Blanca exist? If so, where?—and, finally, if it does—what lies hidden there? Not even the marauding Spanish Conquistadores penetrated this area.

So I flew to Honduras with Frank, who had visited the area of the Black River (or Rio Tinto) on the coast of Honduras on his previous expedition. It was whilst searching for the White City that Frank had made an important discovery. Although it was not the prime objective of the expedition, they had come across evidence of a later settlement. So it was that he led me to a jungle clearing in which lay three enormous cannon. As soon as I saw the 'GR' markings (George Rex), I realised they were British and that this was possibly the site of the Fort set up by the Black River colony in 1732. Digging in the shallow depression, which I fancied might have been the moat, we discovered parts of a musket, a sword and a completely intact glass wine bottle of the early 18th century.

Nearby we found tombstones, including that of William Pitt, leader of the Colony. So we were certain that this was the site of the lost colony of the Black River.

Deeper in the jungle, Frank showed me the overgrown ruins of a pre-Columbian site. There were large columns, mounds, pottery and five huge altar stones, each weighing over 1½ tons. Frank had found a splendid stone owl here and presented it to the Honduran

National Museum in Tegucigalpa. But although this site is fascinating, it is not the White City.

However, the site offered plenty of scope for community and scientific tasks, so we decided to investigate it further as a job for Operation Raleigh.

Thus, in 1982, I asked the well-known explorer, Major Roger Chapman, to return to the area with Frank along with some scientists and young people to excavate the site to discover what we believe is the 18th-century fort, survey and explore the pre-Columbian ruins with a view to finding clues to the site of the lost White City—or even the city itself—and finally to carry out biological studies to guide future scientific research in the region.

Thanks to a lot of kind help from Air Florida, Roger's expedition flew out to San Pedro Sula in September, 1982. But on arrival they found themselves in the midst of a 20th-century conflict, terrorists having seized two hundred businessmen as hostages in the town. This upset all the carefully planned arrangements to get them to the remote Black River. However, eventually they arrived and set to work. Their research showed that the barely discernible mounds where I'd unearthed my prized black bottle was indeed Fort Wellington (as the colony fort had been named). It had been built by the British in 1746 and when the Spanish had taken over the colony in 1787, renamed the Fort of the Immaculate Conception of Honduras. But Frank discovered that it had been destroyed when the Mosquito Indians, formerly allies of the British, had attacked the Spaniards at 2 a.m. on 24 September, 1800.

Apparently there were six English traders and two doctors living in the colony at the time and the Indians thoughtfully advised them to barricade themselves indoors on the fateful night. It all smelled of a spot of 18th-century political intrigue!

In 1839 the British were back in strength, running the settlement for three years. However, thereafter it declined, the sugar estates of the interior died out, leaving little but the great cast-iron boiling-pots to mark their site. William Pitt was reputed to have owned five hundred slaves, so the extent of the plantations may be imagined.

'How about the White City?' I asked Roger and Frank as soon as they returned to our London HQ. They had certainly found something. At the ruins of the pre-Columbian site that Frank had

5. *(left)* Fort St. Andrews. The moat examined by Sgt. Brian Ranner and Flt. Lt. Mike Cameron.

6. *(above)* Fort Wellington. Abandoned cannon, the barrel imbossed GR (probably for George II).

7. (*left*) Bird-eating spider, Central American rain forest. Perched on a mess tin, it measures seven inches across.

8. (*below*) Caledonia Bay. A hammerhead shark which got in the way of the divers, WO 1 Marc Moody, RAOC.

shown me, the expedition had discovered thirty huge mounds and interestingly, some were L-shaped. Clearly Aguacates, as it was named, was a much more important settlement that we had imagined. They had news too of stone petroglyphs found on the nearby Rio Patuca by Honduran archaeologist Francisco Flores. Although time had not enabled Roger to send out a patrol to investigate it, there were reliable reports of a paved road to the south-east of the Black River. Indeed, it would seem to be part of a highly organised network. It was felt that this might lead towards the White City.

However, the new discovery of the mounds at Aguacates may indicate that this was a settlement at the end of a chain of highly developed pre-Columbian cities, the largest and most important being in the interior. If the size of Aguacates was anything to go by, the biggest would be quite something. More clues to the legendary location of the White City? Perhaps. But that will have to wait for Operation Raleigh.

The Black River is a fascinating place for archaeologists, historians and any who seek to solve the unexplained. And I found one intriguing little puzzle when Frank and I visited the area in 1981. Mister Green, a charming old negro who spoke 19th-century English, was a fund of tales. 'Do you know any ghost stories about this place?' I asked him as we sat in his old dugout on the lagoon.

'Weell' he wheezed; then, cocking his wrinkled old head sideways, he said, 'There's mysterious lights here'.

'What sort of light?' I probed.

'Ghostly lights, mister, ghostly lights,' he went on. Mister Green took a long time to tell a tale, simply because he enjoyed it.

'When there's a storm you sees a light, jus' like a lantern on de water off de bar,' he explained, pointing at the sand bank off the river mouth. 'It kind of floats on the surface across de bar—but there's no one there—it's bad news for boats.'

I wrote it down in my log and forgot all about it—for several months.

Later that year, I was doing another reconnaissance for Operation Raleigh in Honduras, but this time on the island of Roatan, not far from Black River. Amongst the expatriates living at the old pirates' haven of Port Royal was an ex-US-Navy veteran, Joe Garrison. Joe, round, smiling with a mass of fair curls above his sunburnt face, was rather like a jolly cherub. But one night as we sat sipping a beer and looking out to sea, he told me a tale of horror and mystery.

Having retired from the Navy, Joe had decided to sail round the world in a brig he'd bought and done up. However, having reached Roatan he reckoned he'd found paradise and settled for a while. One morning he sailed with a friend to the mainland for supplies. However, as the day wore on a strong 'Norther' blew up, driving them eastward along the Honduran coast. The storm strengthened and by nightfall, Joe's old sails had blown out and his engine was faltering as sea water entered the fuel. Knowing they were off a dangerous lee shore, the two men fought to keep the brig out to sea. When the engine stopped, they stripped and cleaned the filters, getting them back just in time to restart the old diesel and beat away from the coast. Throughout the night they battled, struggling to keep themselves upright as the boat pitched and rolled in the mountainous waves.

Joe felt they were winning and had just told Charlie, his faithful tabby cat that they'd made it, when they saw the light. Still some miles astern, one single navigation light was bobbing in the storm. 'Hell, a bloody shrimp boat coming up the coast—probably all boozed out of their minds and no watch,' thought Joe. Shrimp boats often carry only a single hurricane lantern slung amidships and this was exactly what it looked like. Now they had two problems. If their engine stopped seaward of the shrimper, they could drift back across her path. But if they didn't keep beating out to sea, they'd be on the rocks. So they decided to let the other boat pass.

However, minutes later it was still astern and they were drifting rapidly shoreward. Joe decided to chance it and restart the engine. Yelling to his chum, he went below and the diesel was just about going when there was a shuddering thud. Joe went flying and tons of water cascaded over them and down the hatch, killing the motor for good.

'We're in the breakers,' screamed his pal, as another jarring crash shook the brig and Joe knew they were doomed. There was just time to grab Charlie, thrust him into a beer box and seize the compass before the boat began to go over.

Luckily their dinghy slipped easily from its mounting and they
urfed through the roaring waves to ground on a sandy beach. Joe
ound Charlie, who scratched him savagely and scampered for the
ingle. Back on the sand bar, they saw the brig break up in the
noonlight. Joe watched, tears rolling down his salt-stained face—
ie'd lost everything and hadn't even been able to afford insurance
or his floating home. His luck wasn't completely out because his
vallet with some dollars and his passport washed up right beside him
nd, at dawn, some Indians used their dogs to help him find Charlie.

Sitting beside him that warm evening in Port Royal harbour, I
.stened attentively to this moving story. 'Where had you ended up,
oe?' I asked. 'Oh! We'd hit the bar at the mouth of the Rio
'into—the Black River,' he replied. My heart leapt and I remem-
ered Mister Green's story.

'Did you ever see that shrimp boat?' I enquired. 'No, darn it—we
.ever did, just the goddam light,' said Joe.

3

Mysteries of The Desert

'Funny . . . must have been the wind.'

Of all terrains in which I've operated the desert is the most mysterious. The vast empty distances seem to cry out, 'something hidden, go and find it' and few who have not experienced the endless rolling sand dunes, gravel plains and rocky hills can really appreciate the sheer nothingness. And yet if you pause awhile, there is often more to see than you imagine.

In 1959 our squadron of Royal Engineers was sent to Libya to assist in the production of 'going' maps which were to be used for future army exercises and were also of value to the oil exploration companies seeking the precious black liquid far beneath the sun-baked surface.

Apart from intruders like us, the desert was largely a still, silent place. We saw few birds, very little wildlife and no other men or even the sign of any since the prehistoric inhabitants had disappeared. There were no wheel tracks, footprints or litter in the deep south of Libya. We buried our garbage religiously, partly for hygiene, but also because it seemed offensive to desecrate this unspoilt world and I even disapproved of our vehicles moving in line abreast, because it made more scars on the landscape than line ahead. Yet it was sensible because we could motor in comfort out of each other's dust. I have always felt concern for the exploitation of virgin and un-explored territory; nature heals, but in the desert the scars may last a million years.

With these thoughts in mind, I recall one strange incident that happened whilst we were mapping a remote plateau. Our com-mander had produced very thorough emergency instructions and we all knew what to do in the event of a breakdown. We rarely moved in less than two vehicles and each group had a radio. If we broke down pyrotechnics were to be used at night and the rule was that we waited until dark and then climbed on to the highest ground and fired a signal pistol vertically. Anyone seeing the flare, which would shoot up for about 400 feet, could take a bearing on it by compass and then fire an answering flare. At daylight a 'box' search would be mounted. All very simple and, as it had proved on several occasions, pretty effective.

It was not unusual for small parties to be detached from the main camp, and on one particular evening we were seated about the fire, downing the customary gin and lemonade powder and listening to our doctor's thoughts on aphrodisiacs. Suddenly all talk of rhino horn and Spanish Fly ceased abruptly, for there to the east a white flare rose from the featureless plain and dropped back again—a little quickly, I thought; but we leapt to our feet, got the bearing and fired a reply. There were two parties out, although I was surprised at the direction from which the flare had come. Our groups should have been well north of there. At dawn we used the radio and, to our relief, learned that both parties were safe and, strangely, knew nothing of the distress signal. Nevertheless we searched the area just in case. It was a flat stretch of stony desert, without a hill or even a bump on the landscape; you could see for miles. There wasn't even a wheel track.

I offer no explanation, but I did read of a similar incident being reported by the war-time Long Range Desert Group (LRDG) near the coast. We were all disciples of the LRDG and I thought I knew the history of this crack army unit quite well. Previous exploits in the Kufra minefields had caused me to read the accounts of the campaign around the oasis with keen interest and great care. However, on one expedition we were to have a resupply run from our survey teams on a remote plateau to our rear base at Kufra, which was to prove rather interesting.

There were three of us in my Land-Rover when we set out before the glowing orb of the sun rose to destroy the glorious cool of dawn. How I loved those blissful couple of hours! Quite why we went with only one vehicle I cannot recall, but it was an easy run on what was by now a well-trodden trail, and we had a radio. We made good progress and in the afternoon were bowling along at about 70 m.p.h.

on the flat, hard sand. The cars were always piled with kit and, to make more space, panniers of wire-mesh hung out of both sides. In these we carried our rations, sleeping-bags and personal belongings. In the back of the Land-Rover were fitted a dozen tightly packed jerricans of petrol. Water, not petrol, would be carried in the jerricans at the front—in case of a collision. Smoking in or near vehicles was strictly forbidden for obvious reasons. The good old army issue boiled sweets were great thirst-quenchers, and John, my navigator, turned about to locate our stock in a pannier.

'Fire!'—he screamed the dreaded word. If you stop a moving vehicle suddenly, the flames may come back and—woomph! that's the end, but by keeping going, one might just keep the fire away from the fuel cans.

'Where?' I said, looking about for some soft sand for fire quench-ing to stop by, but for once there was none.

'In the pannier—the bedding's alight!' yelled John.

The wind, such as there was, was blowing from behind so I pulled the wheel over to the left to keep the flames away from the cans and we halted gently enough to avoid spilling fuel. Hurling survival gear away from the car, we leapt out, tearing at the burning bedding. 'Get the water from the front,' I shouted to the other crewman, but he had already dragged a can of precious water off and placed it in safety, in case the vehicle blew up with all our supplies. Using the pathetic little fire extinguisher and some hastily-dug sand, we smothered the fire. The cause was simple. A hard bump had damaged our exhaust, pointing it upwards at the bottom of the pannier. Fortunately the only loss was a sleeping-bag, but it had not been a pleasant experi-ence. We stopped shaking, repacked, had a few good gulps of water and drove on in silence.

I'd wanted to make Kufra by dark, but with the delay caused by the fire we obviously hadn't a hope. As dusk fell, we reached some low rocky hills, north of Maaten Bisciara, really just big piles of jumbled broken stones. There were numerous narrow passes running through them. The map wasn't very precise so I chose one at random, which turned out to be a little west of the usual route. The sand was soft, and in the failing light we bogged down several times. Having the sand channels back aboard for the third time I said, 'We should be able to get some shelter amongst these rocks,' and my weary crew readily agreed that it was none too soon to call it a day. None of us felt like cooking, so we ate a few hard-tack biscuits smothered in raspberry jam and washed them down with a mug of coffee. The night was clear and before turning in, I went out with the shovel to commune with nature.

Squatting beneath the stars I swore I heard the sound of a voice twice. The first time, I looked back towards the dull black outline of the Land-Rover. The second time, I said loudly, 'Just a minute,' because I thought one of the men had called out to me. A few moments later, I returned to the car.

'What's the matter?' I enquired.

John was already asleep, his colleague looked up and said, 'Nothing, why?'

'Didn't you call?' I said.

'No,' he replied.

'Funny,' I yawned, 'must have been the wind.' Then, exhausted, I fell asleep.

I woke just after dawn, with a shiver and a bursting bladder. Standing up, I shook off the sand, rubbed my eyes and stretched my stiff limbs in the half-light. I was still only partly awake when I caught sight of something odd. About sixty yards away was a truck, or rather the remains of one, and all around it were scattered bits of equipment, dark against the white surface. I walked over to the Chevrolet, for even at this distance I recognised the familiar shape of the LRDG raiding vehicle. The debris consisted of cartridges, unexploded grenades, mortar bombs, broken rifles and parts of a machine gun. Thirty feet to one side at the head of a low mound, lay a small wooden cross and pieces of splintered wood that would probably have made up another. Other similar vehicles were 'parked' along the black wall of the pass. Some had engines missing, all appeared to have been blasted apart by a single explosion in the back. A self-destruction charge, I guessed.

Combing the area, we made an interesting discovery high amongst the rocks and found a faded canvas British Army haversack, containing the rusty fragments of a Kodak folding camera and a toothbrush. Nearby were scattered a pile of empty .303 cartridge cases. I believe it was here that the LRDG's 'T' Patrol was destroyed by a force from its Italian opposite number, the Auto-Saharan Company based at

Kufra. According to W. B. Kennedy Shaw in his book, *Long Range Desert Group* (Collins), a running fight developed on 31 January 1941, when the Italians, with a heavily armed motorised patrol and three aircraft, caught 'T' Patrol advancing on Kufra, in the valley of the Gebel Sherif.

Following the battle a New Zealander, Trooper R. J. Moore, and three colleagues had remained undetected amongst the rocks of the waterless hills. Almost everything they needed for survival had been destroyed in their vehicle, three of them were wounded and, as all the wells within two hundred miles were either in enemy hands or filled with rocks to prevent access, the situation seemed hopeless. However, somehow they managed to salvage a two-gallon tin of water and, scorning any idea of walking a mere eighty miles north-east to surrender to the Italians at Kufra, they buried the dead then turned and marched south towards their allies. The Free French Army's positions were known to be several hundred miles away across almost waterless desert.

The story of their remarkable and heroic escape over an astonishing distance is a worthy tribute to soldiers of one of the finest special forces ever raised. Three of the men survived and their leader, Trooper Moore, was found by the French walking steadily after ten days, 210 miles from Gebel Sherif. He was awarded the DCM for his leadership and courage.

We tidied up the grave, re-erected the crosses, stood silent for a moment, saluted and drove off towards Kufra. Later I reported the matter to the Headquarters in Benghazi and heard that a detachment from the Imperial War Graves Commission had visited the site. But I never did discover the origin of the strange voice I firmly believed I'd heard whilst squatting in the dunes that night.

Much of our time in the desert was spent in clearing routes through the wartime minefields. Although many of the mines were rusting and useless, some of them were in an extremely unstable condition. We were young and life was exciting. Rumours of Rommel's gold, tunnels full of Nazi loot, and even a U-boat laden with precious metal trapped in its undersea pen were rife. Already professional treasure-hunters were arriving and only recently, two ex-German

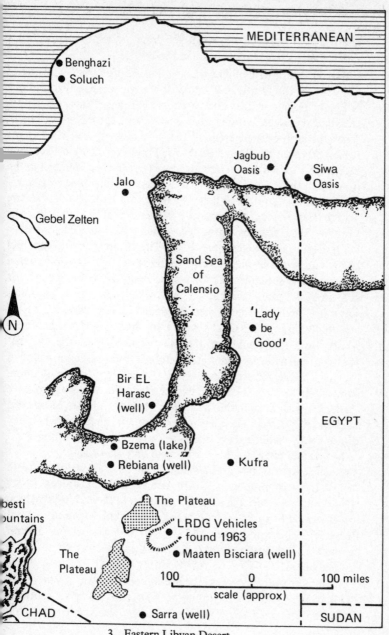

3. Eastern Libyan Desert.

soldiers had been blown up in the huge underground ordnance depot that lay beneath the headland at Tobruk.

To the south-east of Benghazi there lies the great sand sea of Calensio, or the Desert of Thirst as it is sometimes known. No-one willingly travels in the area, which in the late 1950s was hardly explored or visited; no-one, that is to say, except the oil explorers, who constantly begged our going maps. At that time I was acting as a liaison officer at the United States Air Force base at Wheelus on the North African coast. Our squadron was engaged in exercises in the desert and the Americans, with their usual hospitality and generosity, were doing much to help us. It was whilst working with the Search and Rescue Squadron at Wheelus that I first heard the rumour that some geologists had seen a Liberator (B24) bomber lying deep in the Calensio Sand Sea. The oil prospecting team had been flying over the lifeless wastes of the desert for many hours when they reached the almost unknown, inaccessible and unmapped Serir of Calensio. This is a flat, gravel plain which starts some 350 miles south of Benghazi. The oil men, hardened as they were, must have felt something of the thrill that we so often experienced as they passed over this remote arid region which it was unlikely that Western man had ever penetrated before. The ground shimmered in the heat rising from the waterless plateau, but suddenly there beneath them lay a huge four-engine plane that appeared to have made a belly landing on the desert floor some 25 miles south-east of a stark, solitary limestone pillar we knew as Blockhouse Rock. They could hardly believe their eyes—the plane looked in quite good condition and might have been there for only a few days.

Crashed aircraft, burnt-out tanks and all the wreckage of war were still fairly common along the North African coasts and indeed, in our wanderings we seldom paid much attention to them. Nevertheless, it was very odd to find a bomber 426 miles inland, south-east of Benghazi. The war plane's faded pink colour gave it a natural camouflage and indicated that it had been designed to operate from a desert airstrip.

Flying low over the wreck, the geologists could see no sign of life and marking the position on their chart, returned to base. Immediately they informed the USAF at Wheelus, where I heard of the discovery.

At first my American friends were inclined to dismiss it. They pointed out that the B24 Liberator bomber was an obsolete aircraft and that they had none of that type operating in Libya. Furthermore none had been reported lost that far into the desert—even in the last war.

The mystery remained. How had the plane got there? Whose was it? What had happened to the crew? Why were there no distress signals beside the plane that was relatively intact? Few people were inclined to mount an expedition so far into that living furnace. However, I did my best to persuade my superiors that perhaps we should go and have a look. Sadly there were more important duties which intervened.

We later learned that an oil company convoy had reached the bomber. As they had pushed forward through the sand sea, they kept a sharp lookout and one could imagine their excitement when they found it glistening in the heat waves.

The fuselage had been smashed off behind the wing as the bomber slid to a halt; the right-hand engine had come away on impact. On the aircraft's nose was a clearly written '64'. The oil men made note of all other identification numbers and on closer investigation, were surprised to see how well the bone-dry desert air had preserved the wreck. Beneath the wings of the aircraft, the searchers found mummified carcasses of birds who had sheltered there from the sun. Immediately they began to look for clues as to what had happened to the crew. They realised that unless the men had been found soon after the crash they would all have died. One of the geologists suggested that desert nomads might have captured the airmen and sold them as slaves deep in the Sahara. Perhaps they might still be alive in some desert city. However, a local guide rejected this theory, pointing out that it was so uninhabitable that even the tribesmen avoided it. He said, 'They say it has been cursed by God.' Indeed, to the best of my knowledge, the nearest water was at Bir El Harasa, 160 miles to the south-west. The land was virtually flat, featureless desert, hard-packed sand with a few pebbles on the surface. Only migrating birds would pass this way and even they would avoid landing on the lifeless surface.

As the explorers looked around the wreck, they noticed that the skin of the fuselage was still polished and shining in the sun.

Corrosion had not yet set in and they concluded that the plane must have crashed fairly recently. The fact that the United States Air Force had not claimed it as one of theirs led to a suggestion that it might have been used for some clandestine mission by a developing African country. However, this was considered unlikely as there, for all to see, was the white star on the deep blue surround of the United States Air Force. There seemed no doubt that it was an American bomber. There too was the name of the stricken plane—'Lady Be Good'. The oil men recognised the connection with the Gershwin song and, climbing into the body of the plane, they met a wall of heat. It was like stepping into an oven. To their surprise, they found no bodies nor indeed anything to suggest that there had been any casualties when the plane had crashed into the desert. Indeed, it seemed that everything was ready for flight. Machine guns were loaded and workable, the crew's clothing hung neatly on their hooks, and when the taps of various water containers were turned, water poured out—they were well sealed against evaporation. They even found a flask of drinkable coffee. There was no doubt, however, that the crew had left in some haste.

As they moved into the forward compartment they found themselves in a ghostly hothouse. The pilot's cockpit seemed almost normal, with the aircraft instruments registering nothing. On the navigator's table they found the log and from this, quickly discovered the date of 'Lady Be Good's' arrival in this God-forsaken place. The last entry recorded a bombing mission to Naples on 4 April 1943. There was no doubt that the crippled Liberator had lain on this burning plateau for sixteen years. But they all asked each other what had happened to her crew? Had there even been anyone on board when the aircraft crashed? Was it a crash-landing?

When the news reached Wheelus Air Force base all of us who were involved in exploring the desert were itching for an opportunity to get to the site of the mystery bomber. However, it lay over a thousand miles away and my unit had a great deal of work to do at the time. So I had to content myself with listening as the story unfolded from the men of the 58th Air Rescue Squadron who by now were flying regular missions to 'Lady Be Good'.

The information provided by the oil men soon enabled the US Air Force to discover the history of this unfortunate plane. It was identified as being a member of the 376th Bomber Group, US Air Force, which had been based at Soluch in April 1943. This airstrip was some thirty miles south of Benghazi, and I had passed through it on several of our reconnaissance trips. Now in 1959 it was deserted but at one time, it had been a busy base on what was little more than burning red-brown desert packed hard and swept by the fierce *ghiblis*—a strong sandstorm which we knew only too well. It must have been a pretty uncomfortable place for the aircrews: they would return from their bombing missions across the Mediterranean to face disease, sand in everything they ate and drank, and the same broiling heat that we were now suffering.

The pilot for the Liberator's final raid had been First Lieutenant William J. Hatton, from New York. He and his crew had all come from the north-eastern states of the USA, and their home towns stretched from Massachusetts to New York, Pennsylvania, Ohio, Michigan and Illinois. The co-pilot was Second Lieutenant Robert F. Toner. Apparently he was a fatalistic man who did not believe too much in the future. The navigator was another Second Lieutenant, Hayes, who was also the shortest man in the crew, going bald and known to be the comedian of the team. The bombardier was Second Lieutenant John S. Woravka. The aircraft's flight engineer was Technical Sergeant Harold S. Ripslinger who, together with Staff Sergeant Guy E. Shelley, was the tallest member of the team. The other crew were radio operator Staff Sergeant Vernon L. Moore and the airgunners Staff Sergeants Samuel E. Adams and Robert La Motte. They had originally formed up for crew training in late 1942 at Topeka, Kansas, and from here had flown over the South Atlantic to arrive at Soluch on 27 March 1943. By the standards of the Second World War this crew were already old men; by 1943 most bomber crews were in their early twenties. Their arrival at the desert base of 376 Group was the start of an extraordinary run of ill fortune for Lieutenant Hatton and his men. Whether it was them or the plane in which they were to fly that had a jinx we shall never know, but for these young Yankee airmen it was to end in horror some seventeen days later, four hundred miles deep in the Libyan desert.

My friends at Wheelus discovered from Air Force records that when William Hatton arrived at Soluch his new unit, the 514th Squadron, was extremely short of serviceable aircraft. As a result the bomber that Hatton had flown over from the United States was passed to a veteran team and for nine days they waited around in the hell hole at Soluch and 'acclimatised'. However, on 4 April they got their chance to go into action at last. The crew of another Liberator, 'Lady Be Good', had been stranded in Malta when the engine on a spare plane they had been flying temporarily, had given trouble. Their own aircraft was still at Soluch being checked over, but now she was ready for action. Thus it was that Hatton's team found themselves boarding 'Lady Be Good' to take part in an unescorted high-altitude bombing mission that day. The target was set as the railway marshalling yards and port installations at Naples. There were to be twenty-five aircraft from Soluch on this particular operation. The plan was that they would be divided into two sections which would strike the target area at last light, then scatter and return to base singly to avoid enemy fighter planes. In Section A there were twelve aircraft while Section B, of which 'Lady Be Good' was a member, had, rather significantly, thirteen. As Section A roared off the desert strip they hurled back a whirling cloud of sand and dust into the waiting aircraft of Section B, whose air filters and engine air intakes received the full blast. This was to take its toll during the day as Section B suffered one casualty after another due to engine failure and in the end, seven of the thirteen B24s had to turn back. As they approached the target two of the remainder lost the formation when they were forced to dive to revive the waist gunners, whose oxygen masks had frozen at high altitude, causing them to black out. Now there were only four of the original Section B left.

As the section leader and deputy leader were amongst the casualties it was 'Lady Be Good' that moved up to the front position. However, they had never really caught up the time they had lost through their delayed take-off, and when they were still a few miles from the target the sun set. Section A had already dropped their bombs but Hatton found the ground deep in shadow which made the use of their Norden bomb sights impracticable. In view of Italy's impending decision to change sides, bomber crews had been given strict orders that they were not to risk unnecessary slaughter of civilians. B24 crews normally bombed in daylight and it was the opinion of the pilots that it was now too dark to risk bombing their target. Naples Harbour was just too near the densely inhabited city for safety and Hatton broke off the attack and headed south for base. On the way home the Liberators dropped their bombs on alternative military targets or simply jettisoned them into the sea.

The researchers found that of these four aircraft, one ran out of fuel but made it to Malta, another two returned safely to their base at Soluch and that left only one plane that could not be accounted for. This was 'Lady Be Good'.

The bombers were under strict orders that radio silence was to be maintained at all times except in an emergency. However, at 0012 hours, with fuel beginning to run low and no sign of the Libyan coast, Lieutenant Hatton decided to call Benghazi. 'Benina Tower from Six Four. Do you read?' 'Five by five. Over.' 'Request an inbound bearing. Over.' Whilst the pilot kept his transmitter switch pressed, the operator at Benghazi's Radio Direction Finding (RDF) station calculated 'Lady Be Good's' bearing and answered back. 'Six Four from Benina Tower. Your bearing from us is three three zero.' 'Roger three three zero. Out.'

A feeling of great relief must have swept through the young pilot for it seemed he was on course after all. Clearly, he thought, he must have been flying against a head wind and could not yet have reached the coast, so he accepted the bearing as it was given; 330 degrees which meant that he must continue to fly on his present course of 150 degrees (the reciprocal bearing) to reach home safely.

But 'Lady Be Good' never did come home. One fact had been tragically overlooked. In 1943 RDF stations were only equipped with a simple rotating antenna which, although it gave an accurate bearing of the aircraft from the station, could not tell whether the plane was approaching or flying away. William Hatton had asked for an inbound bearing and the RDF operator had assumed he was approaching from the north. But he could have just as easily been approaching from the south and the desert; or for that matter, flying away into the great sand sea to the south. In fact that was just what 'Lady Be Good' was doing. Had the pilot been dissatisfied with the bearing he could have got Sergeant La Motte to tune in their own Automatic Directional Finder on Benina.

Normally returning bomber crews would hope to spot the thin white line of breakers on the beach as they crossed the Libyan coastline. However, having flown over this many times at night in bad weather, I can understand just how they missed it. The coast was blacked out, it was a moonless night and the sand storms had left a haze which may well have helped to obscure this landmark. It is also thought that the *ghibli*, which had been with them all the way to their target, had also turned back with them and thus they had reached the North African coast ahead of the expected time. Somehow they also missed noticing the collapse of the needle in their radio compass as they passed over their base. We know that the pilot did try to call Benghazi again but by now the four powerful engines of the B24 had taken him out of range.

As they looked down for a sign of the coast they would now only have seen the gently undulating sand dunes of the desert. These can look very like the wave motion of a relatively calm Mediterranean.

Shortly before midnight on the ground at Soluch an over-flying B24 had been heard. However, there were many aircraft about and many airfields, and there was nothing that would necessarily identify this sound with 'Lady Be Good'. Another pilot in Section B had said on return that he thought that the leader at the target was number 64 and indeed if that had been the case, why should 'Lady Be Good' be coming back so late? Nobody paid a great deal of attention to this at the time and the USAF concluded eventually that Hatton and his ill-fated team had ditched in the Mediterranean.

At approximately 0130 hours 'Lady Be Good' would have passed clear of the rolling sand dunes and begun to fly above a vast flat plateau, more than a hundred miles long and another hundred miles wide and some three hundred miles south of their base. They were over the Serir of Calensio. They probably thought in the beginning that it was nothing more than a smooth stretch of water and that they could expect to reach land soon, but somewhere along this route the crew may well have realised, perhaps with relief and then dismay, that they were now flying deep into the desert. At this point their fuel would have been running dangerously low and as they circled lower and lower it seems that the pilot closed down the engines one by one, losing height gently and so eventually the fuel ran out. Shortly before this Hatton must have given the order to bale out. Second Lieutenant Toner and Sergeant Ripslinger carried small diaries and from these we were eventually able to glean much of the story.

For a few minutes the bomber flew onwards on its last engine, gradually sinking towards the desert. Finally, quite unaided it made a remarkable belly landing on the hard-packed sand, careering this way and that, before it finally slid round, broke its fuselage in half and stopped. No-one heard the crash of 'Lady Be Good' and her ill-fated crew had come down in one of the most desolate areas on this earth.

It is interesting to surmise that Hatton might have believed that they were still over the sea, but it seems likely that he knew they were now over the land. To parachute into the water at night does not give one a great chance of survival and they would have been far better to have remained with the bomber and try for a ditching on the water. This would have given them the use of their rubber dinghies and various emergency radios, water, rations and other survival equipment. So I feel that they probably realised they were over the desert. Had they only known it they were flying over one of the flattest, most featureless areas in the world which was ideally suited to a landing almost anywhere they might have chosen.

In 1959 the reports by the oil explorers had been digested and at Wheelus Air Base preparations were made for a thorough search for the crew of 'Lady Be Good'. So it was that on 11 May a party including two mortuary officers and an Air Force surgeon, plus an expert on desert survival, set out with C47 transport and an L19 light aircraft. It was now seven months since the oil company had first sighted the wreck, but the US Air Force search party found everything to be as the oil men's later ground party had described. They were amazed at the incredibly good state of preservation of the bomber.

Inside the fuselage they noted with interest that two items were missing: the life jackets and the hand-cranked emergency radio. They also noted that the B24's controls were not set on auto-pilot. During their short stay—they were only there for two days—their C47 transport suffered from a failure in its high-frequency radio but their technician discovered that 'Lady Be Good' was fitted with the same model so, with little choice, he removed it and installed it in the transport, and you can imagine his surprise when it worked perfectly. They knew then that radio failure was not the reason for the crash. They also found that the bomber's magnetic compasses and the radio compass were working perfectly.

The absence of any parachutes indicated that the crew must have baled out, but the question was, where? At this stage it was still a mystery as to why they'd baled out when the chances of an emergency landing were so good.

It was clear that a much larger-scale expedition was needed to solve the problem and so a party equipped with special desert vehicles, guides and eight expert navigators set off in July. They worked on the assumption that the crew had baled out to the north of the wreck site and so the search was concentrated in that direction. Eight miles from the bomber they came across tyre marks of Italian Army vehicles made during the war and heading north-north-west. It seemed likely that these tracks would have been there at the time when 'Lady Be Good' had crashed and it was therefore possible that the crew might have found these and attempted to follow them. The searchers only had to go another couple of miles along the tracks to find the answer. Here, squinting through their goggles, they spotted a pair of flying boots weighed down with stones. The toes pointed towards the north in a V shape. They wondered how many of the crew this single pair of boots represented and they could not tell whether the airmen were marching as a group or singly.

Moving on in the scorching midsummer temperature which climbs to over 130 degrees Fahrenheit at midday, they could imagine the sheer horror that had faced the luckless fliers. They guessed that they could not have survived for any length of time with the water that they must have carried when they baled out.

Next day the search party set out just after dawn and whilst it was still cool and found the first of eight markers; these were made from strips of parachute cloth arranged in a V pointing along the track. Clearly the crew had remembered its desert survival instructions. These successes elated the searchers and further down the track they came on six old life jackets. These were of the type that can be inflated with carbon dioxide cartridges. All cartridges had been used and this showed that 'Lady Be Good's' crew may have thought they were baling out over the sea or perhaps they inflated them to give added protection against the bitterly cold nights. The search team continued to find parachute cloth markers at regular intervals and felt sure they would discover the bodies quickly. However, 28 miles along this vehicle track they found a mass of British army vehicle tracks crossing those of the Italians. They came from the north-east and were probably part of the British force who in 1942 had converged with the Free French forces in an attack on the Italians at Kufra. However, the searchers were now in something of a quandary as to which track the survivors might have taken, but the next day they found another parachute silk marker a little distance up the Italian track. So they went on, finding another three markers in all. Then there was nothing so they simply spread out and searched a circular pattern. And it was during this sweep that they came across the eighth marker—surprisingly some way up the British track and pointing north-north-east. Did this mean that the crew had split up? All they found was the grisly remains of a desert nomad who had perished many years before with his five camels. Their mummified carcasses lay where they had fallen in the unforgiving sun. Under such arid conditions the moisture in the body evaporates quickly and as bacteria do not easily survive in this dry sterile region, human remains quickly become petrified.

From the few belongings of this lone traveller they deduced that he had died some time in the last century and it gave them a preview of what they might expect when they found Hatton and his men.

However, in spite of every effort and a costly three-month search that covered over 5,500 square miles of desert, nothing was found. The searchers gave up and the mystery remained. Where had those men gone?

In 1960, my squadron was again engaged in desert training and exercises and, like all units in this region, were asked to keep a sharp look out for any sign of human remains in the area where 'Lady Be Good' had crashed. However, on 11 February that year it was reported that the British Petroleum Company operating to the north of the wreck had found five skeletons. Immediately a C47 transport was dispatched from Wheelus Air Base and the US airmen were able to identify the final encampment of Hayes, Hatton, La Motte, Adams and Toner. They were lying together amongst the remains of their equipment, parachutes, clothing and their empty water bottles. The searchers found their silk escape maps which sadly did not even show the area where they had crashed. Had the maps continued for a further 120 miles to the south, they might have shown the survivors the Blockhouse Rock and the site of Kufra

Oasis, some 170 miles to the south. They found a sunglasses case with the name 'Dp Hayes' on it and this, of course, left no doubt to at least one of the crew's identity. However there was no sign of Moore, Shelley or Ripslinger. By far the most important discovery they made was Second Lieutenant Robert F. Toner's diary and from this they were able to learn what had happened from the moment the crew had baled out. Apparently, by using their distress flares and firing their pistols, eight of the crew had managed to join up by first light on 5 April 1943. Second Lieutenant John Woravka, though, was nowhere to be found. Although they searched for several hours, they had to assume that he had landed a very long way away. Of course, they had no knowledge of how far to the south the bomber might have crashed, but they presumed that it would have exploded on impact and the little that remained would not be of much value to them. They had no choice but to walk north towards the coast. The ill-fated crew could not be expected to know that their Liberator had made an amazing belly-landing all by herself some twenty-five miles away and that the survival equipment on board was in perfect condition. They had no idea that they were more than four hundred miles from Benghazi and were located in the centre of the most remote stretch of desert in North Africa. Ahead of them and to either side lay the rolling dunes of the Calensio Sand Sea through which it was impossible to march. Fifty miles to their rear was a range of rocky mountains that was just as difficult. In fact they were trapped and but for some outside help they would surely die. Had they been able to stay with their aircraft, the survival kit would only have prolonged the excruciatingly agonising death. Perhaps it was as well that they were not aware of the situation.

It seems that the survivors imagined that they were only fifty miles from the coast or, at the most, a hundred. Thus, early on 5 April they began to walk and at the same time they spread out in the hope that they might find John Woravka. They only had a single water bottle and a few rations plus their parachutes to give them some shade. These would also help to give them some warmth during the cold nights and they could make markers to aid searchers and trap water if, by some miracle, it rained. Of course, they would not realise that in this area of pure desert, dew does not fall and it had not rained for a very long time.

They limited themselves to a mere mouthful of water per day, measuring it out in the metal top of the water bottle. It would have been barely enough to wet the tongue. John Woravka had carried a second flask and this they were to miss dearly.

At first they pressed on in hope and a north-westerly wind cooled their faces as they tramped beneath the burning sun. All the time they watched the sky for the searching aircraft they believed must come soon. They felt the searchers would look for the wreck of the bomber and then try to pick up their tracks and so they stopped from time to time to lay out markers of stones and coloured these with strips of parachute silk.

The plateau that seemed so lifeless had in fact been crossed on a number of occasions by army vehicles. There was the Italian-made track which came up from Kufra heading for Benghazi. A British trail passed through the great sand sea from the El Zighen Oasis just over 120 miles to the south-west. As the searchers discovered 17 years later, these trails intersected near where the crew had parachuted down. They quickly came across the Italian track. It led to the north and after consulting their silk escape maps, they noticed that there were three desert trails leading in that direction. They therefore concluded that this must be one headed towards Benghazi. Of course, it never occurred to them that they were so far south that their maps did not even cover the area.

At night they wrapped themselves in their parachutes and tried to keep warm, but the temperatures plummeted to only a few degrees above freezing point. Huddled together, with chattering teeth, they could not sleep. In the end they decided it was best to walk by night, occasionally resting, but not sleeping. The next day the Italian track reached the British trail which headed to the north-east and would eventually take them to the oasis of Jagbub and Siwa. They had no idea how far help might be. Two of the men tried the new trail for a short distance but, finding nothing, rejoined their colleagues and they all continued on the main track which at least led in the direction of Soluch and Benghazi.

By now, the breeze that had spared them the heat of the previous day had died down and as the temperature soared, they began to suffer. Doubtless their survival training would have warned them of the effects of the intense desert sun on unprotected heads and eyes.

They all complained of their eyes, for few of them had any sunglasses and they attempted to shield them as best they could. The glare of the sun soon began to affect their retinas and as they sank into despair, they began to pray. They felt certain that help must be coming but there was still no sign of any searching aircraft. And yet, driven on by superhuman effort, they marched forward. They were still on one capful of water a day and half the water bottle had been drunk. Nevertheless, their desert survival training held good and as they advanced they laid out ground markers at regular intervals. The diaries began to talk of prayer every day.

It came as a happy surprise when they sighted dunes of the great sand sea and indeed, they may have thought that behind these lay the coast. However, sadly when they reached the sand hills, their plight increased. The track had disappeared, wiped clean by the ever-shifting sands. Staggering on, often knee deep in the fine sand, it is amazing that they were able to march as they did. For already they had walked for about a hundred miles on almost no water. Their bodies racked with pain, they plodded forward. Sergeant La Motte had almost lost his sight and he moved slowly, hardly seeing the way ahead. They were now all terribly weak, for it is doubtful that they had any food, and both Adams and Moore kept lagging behind. There must have been something very special about these men because they kept together and crawled painfully northward. By now they had no strength left to leave markers for the searchers to follow but they still prayed fervently for rescue.

On 9 April only three of them could go on. Guy Shelley, and his friend, Ripslinger, were the giants of the team and Vernon Moore had somehow raised an inner strength to continue, but the rest were too exhausted to move and sought no more than to be left to die in the sand. Speaking in croaking whispers they held a conference and it was decided that the three men who could still march should try to reach the coast. The water bottle was left with the five who could not move and anyway, there was hardly any water left in it. At first light the five in the sand said farewell to the three marchers who set off once again into a cool breeze. The day was every bit as bad as the previous one and the bitter cold of the night was now more noticeable because only one parachute remained to cover their bodies. All the others had been torn up for markers or simply left behind when the carriers became exhausted. The next day the five prayed again and again; watched the sky for searching aircraft and wondered how their three colleagues were getting on. The sight of a pair of migrating birds gave them momentary hope but by now they hardly had the strength to stand up. In that terrible furnace they prayed for death and that night, they drank almost the last drop of water. The next day they moistened their tongues with the last of the precious liquid and looking at each other, realised that they were already virtually skeletons.

Robert Toner still managed to write his daily few words in the diary. But eventually his strength gave out on Monday, 12 April. It was eight days after they had parachuted into this living hell, but Toner still hoped for rescue. He wrote briefly of the intense cold of the night and it was probably this that killed them, as opposed to the searing heat of the day.

In 1960 the five skeletons had been found by the geologists, lying in the sand dunes as if they had collapsed whilst trying to reach the top of the next dune. Toner's entry for 9 April had said, 'Shelley, Rip, Moore separate and try to go for help, rest of us all very weak, eyes bad. Not any travel, all want to die, still very little water, nites are about 35°, good N wind, no shelter, 1 parachute left.'

So it was years later that the US Air Force continued the search to the north, but once again in spite of a well-organised attempt they failed to find any evidence of the missing men. Nor for that matter had they found any sign of John Woravka. As they were about to call off operations the British Petroleum geologists were again lucky and found Ripslinger and Shelley, incredibly, 21 and 27 miles respectively from the five skeletons that they had originally discovered. Shelley had actually managed to cover ninety miles from the point at which he had parachuted into the desert! Ripslinger's diary was also with him and against Palm Sunday it read . . . 'Palm Sun. Still struggling to get out of the dune to find water.' This was his final entry. How these men had achieved such a feat was beyond our comprehension as we sat back discussing it in our Mess on the coast. It seemed clear that under such conditions of adversity they must have drawn upon some extraordinary source of power and endurance.

To the best of my knowledge, Vernon Moore's body was never

found, although some day, when one of those great dunes moves on, it may well be revealed.

If only they had known where they were and their escape maps had covered that area, one may imagine that all eight men, and especially Shelley and Ripslinger, could have reached water by marching in a south-westerly direction. Indeed it is likely that they might have come across their bomber on the way, with its life-giving supply of water, which was still found to be drinkable seventeen years later. Only one mystery remained, and that was the whereabouts of Second Lieutenant Woravka. Eventually he too was found by another group from the British Petroleum Company who were working in the area of 'Lady Be Good'. The skeleton was discovered twelve miles north-east, fully dressed and wrapped in his parachute harness. Apparently the parachute had not functioned properly and as a result he had died on impact. His water bottle was three-quarters full and it was still drinkable. Perhaps he had been the luckiest of them all. So the remains were flown back to the United States for burial and the scientists and technicians moved in on 'Lady Be Good's' wreckage. Everyone was anxious to see how the oils, fabrics, ammunition, and fittings of this luckless bomber had withstood seventeen years in the Sahara. In 1968 the RAF El Adem Desert Rescue Team recovered an engine from the B24 for examination by the McDonnell-Douglas Aircraft Corporation. When they had stripped it down they discovered a piece of 20mm cannon shell inside one of the rocker boxes. This indicated that 'Lady Be Good' had been attacked in the air during her mission.

The march by the survivors is not the longest across a desert on record and in fact Trooper Moore, who had set out from the Gebel Sherif with his colleagues, had covered 210 miles in ten days. Nevertheless it was an amazing achievement, and the epic struggle of 'Lady Be Good's' survivors remains one of the most tragic stories of the desert war.

The tale has a strange twist to it, because if ever an aircraft had reason to be branded as jinxed, that was the 'Lady Be Good'. Behind her she left a terrible trail of disaster. Before she joined them, the 376th Bomber Group had been going from success to success. However, when this particular Liberator arrived they aborted their first mission and finished up with only three of the thirteen planes to start out. Her crew were all to die in the most terrible circumstances in the Sahara. Eighteen days later Lieutenant Swarner, one of the pilots of Section B on that fateful attack, was dead, and two months afterwards, Lieutenant Worley and his entire crew were missing. They were never seen again.

In August 1943 the 376th was leading a raid of 175 aircraft on the Ploesti Oilfield. This became the most disastrous single American air-raid of the Second World War. The first plane to take off crashed almost immediately in the Mediterranean killing everyone aboard. Another twelve became casualties due to a number of mechanical faults, and never reached their target. No fewer than 41 of the Liberators were lost over the target area and a further thirteen more on their way back to base. Some 440 airmen were killed or listed as missing. But the jinx on 'Lady Be Good' did not stop there. The radio that was installed in the Wheelus Air Base C47 was still aboard a month afterwards when the transport was caught by a severe *ghibli* and had to ditch in the sea. The propeller broke off on striking the water, sliced through the cockpit and killed the pilot. A US Army Otter light aircraft also visited the crash site of 'Lady Be Good'. Some of its crew took the Lady's armrests as a souvenir and fitted them in their own aircraft. Eight months later this Otter, carrying ten passengers, struck another *ghibli* and disappeared. There were no survivors, but amongst the wreckage that drifted on to the North African coast were the armrests. I was also told of a helicopter that had been fitted with one of the bomber's fire extinguishers, and this had crashed in flames. Some of the mystery still remains. Where was the bomber's emergency radio transmitter? Who was it who placed the parachute marker pointing north-east on the British trail? And where is Sergeant Moore? Perhaps we shall never know, but I for one will never forget the mystery of 'Lady Be Good'.

However I did solve one curious desert mystery. We'd been clearing war-time mines near Tobruk and as the day ended one of our number, a large taciturn Lancashire sapper, had strolled out into the sand dunes to relieve himself. He headed off towards a huge war-time rubbish dump that lay dark and sinister in the moonlight. The piles of rusty equipment assumed strange shapes at night and the previous day we'd found a couple of nasty little sand vipers sheltering from the blistering heat beneath some old corrugated iron. 'Watch out for the snakes,' we yelled after him as his bulky figure disappeared.

A chill breeze blew through our camp, sending fine powdery sand into the brew of tea that was just coming to the boil on the petrol stove. Above us a carpet of twinkling stars stretched from one horizon to the other. Sitting with my back against the warm rubber of the Land-Rover wheel, I shivered and reached over for the heavy wool pullover on my bed roll. It was half way over my head when I heard running feet and peered out to see the sapper racing towards us as fast as his legs would carry him. 'What's up?' grunted Harry, my driver. 'Bloody snakes get you then?'

'There's summat over there,' gasped the runner—clearly terrified.

'What do you mean?' I asked.

'T'dump's moving,' he replied with a wild-eyed look. After he'd had a swig or two of warm, sweet tea he calmed down and told us that whilst quietly squatting in the dump he'd seen things coming at him over the desert. As he jumped to his feet he realised they were old tin cans. Apparently they'd advanced, retreated, circled and all the time made a gentle rattling sound. 'How many beers you had, Prescott?' asked the beady-eyed Troop Sergeant.

'Only one—honest, Sarge,' replied Prescott.

'It's probably the wind blowing the cans about,' I advised—but he'd have none of it. 'Weren't no wind blowing when they started coming, sir.' So warily I pulled on my Chukka boots and slipped my shotgun out of its battered canvas case, fed in a couple of rounds of SG and strolled over to the dump.

The twisted metal threw curious shadows in the bright moonlight and the occasional puff of wind rattled the odd strand of barbed wire—but nothing moved. Back in camp I put Prescott's mind to rest and made a mental note to give him an administrative job next day, as a change from mine lifting. However, a week later I heard a similar tale from Arabs who alleged the spirits of dead soldiers moved old food cans around at night.

I'd quite forgotten about the strange case of the haunted tin cans until I found myself in a most difficult situation a few years later. It was 1961 and we were on an expedition near Kufra oasis. We'd been held up awaiting spares for a broken-down truck. At last they arrived and we all turned for home and a big party in Benghazi.

'Do you mind if I go on ahead?' I asked the expedition leader.

'No, by all means,' said Bob in his usual cheerful tone.

'I'll keep to the main track and come up on the radio schedules as usual,' I assured him. So saying, I set off in my well-laden Land-Rover with Sapper Smart at the wheel and Lance Corporal Smith as navigator. We made good time and by lunch had cleared one hundred and thirty miles. Hisss! went our nearside front tyre. 'Oh, hell!' said Smart, as we pulled to a halt.

'I'll get the spare down,' I said and unbuckling the reserve, rolled it towards the punctured tyre. Smart was standing silent and grim. 'Well,' I said, 'let's get on with it.'

Our driver was looking very dejected as he uttered the awful words, 'Sir, I lent my box spanner to Higgins last night.'

It took several seconds for the full meaning of this statement to become clear. The desert Land-Rovers were fitted with a special type of hub to which a rope could be attached and thus provide the vehicle with a simple capstan. However, with these hubs fitted, it required a long box spanner to undo the wheel nuts. Now, without the necessary box spanners, we could not change the wheel.

'There must be another way,' I protested. We turned out every item of kit, but there was no way we could unscrew even one nut. To attempt to drive on with the flat tyre would have been virtually useless as we'd have sunk deep into the soft sand patches. We were stranded, not so far from 'Lady Be Good'.

'Got about three gallons left,' said Lance Corporal Smith and I knew he was talking about water. 'Plus the water bottles,' I added, trying not to sound too concerned.

Silently and avoiding unnecessary activity, we laid out the fluorescent air identification panels in the form of the emergency signal, prepared the flares, made a shelter projecting from the side of the Land-Rover and crawled beneath it. Our radio was not working terribly well and therefore it was no surprise when we failed to make contact at dusk. After the scorching heat of the day, the blissful cool of the night was a welcome relief. I began to think of Hatton and his airmen.

After the first flush of panic, I had wanted to call Smart every name under the sun. However, eight hours later my anger had subsided and I concentrated on trying to evolve a plan that would save us. We had broken down on the edge of the mile-wide track and it was quite possible that the convoy would find us. But they only had to be five hundred yards eastward and they would pass behind a low ridge, missing us completely.

We drifted into an uneasy sleep as night fell. Lying in the open grave I had dug in the sand, I awoke suddenly to hear a rattling metallic noise nearby. There was no wind, and when my eyes peered out across the desert bathed in moonlight, I could see nothing. That's strange, I thought, and there it was again. Instinctively I drew my Walther pistol from my pack and, thus armed, prepared to meet whatever it was making the noise. Raising myself on my elbows, I scanned the moonlit sand. From behind a low hillock, one of our discarded tin cans rolled into view. It was rolling over and over as if being pushed by a strong wind, but the night was still and there was certainly nothing visible pushing it. As I pondered this, the can suddenly stopped and then rolled back the way it had come. Must be going mad, I thought. Then it changed direction and came towards me.

'My God, a haunted tin can!' I remembered the incident at Tobruk, but before I had time to think, the shining object advanced and now it was only ten feet away, rolling this way and that. I raised my pistol. The sharp crack rang out in the still air, the bullet threw up a spurt of sand a couple of inches from the can, which instantly accelerated away as if it had been frightened off. I fired again. The can stopped rolling and, to my amazement, a desert rat hopped out—clearly annoyed at having his feast disturbed. We all burst out laughing almost hysterically. 'Well, that's one mystery solved,' I thought, but I wondered if I'd ever get out to record it.

At daylight, I rose stiffly from the sandy bed. The radio still remained silent and although I went through all the drills a dozen times, I could get nothing; altering the setting of the skywave aerial didn't help either. However, just in case others could hear us, I sent an SOS signal giving our position. The sun was well above the horizon when I gave up fiddling with the knobs.

'What shall we have for breakfast?' asked Smith.

'I don't mind,' I replied, 'but let's have it quickly before the heat hits us.'

92

Lying under the shelter I made a mental check of our emergency actions. Flares ready, ears alert for noise of aircraft or vehicles, air identification panels out. Remaining water, now down to two and a half gallons, carefully stowed in the shade. All other sources of liquid checked, we lay in silence, the beads of sweat grew on our filthy skin and turned into rivulets which ran into the sand. God, how we smelt! On the move we had not noticed it, but now it was becoming unpleasant to be near anyone else. Somehow one's own odour was bearable, almost fascinating, but anyone else's was disgusting. Sleep was impossible, so I tried to read, but a voice in my head kept saying, 'There must be a way out.' Rather like shipwrecked sailors on a raft, I mused. It's the waiting that is the worst.

Then an idea struck me. If we could catch some desert rats, we might live a little longer on the liquid their bodies contained. I began to consider ways of doing this.

'Water, sir?' said Smart, handing me a plastic mug of luke-warm fluid. 'What precious stuff this is,' said Smith. 'We always take it for granted in Blighty—just turn on the bloody tap and there it is.'

At noon the sun was right overhead, and to reassure ourselves we took a fix with the bubble sextant. It simply confirmed that we were about 120 miles south of the coast. The nearest water was 75 miles away. We discussed walking out, but we realized this was hopeless. Stay with your vehicle, was the great cry and we all knew the story of 'Lady Be Good'. I doubted if we could equal their feat.

Smart was looking very sorry for himself. After all, it was his fault we were in this predicament. But then I was the one who had asked if we could go on ahead and alone. Corporal Smith was truly without any blame and looked the most cheerful of us all. We delayed lunch until mid-afternoon to avoid working in the full heat.

'These boiled sweets certainly help to lessen the thirst,' I remarked, but already my tongue felt like leather. Smart passed another, and I began to remove the paper. We all heard it together, like a distant rumble of thunder, but with a note that rose and fell. I sat up, straining my ears and searching the horizon.

'Three-tonners,' yelled Smart. 'It's the convoy, I knew they'd find us.'

In a few seconds the flares were streaking upward. I still couldn't see the trucks, but the noise of their engines was quite clear. They must be just the other side of the ridge. An awful feeling gripped me—would they miss us? Corporal Smith was already tearing towards the ridge, his pounding feet throwing up the sand, when I heard another engine and spinning round, saw a pale yellow Land-Rover bearing down on us. The goggle-clad face grinned.

'Having a spot of bother?' Bob enquired.

We all learned a lesson. There must be many deaths kinder than dying of thirst.

4

The Mysterious Gorge

Sinister canyons, through which no white man had sailed.

The mile-deep gorge that cuts through the highlands of Ethiopia is the home of the infamous Blue Nile; here this great natural feature forces its way through the mountain fastness and leads the river to spill out into the sun-soaked plains of the Sudan. Until 1968 it remained virtually unexplored, although the actual source is a spring that bubbles up in a bog south of Lake Tana and is not difficult to reach. Following our successful earlier expedition in Ethiopia, Emperor Haile Selassie had suggested that I explore his Blue Nile. His Imperial Majesty had plenty of reasons for wanting to fill in the blanks on the map of his domains—security was no doubt one of them. I accepted his challenge and began seeking what information I could about this unknown tract of the Blue Nile.

From my research I learned that the first Briton to view this spring was the adventurer James Bruce. Visiting Ethiopia in 1771 he wrote of 'people who anointed themselves not with bear's grease of pomatum, but with the blood of cows, who instead of playing tunes upon them, wore the entrails of animals as ornaments and who, instead of eating hog meat, licked their lips over bleeding living flesh'. For my part, whilst seeking an elusive swamp rat, I had tramped many miles on a previous expedition and been eaten alive by mosquitoes in this region.

The stream that runs from this spring becomes the Little Abbai, which it is said flows through Lake Tana and becomes the Great Abbai or Blue Nile near the town of Bahar Dar.

For its first eighteen miles after Lake Tana, the Blue Nile is wide and shallow, flowing through swampy water-meadows and around numerous islands. But there are long stretches of dangerous white water and several small waterfalls.

At Tississat the river suddenly drops with a thunderous booming over the second-biggest falls in Africa. There, the huge volume of water is compressed into the narrow sheer-sided gorge, and for almost a hundred miles the torrent races through this cleft before the valley opens out. However, the river is still at the bottom of a great gutter in the Ethiopian Highlands and 10,000 feet above it towers the cloud-swathed Mount Chokai. From here on, the river alternates between rocky cataracts, dangerous shallows and stretches of flat water populated by hippo and large aggressive crocodiles.

As far as I could tell the first attempt at navigation was made in 1902 by an American big-game hunter with three specially designed steel boats. However, after only three miles these were swamped in a cataract and the expedition abandoned. In 1905, a Swede called Jesson came upstream from the Sudan. He could only get his boats to the Azir River where he met hostile natives and marched back to the Sudan. Later he reported that it would have been suicidal to attempt to force a passage in steel boats over the rocks and rapids.

In 1926, Major R. E. Cheeseman, the British Consul in north-west Ethiopia, tried to follow the course of the river on foot. His survey work was invaluable, but due to great difficulty experienced in moving along the banks of the gorge, he was soon forced up onto the high plateau (see his book, *Lake Tana and the Blue Nile*, 1968).

In 1955, Herbert Rittlinger and his wife, Aveckle, and a small party of German friends attempted to canoe down the river. They had with them a number of ladies who, by all accounts, were rather attractive. However, crocodiles are no respecters of persons. Their canoes were attacked and the party driven from the river.

One of the best-organised expeditions, I discovered, was mounted in 1962 by the Canoe Club of Geneva. Six tough, experienced canoeists set out in two large Canadian-style boats. They started, as have many expeditions, from the Blue Nile bridge at Shafartak and after a great effort they reached a point near the Sudan border. There they camped on an island and whilst asleep were attacked by bandits. In the fight two died but the rest escaped in one canoe.

The next attempt was by Arne Rubin who became the first man to travel along the Blue Nile from Shafartak bridge to Rosiares. During our research, we corresponded with this plucky Swede, who in 1965

9. Caledonia Bay. Giant inflatable diving platform *David Gestetner* over the site of the *Olive Branch* wreck. Fort St. Andrews in the background.

10. Sand Sea of Calensio, Libyan desert. The author's Land-Rover.

11. (*above*) 'Lady Be Good',
U.S. Air Force B24 Liberato
found wrecked in the Sahara
sixteen years after it crashed.
12. (*left*) 'Lady Be Good'. C
of the five skeletons of aircr
found in the sand dunes.

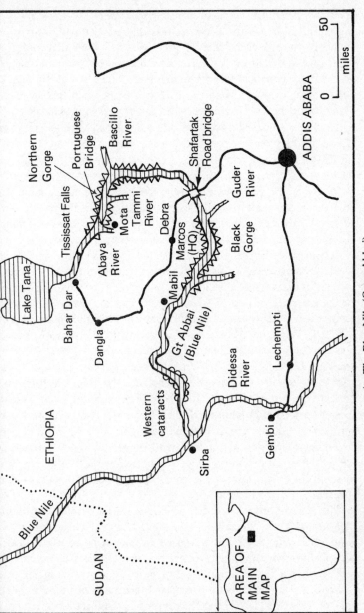

4. The Blue Nile (Great Abbai).

had navigated this stretch in a Kleeper canoe, alone! It was a splendid achievement. The next year, he returned with a friend to attempt the upper reaches of the river, but after fifty miles of hair-raising adventure their canoe was smashed to bits on jagged rocks in the Northern Gorge and they were forced to walk out. There were other expeditions and in March 1968, a small British team, attempting the river in rubber boats, came to grief in a short distance after the bottoms had been torn off their craft and Ethiopian police had forbidden them to proceed. It was a salutary warning to us and, studying the reports of the disaster, I realised that if one was to navigate this river it must be done when there was plenty of water.

None of the previous explorers had been able to examine the banks or carry out any scientific research, so we hoped that our expedition would not only be adventurous, but would be of value both to science and to the people of the region.

There was surprisingly little reliable local knowledge, but on an early reconnaissance visit to Ethiopia, I met numerous 'experts', who told me some of the elements of mystery that surrounded this fearsome river. There was said to be a great swamp alive with crocodiles—'Crocodilicus Niliticos', the most terrible man-eater of all Africa! Had not the Queen of Sheba sought the advice of Solomon because of the depredations of a monster croc? And it was a fact that an Austrian gentleman had recently been seized by one of these powerful reptiles and dragged down into the Nile, bleeding and screaming, under the eyes of his wife. The crocodiles were said to reach 10 metres in length, but this I considered an exaggeration. However, if there were such giants, where did they hide? Where was the legendary swamp, infested with mosquitoes and leviathans? Much of the river was unmapped, but the towering cliffs that rose steeply on either side of the gorge did not seem to indicate the presence of a large marsh.

There were many, including white men, who told tales of radio-active gas. They claimed the intense sun heated the black basalt, so much that radio-active vapours oozed out and, being heavier than air, dropped to the bottom of the canyon. There the gas was thought to collect in pockets, bringing a slow death to every living thing it touched. Dead animals were reported to have been found in such places. However, if the Blue Nile Gorge had radio-active gas, it must have radio-active minerals. Were there great deposits of uranium awaiting discovery?

Geologists told of extensive lakes being formed when landslides of rock, loosened by erosion and earthquake, crashed into the river, forming instant dams and creating waterfalls over which a frightening volume of water cascaded, making it totally unnavigable. Yet if valuable minerals were present in the gorge, it would be extremely useful if mining companies could use the river as a road. Doubtless this thought had occurred to the Emperor when he asked us to explore his Blue Nile. I wondered how frequently these avalanches occurred.

Apparently wildlife was plentiful and dangerous. There were rumours of huge leopards, and the lions, Ethiopia's national beast, were said to be the biggest in the world. Herds of buffalo and elephant were reported to abound to such an extent that the Ethiopian Wildlife Department was eager to see if there really was a mysterious untouched Nature Reserve.

Snakes were another hazard. One species, a small grey viper, was thought to be present, in millions! The little reptiles were said to attack humans (very unusual)—the bite, a neuro-toxin, brought immediate paralysis and a painful death. Local hunters advised that we should wear strong breeches and high leather boots whilst smearing our legs with an ointment of dubbin and tar! I had come across an island in a swamp near Laka Tana in 1964 on which we'd captured several dozen little grey snakes, so perhaps there was something to this tale.

Giant pythons were said to abound in the Northern Gorge and an earlier explorer had apparently grabbed one by the tail in error whilst following a path beneath the Tississat Falls.

As our research into the nature of the mysterious gorge continued, the number of intriguing rumours grew. The legend of the Queen of Sheba popped up all the time. It was said that following the 1914–18 war, an ex-Royal Engineers officer had discovered an amazing cave system full of gems that could only be reached by overcoming a forceful underground river. The Ethiopians are well known for carving churches and dwellings from solid rock and one tale told of a 'lost' tribe of white people living in a subterranean town—somewhere in the gorge. There were also rumours of ape men who attacked travellers.

My friends at the British Museum (Natural History) reckoned the hippo might be more dangerous. 'Give them a wide berth, my boy,' cautioned one scientist.

'How far away should we be?' I asked.

'Oh! about a quarter of a mile,' he suggested. As the river is rarely more than 150 yards wide in its upper reaches, this would not be easy. 'And avoid them in the mating season,' my friend said, but he wasn't too sure when that would be, and added that he'd be grateful for any information on the sex lives of the Blue Nile hippo.

The water was said to be full of the dreaded Bilharzia which the river carried down from Lake Tana, but some experts were unsure if it really did exist in the turbulent waters of the river, and we were asked to investigate.

Everyone talked of the Blue Nile Gorge as the home of the most murderous bandits in all Ethiopia and several travellers reported hearing spine-chilling voices and even screams echoing about within the walls during darkness.

Rumours of alluvial gold and great deposits of copper all added to the reputation of the area and I wondered why the Ethiopian police had made such an effort to prevent a small British expedition from entering the Northern Gorge. All this only served to heighten my curiosity. 'There must be something there,' I said to myself.

Accurate information on river conditions was not readily available. But as up to 80 inches of rain falls annually in the mountains, mainly in the summer, I expected the Nile would be in flood in August and the level beginning to drop in September. On the plateau at this time the rain would be heavy and vehicle tracks extremely difficult to say the least. At the higher altitude the temperature would be around 60°F at midday, but down on the gorge bottom it would rise to at least 80°F. We could expect nights in the mountains to be extremely cold, but the great advantage of attempting a navigation at this time was that the high water should cover the dangerous rocks.

Chris Bonington, the British mountaineer, who was to accompany us as photo-journalist on behalf of the *Telegraph Sunday Magazine*, described the area as 'the last unconquered hell on earth'. This caused some mirth at the time, but we were later to discover that it was not so much of an exaggeration after all.

To organise a scientific investigation of the area presented me with something of a dilemma. It would cost a great deal of money to get the scientists into the difficult region, enable them to work, keep them alive and get them and their specimens out again in one piece. It would also mean sending a lot of people there just to back them up and see that they got the assistance they needed. To get the money, the resources and the necessary backing for the project we had to catch the imagination of the Army, the Press and Industry. At the same time, I would have to recruit servicemen and civilians who would understand the needs of the scientists, and their idiosyncrasies and demands.

But most important of all, I realised the whole team would have to consist of people who were as compatible as I could assemble, for undoubtedly we were going to be under very great stress and there was no certainty that the expedition would fare any better than the many that had preceded it.

My first recruit was Richard Snailham, a civilian lecturer at Sandhurst. I knew him well from a previous expedition and found him one of the most amusing and likeable men I had met. It was Richard who was to become the Chief Nilographer, reading up everything he could find about the area and helping to write the various prospectuses and begging letters that we had to put out to gain sponsorship and support. He would also write the official history of the expedition (*The Blue Nile Revealed*, Chatto & Windus) and act as Treasurer.

My second-in-command was to be Nigel Sale, of the Royal Green Jackets. I had known him for some years and believed that this thorough, slightly serious, and efficient officer was just the sort of chap I needed to balance my own character.

One of the most important people would be the Chief Engineer. Here we required, not a fresh-faced, Sandhurst-trained subaltern with bags of enthusiasm, but an experienced, bold and imaginative engineer who would be prepared to tackle any obstacle with the minimum of resources and manpower. For this post I selected Jim Masters, a quiet forty-year-old officer from Somerset whom I knew I could depend on at all times. We had served together in Cyprus and I respected his depth of experience and expert knowledge.

To organise and lead the White Water Team, I chose Roger

Chapman, an instructor at Sandhurst. Roger, a Captain in the Green Howards, was a likeable muscular officer who possessed boundless vitality and dogged determination. It was he who would have the unenviable task of navigating the most difficult stretches.

In total the team would consist of seventy servicemen and civilians from Britain and Ethiopia and the scientists were to include an archaeologist, an ornithologist, a veterinary surgeon, the medical officers and a host of zoologists. I was simply the conductor of a large, highly motivated orchestra. Now we had to start playing.

My plan was to set up a base on the plateau at Debra Marcos roughly at the centre point of the expedition area and with the gorge running on three sides. From here we could radiate outwards, attempting to navigate the river first from Shafartak to Sirba, when the water level was at the highest. On that phase we should use Army alloy assault boats powered by 40-hp Johnson outboards.

For the second part of the expedition we needed boats that would stand up to the tumbling white water in the narrow gorges at the head of the river. Arne Rubin told me he believed that only inflatable craft could survive these terrible rapids. So I planned to navigate the head of the river with special Avon rubber boats.

Re-supply would be by small overland parties dragging mules through the mud on the high plateau, before descending into the baking hot gorge. More supplies would arrive by parachute from an Army Beaver aircraft.

Some of the Army members were to be from the Royal Military College of Science at Shrivenham, where we planned the project. Here lived our patron, Major General Napier Crookenden. The General was the energetic and fiery Commandant of the College, and his active support was to prove especially valuable.

Shrivenham was an ideal place to launch an expedition. Judith and I moved into a tumbledown camp nearby, took over a host of buildings and, together with the amusing Lance Corporal Henry of the Royal Engineers who had volunteered to accompany me, we made up the expedition headquarters. The excellent scientific and technical facilities at the College were of great value. A computer was used in design problems and the Fluids Laboratory staff kindly reproduced a simulated section of the river, complete with an adjustable cataract. Here we could create various wave formations and test different types of model boats. One day I came to see how the experiments were progressing.

'Splendidly, splendidly!' enthused the white-coated assistant. 'There is only one problem.'

'What's that?' I asked.

'The cataract works perfectly and the boat goes down the centre, but it always turns over!'

Months of training and preparation now followed. Every spare moment was taken up by the expedition and the thankless task of raising £15,000 in cash, which was needed in addition to the items the Army and sponsors could supply. We tested boats on the wild rivers and the sandy areas of Aldershot, we trained with Army pack horses. Boats were selected, boats were rejected, boats were modified and finally, with days to go, boats were packed. Under the eagle eye of the quartermaster, a mass of stores was prepared in an old hangar at the camp.

In March, 1968, I was able to visit the river and carry out an air reconnaissance. Flying in a small single-engine plane, I went the length of the lower gorges. It was certainly impressive. We were seeing it in the dry season, and although we found no large swamps, I observed whole regiments of crocodiles rushing into the water as the aircraft roared overhead. There did not appear to be any obstacles in the river itself that we could not overcome in the wet season although there'd be some challenging rapids. However, weather did not permit an air reconnaissance of the unknown Northern Gorge.

By the end of July we had completed our preparations. Then, at the eleventh hour, I had an accident that almost knocked me out of the expedition. During the boat training in Wales, I fell heavily onto my right knee. Within a day it was swollen, excruciatingly painful and I could hardly walk. 'Rest it for a month and then start taking gentle exercise,' said the doctor. I acquired a stout walking-stick and a supply of crêpe bandages and prayed hard.

We flew into Addis Ababa on 31 July. Our advance party had come out a few days earlier to pave the way. Considerable help was forthcoming from the United States Army Mapping Mission and various Ethiopian Government Departments. We were able to move our personnel and stores to Debra Marcos on 2 August. Here we set up the base in pouring rain. Flying ahead of the main column, I went forward with our cheerful chief pilot, Major Alan Calder, in the Beaver. We reached the grassy airstrip above the town at the same time as a tropical squall. High winds and rain clouds were sweeping across the flat green landscape as Alan fought with the controls and tried to land. Six times he made his approach and six times pulled away again at the last minute. Fuel was beginning to run low and there was not enough to get us back to Addis Ababa. 'Here we go!' he yelled through the intercom as we went in for the seventh time. Ahead, strolling slowly across the strip, a herd of white cows appeared. Alan swore and the next moment we were over the top of the cattle by a hair's breadth and with a bump, our wheels hit the ground.

At once, we felt the full force of the crosswind swing the Beaver from one side of the strip to the other. Fortunately, there was nothing in the way and we taxied to a halt. The true violence of the storm was now apparent for as we tried to open the doors, they were almost wrenched off in our hands. At the other end of the airfield sat a silver and red Ethiopian Army helicopter, rocking in the heavy gusts. Climbing out to meet our allies, I ran across in the torrential downpour. Huddled inside the chopper were half a dozen soldiers, with bandaged heads and limbs. The pilot, a young Amhara in a bright orange flying-suit, grinned and slid open a small panel of perspex. 'Good morning,' I shouted above the noise of the wind. 'Hi,' he replied, with an American accent, 'Who are you?' I explained that we were a British Army expedition, come to examine the Blue Nile Gorge. 'Gee, I thought you were reinforcements,' he added. 'Say, don't you guys know there's a war going on?' He pointed to the wounded soldiers whom he was about to evacuate when the storm abated. I had heard that there was some minor internal problem in the province of Gojjam, but I had not been informed of the serious nature of the conflict. It seemed that the people of the region had risen up with one accord against what they considered the dastardly imposition of something called Income Tax. Clearly, we had some sympathy with the rebels. But in protest they had turned to slaughtering the Tax Collectors and now the Army were trying to sort out the rebels. We had landed in the middle of a small civil war.

As soon as the rest of the party arrived, I went down to visit my old friend the Governor. I had last seen him four years ago in his mud-walled palace in the town. On arrival at his offices I noticed how very few people were around. There was not even a guard on the main gate. Walking up to his office I found the door open and to my surprise saw a Corporal of Police seated at the Governor's desk smoking a cigar. I greeted him and he looked up equally surprised and said in halting English, 'Good morning.'

'Where's the Governor?' I enquired.

'He's gone,' said the Corporal, 'and I go too.' He hastened to explain to me that the town was soon to be attacked by some 3,000 well-armed rebels who were out for the Governor's blood and, indeed, that of anyone connected with the Administration.

'Well, before you go,' I asked him, 'will you be so kind as to let me have some letters that I can send out to the various chiefs to grant us assistance and passage through their tribal areas?'

'Ah yes,' he said, 'I have these here—the Governor left them,' and to my astonishment produced a sheaf of letters which he proceeded to stamp with the official rubber stamp. Messengers were sent for and each one was handed a letter for an appropriate Chief. Bowing their way out from the Corporal's presence they made off at high speed towards the great river. I was given more letters of authority and assured that all would be well.

Back at camp, I explained to the bewildered expedition that we were in a very hostile area and that the town was likely to be surrounded by a large number of armed tribesmen, hell-bent on blood, who would undoubtedly sack it and having done so, might turn their attentions to us. 'Ah well,' said the quartermaster, 'we'll build a *zoriba*, that'll keep them out.' The *zoriba*, all of two feet high, was made of thorns, and I noted with interest that even the small boys who plagued our camp, had no difficulty in hopping over it. The effect was undoubtedly intended to be psychological.

The final preparations and air reconnaissance took a few days and then we moved down the Nile. Obstacles had been photographed with polaroid cameras and I used these pictures at the various briefings. Mules and donkeys for the re-supply teams had been made available as a result of the Governor's letters, stores were packed, the aircraft flying schedule was detailed and all was made ready. The die was cast.

The plan was that the scientists and their immediate supporters should move along the river in boats. Another group under my second-in-command, Nigel Sale, was to march to the river from the south, through the Didessa Basin and carry out a game survey en route. Because of the river conditions necessary for safe passage, the first part of the expedition would be from the great bridge at Shafartak to the Missionary Air Strip 275 miles downstream at Sirba. Having successfully completed this phase the teams were to be re-organised to explore the river from Lake Tana back to the original starting-point at Shafartak. At the outset the river was too low and I knew that we must wait until the water level had risen. However, on 7 August, two of us in four assault boats started on the voyage to Sirba.

For three weeks we battled through the cataracts of the mighty river, stopping at selected points for scientific investigation. Specimens were taken out of the gorge by mule parties, who likened their journey to the ascent of a never-ending ladder in a Turkish bath. Rising for almost a mile, the steep, trackless slopes were covered in loose rocks, concealed by elephant grass up to twelve feet high. Midday temperatures could soar to around 90°F and the humidity could go to 85 per cent. At night we shivered as the damp air cooled to around 60°F. On many mornings, low cloud hung in the gorge blocking out the warming sunlight.

The cataracts were certainly pretty challenging and we found places where enormous chunks of rock, weighing thousands of tons, had crashed down into the gorge, but there were no waterfalls.

Between the cataracts were large pools of water, laden with brown sediment. The Nile was anything but blue in the wet season. Welcome swimming breaks cooled our perspiring bodies, but armed sentries kept a careful watch for crocodiles. Although they were large, they never exceeded 18 feet and only displayed aggression on one occasion when a basking croc shattered a few teeth on the bow of an assault boat that almost ran it down. Beaches littered with mica and 'fool's gold' caused momentary excitement, but we found no caves full of gems. The tribesmen were generally friendly and even a couple of bandits who we found spying on us turned out to be amicable.

It happened at the first camp made at the junction with the Guder

River and whilst our scientists ranged about their demi-paradise on the sides of the gorge we met our first locals. Two tall upright bronzed men stalked one of our patrols for several hours until our men, tiring of the game, reversed the process and herded them down to our camp. Attired in old Italian Army tunics festooned with accoutrements of leather worn over faded loin cloths, they spoke no English. On their right shoulder they carried a blanket and in their left hand a thin five-foot staff. On the other shoulder was slung a heavy Russian rifle (circa 1898), almost certainly captured at the battle of Adowa. Their hair was anointed with rancid butter which smelt revolting.

Taken off guard, I couldn't think of anything suitable to say to a couple of apparently amicable bandits. So I offered them a Mars bar. They eyed it suspiciously, as a pair of black carrion crows might examine an unusual but possibly tasty morsel in an English field. I urged them to eat and eventually one of them shot out a long scrawny hand and grasped the confectionery. He sniffed it without expression and handed it to his comrade who did the same. They looked at each other and then eyeing me, nodded their approval before handing the bar back again. I broke it in half and gave them a piece each, at the same time eating some myself. They tasted it with care and then nodded again. So I gave them the rest of the bar. At this point, the doctor arrived and seeing him carrying his medical kit one of the bandits said, 'Cannunie.' 'I think they want quinine,' said the Doc, 'but I'll give them some paludrine tablets.'

In the middle of the interview Lieutenant Telahoun Mekonnen, our liaison officer from the Ethiopian Navy, came in from a reconnaissance up river. Immaculately dressed in his uniform he stepped ashore and, sighting our visitors, his jaw dropped noticeably. 'I must speak to you,' he whispered and leading me to one side explained that it was his painful duty to shoot these men immediately. Could I lend him my gun as his own pistol had not yet arrived from Naval Headquarters. I felt sorry that we should need to despatch our two visitors so soon as it was quite possible we would learn much about the mysterious river and the flora from these two wanderers in this lost world. Telahoun insisted that he should shoot them and one of our police guides urged him to take off their ears to return as evidence to Addis Ababa. But in the end I prevailed on him to spare us the embarrassment of an incident so early in the expedition. The two policemen who had accompanied us from the bridge looked positively terrified by our visitors and I noticed that the swarthy bandits regarded our other Ethiopian friends with nothing short of contempt and scorn. Anyway it was time to sail so I took the opportunity of shaking them both by the hand and giving them some old plastic bags. They bowed politely and, thanking me in Amharic, strode back up the slope—smiling and clutching the gifts.

We scoured the precipitous sides of the canyon, but detected no smell of any gas, radio active or otherwise. However, the zoologists made many important discoveries, but although we saw no giant leopard or lions, we heard these cats giving tongue at night. As far as any lost tribes were concerned, all the rumours pointed to the Northern Gorge. However, we did come across a strange cult of hyena worshippers.

While my second in command, Nigel Sale, had been marching in with a survey party through the undulating Didessa valley, they had come upon a man badly wounded in a shooting accident. Apparently he and his friends had been out hunting jackal near their village. The wounded man had shot a jackal but at the same moment a friend's gun had gone off and drilled him through both thighs and the scrotum. He was in a bad way and Nigel did what he could for the poor fellow, but the villagers would not permit the white men to carry him into the shelter of one of their huts. They believed that he had been shot because the bullet fired by him at the jackal had later been thrown back by magic. The Senior Medical Officer flew to the scene in the Beaver and, unable to land, circled overhead for some time giving instructions to Nigel by radio. Next day they had to leave the man and later heard with some sadness that he had died shortly afterwards.

There are many interesting tribal stories about the mysterious cult of the hyena and perhaps one day I can go further west into the Dabus region in search of some of these tribes.

My plans for the second and most difficult phase of the expedition were already made when I flew out of Sirba. It was only a matter of time for the various group leaders to reorganise and re-equip themselves before we tackled the northern portion of the river. Perhaps the answers to many of the Blue Nile's mysteries lay in those unmapped vertical-sided canyons which no white man had seen.

The second phase of the expedition was the descent from Lake Tana to Shafartak. The first fifty miles were obstructed by raging white water cataracts and the river party would move in special inflatables. We were all novices at this game, learning as we went. Looking back on those days it is interesting that all our river-exploring techniques developed from that expedition.

While we made our preparations the archaeological team made an exciting discovery. On the southern shore of Lake Tana they found a small fortress which defended a peninsula from the main land. The moat, ramparts, and gate house were soon revealed from beneath the tangled growth that had gradually crept over them in the passing years. It had undoubtedly been constructed at about the time of the Portuguese arrival in Ethiopia in the 15th century. But the inhabitants had long died—there was no lost tribe here.

Meanwhile, the white-water team under Roger Chapman was anxious to get started on its journey into the Northern Gorge. They had quickly formed a small corps d'élite of nine men in three boats and I gave them as much rein as possible because I knew that they would need all their initiative in the task that lay ahead. In *Faith* Roger had with him Alastair Newman, a nuclear physicist with a thirst for action, and Peter O'Mahony, a tough soldier. Jim Masters, respected by all, commanded *Hope* with John Fletcher, a most skilled engineer, and John Huckstep, another experienced soldier. Then came *Charity* with Chris Bonington, there to record the journey for the *Telegraph Sunday Magazine*, and Chris Edwards and Ian Macleod, both competent, practical soldiers. It was a formidable group.

Flying over their route, Alan Calder reported that there were many more crocodiles than we had expected. They were lying in the relatively still water between rapids, some of them seemed to be 'huge', and therefore we decided that Captain John Wilsey, a tall, cheerful officer in the Devon and Dorsets, should take an assault boat and come upstream from the Blue Nile bridge to meet us somewhere near the junction with the Bascillo River. This metal craft should be able to withstand attack by a crocodile. He could then escort us in his alloy boat through the most heavily infested area.

The way ahead of the Avons was foaming white water for many miles, where outboard engines would be virtually useless, but the first day they found fairly easy and exhilarating. However, by that afternoon they had met the full force of the cataracts and realised that with only paddles, they were powerless to do more than keep the boat's bow head-on to the waves. The fury of this untamed river was more powerful than even the leader, Roger Chapman, had imagined and very soon the team was battered, bruised and often half drowned. To make life more difficult, there were parts of the river where it widened out and flowed through hundreds of channels. The problem was to know which one to take. The edge of the river was a swamp with no firm ground for some distance and this meant that setting up camp for the night was a long and laborious business.

While the team continued downstream, I flew to the hill-top shanty town of Mota and prepared a new group to meet them at an old Portuguese bridge that carried the trade route from west to east, deep in the sinister Northern Gorge. This bridge had been built in the 15th century, its two arches spanning the river and three increasingly smaller ones on each side. The white-water boat crews had more than their fair share of thrills and spills and I discovered some of them, far from being stimulated, were becoming very frightened. Dividing themselves into hawks and doves, some wanted to go on, others to pull back and they argued amongst themselves nonsensically. All I could do was to make one or two unpopular decisions and try to help them sort themselves out. Having done this, they then pressed on with much more caution towards the great falls at Tississat where the boats were roped over.

Once over the falls, the boats were in the Northern Gorge where the cataracts became even more dangerous and I sent Nigel on ahead to run the re-supply groups who were now stationed along the lip of the gorge ready to give help when needed. It was soon found that the big problem was that the boats could not stop and therefore they needed early warning to pull into the bank before a cataract. Then, if there was sufficient water, they would ride it down, but if the rocks showed up they had to portage the boat round the side, a laborious and difficult task especially in the bottom of this vertical-sided chasm.

Leaving the town in the cool of early morning we went down into the gorge, a long straggling column of mules and men taking with us fresh boats, engines, stores, weapons, ammunition and everything else we needed for the final part of this epic exploration.

The last few kilometres of the descent were an interesting example of how mules can be used successfully in this terrain. The path was barely wide enough for a man to walk and yet these sturdy beasts carried on with their heavy loads. Suddenly we came to the edge of a cliff and saw a narrow little path plunging down to the river. Going to the edge, I could see beneath me the rickety structure of the old bridge. The central stone arch had been replaced with local timber and as I watched, a small herd of cows was driven across. Some masonry tumbled away into the swirling brown water. I was amazed that it had stood so long. There was something eerie about the gorge at this point. It was damp, dark and silent, except for the swish of the river racing under the bridge. We had been forced to come here because it was the only place for many miles where there was a track that led down to the Nile and a bridge across it, however rickety.

All we had to do now was to set up camp, await the arrival of the white-water team and then form up the new group to proceed into the most interesting area of all.

Each evening the radio brought news of the various sections of our widespread expedition and I knew that Roger Chapman's boys were only a few miles away. I could tell from their tone that they were very tired and many were suffering from infected bites and cuts. It would be a relief to have them back with me as I felt that one or two, lacking imagination, were allowing their courage to lead to rashness. The tiresome reconnaissances that had to be made at each bend were taking their toll of the men's patience and it would not be long before a boat's crew decided to 'bash on regardless' into what might be a fatal cataract.

However at the old bridge we had plenty of problems to occupy our time. The tribesmen clearly resented our presence and each day grew more insistent that we should leave. Stores were in short supply and money was running out. I was more than a little worried about the rains, for if they stopped early, the river would dry up rapidly and maroon us. Time was not on our side.

Some of the men had persistent sores and the expedition was showing signs of general nervous strain. We had also learned the limitations of life jackets in these turbulent waters. Whilst working a simple flying ferry across the torrent, I was swept overboard and came close to being drowned. 'Our luck seems to be running out,' muttered one of my friends round the fire that night.

It was early in the morning and the sun had not yet reached into the gorge.

'Ian's dead,' said Roger Chapman, leader of the white-water team. Strangely the words did not surprise me. 'Swept away, nothing we could do.'

All around me the group gathered to hear the terrible news. I took Roger aside and we sat quietly on a great, black basalt slab in the shade of the high cliffs, while he told me the story. He spoke in a low voice, his tanned, muscular body glistening with sweat; he had run most of the way to bring me the news, when he found he could not get through on the radio.

The story was simple. It was late on the previous day when the battered and exhausted members of his team had reached the Abaya Gorge. Here the mountain torrent carves a thousand-foot-deep gash in the highlands and cascades down a tortuous rock-strewn path to join the Blue Nile near the ancient bridge.

The white-water team had been the nine toughest and most experienced men I could assemble to tackle the worst cataracts of the upper river. Their three specially constructed Avon Redshank inflatable boats were aptly named *Faith*, *Hope* and *Charity*.

For weeks they had struggled with the mighty river and at last, in the Northern Gorge, they had come upon a stretch of rapids too fearsome for even these stalwarts. On my orders they had let the boats go through the raging water unmanned, to be collected by my own group a short distance downstream, at the crumbling, old bridge. The towering, vertical sides of the gorge had forced them to march west to find a path that would take them to my position. Alas, this narrow route had led across a tributary to the Blue Nile—the Abaya. Now it was a racing brown torrent, swollen by the rains, cascading over black eroded rocks, swirling and eddying with an ominous hiss.

Thus in the late afternoon they had started to cross. Alastair Newman, known for his nerves of steel and lack of emotion, had been the first in and taking a great leap had swum with fast, powerful strokes to the far side. He carried with him a line of red climbing rope and clambering out onto the rock ledge on the far bank, called out for another man to cross and assist him. It did not look difficult and they were anxious to cross before dark. After all, they knew that I was only a few miles ahead with fresh men, new boats, rations and supplies.

Corporal Ian Macleod of the Black Watch and SAS volunteered to go next. I had known Ian from years before when I had taught him to swim underwater in the sheltered coves of Cyprus. He was a wiry and popular Glaswegian, who was one of our toughest and most resourceful members. As well as being a thoroughly professional soldier, he had a scholarly air and was an accomplished linguist. Ian was a man who spoke no ill of any other and a man of whom no-one spoke ill. Lately he had not been well, following a narrow escape and bad battering in the rapids near Tississat, a week earlier. However, apart from a bandaged knee, he showed no sign of his ailments. It was typical of this rugged Scot that he would always volunteer for the dirtiest job. With a rope lashed securely to his waist, he lowered himself into the rushing water and struck out for the far shore, only some forty feet away. On the warm rocks his colleagues rested their aching limbs and waited for the ropeway to be completed.

At first all went well, but suddenly as Ian was about to reach the bank the rope went taut and he disappeared beneath the surface. Seconds later he bobbed up. His friends, aghast and realising his plight, gave more slack to enable him to reach the far side, but almost at once the line went taut again. The rope was being carried downstream by the speeding current, or perhaps a submerged tree had struck it and was dragging it along the river bed. Whatever the cause, Ian was drowning, being pulled under by the length of rope that he had used as a life-line. On the bank they tried to pay out more line praying he could reach the far bank. For a moment it seemed as if he had made it, but then the river washed over him and he disappeared, still struggling for his life.

Roger Chapman was already ripping off his clothes and equipment, someone hurled a semi-inflated life jacket to Ian, it missed and floated away tossing in the turbulent waves. Others, realising that he desperately needed just a few feet more of slack line, yelled, 'Cut the rope'. A jacknife was tossed across the river to Alastair who stood next to the end of the rope and he began to saw through the tough fibres. Roger dived in and reached Ian, forcing the drowning Corporal above the surface. Still the rope anchored them against the jetting current. Then it parted and at once the two men spun downstream through the tossing brown waves of the cataract. Roger, fighting with all his massive strength to gain a grip on the bank, could be seen struggling as he was swept along beside the polished, ebony boulders, his one arm, muscles bulging, crooked around Ian. Dashing along the bank, the men leapt from rock to rock trying to keep pace. Now Roger had an arm around a finger of rock and was trying to pull Ian from the water. But the current pounded them relentlessly and Ian was unconscious. Ahead was a small waterfall, only a ten-foot drop, but with abundant rocks at its base; everyone knew survival chances would not be high if they were swept over this obstacle. Roger's face was red and contorted with effort, Ian's ashen and grey. At this point the vertical sides of the gorge reached almost to the water's edge and the would-be rescuers were having great difficulty in reaching the men. On the bank where Roger was holding on, there was only Alastair and he was moving as fast as humanly possible. On the other side, the rest of the team stood impotently unable to assist.

Suddenly Ian's limp body was seized by some unseen force and he was dragged relentlessly downward from Roger's desperate grip. In a second he had gone. Once his head bobbed above the surface, but after that he disappeared over the waterfall and was never seen again.

On the bank the exhausted men summoned every last ounce of energy and raced down the narrowing, boulder-strewn ledge, desperately hoping to catch a glimpse of Ian and be able to reach him. It was all in vain. The ledge soon ended and they were forced up the side of the gorge. Ahead they could see the river disappearing into a black abyss, into which the water tumbled with a terrible roar.

Chris Bonington, his voice broken with emotion, said, 'We can't get any further, he's gone.' Gulping in the warm humid air, his weary companions nodded agreement and all turned back. As darkness fell, they rigged up an aerial ropeway and crossed to spend a damp, cold night huddled amongst the rocks. Their minds and bodies had reached a point of exhaustion, which sleep would barely alleviate. To make matters worse, the deep canyon prevented radio contact with the rest of the expedition. Roger knew I was only about five miles ahead, but he also knew that we were virtually captives of the local tribesmen. To the dispirited white-water men, it seemed that the bottom had fallen out of their world. Any hope of continuing the expedition seemed out of the question—indeed some even wondered if they would survive.

This was the story Roger told me. I found myself issuing the orders for an emergency helicopter search. I seemed to do it almost mechanically and after a moment, realised that my mind was running on two tracks at once. One of the signals officers was already calling base and our intelligence officer was asking me short, sharp questions, to which I gave automatic answers, which must have been subconsciously thought out minutes or perhaps days before. The other part of my mind was saying, 'Poor Ian, a search is hopeless.' I remembered my own desperate struggle in the grip of the river when I had been swept overboard only the previous morning. There were the fearsome crocodiles to consider, and I expected the tribesmen to shoot up any helicopter that was seen hovering over their territory. I finished giving orders and stood deep in thought, looking at the milk-chocolate-coloured water racing under the old bridge. How many disasters had this awful place seen, I wondered.

'Would you like some of my special porridge, Surr?' a deep Wiltshire voice asked. It was Corporal Michael Henry, our general factotum/chief clerk/expedition joker. I thanked him, taking the smoke-blackened, warm mess-tin and the unwashed spoon he offered. In his simple way, Henry realised something must be done to bring us back to reality and he had cooked up a great dish of burnt porridge! The other members of the white-water team came in during the morning, physically shattered and despondent. The Beaver was overhead by mid-morning and searched the river bed and the Abaya Gorge. Alan Calder called me on the radio and said quite simply that he could see nothing.

In the early afternoon an American Army sergeant landed a small helicopter on a broad ledge above our camp. This caused a great stir amongst the locals, but we were extremely glad to see him; leaving his crewman at our camp, the American sergeant flew me up and down the gorge, travelling as slowly as possible so that I could scan the innocuous-looking water and the rocky banks for any sign of Ian. Once something did catch my eye. It was a football bladder, obviously released from a wrecked Redshank, whose tubes were filled with such bladders as a safety measure. It could only have escaped if the tube had been torn open and this could only have been done by a crocodile. There were several huge log-like reptiles sleeping on the sandbanks.

Turning up the Abaya Gorge, we saw the terrible conditions into which Ian had disappeared and there, still camped on the ledge, were Alastair and Garth. They waved slowly, as if to say, 'It's no good, you're wasting your time.' We made a final sweep of the immediate area and with fuel running low, turned for Mota. As we rose out of the chasm the engine gave an unhealthy cough, rather a worrying noise in a helicopter. We dropped a few feet and I noticed that the sergeant had started to sweat profusely, although it was quite cool in the aircraft. We were too low for safety, only a hundred feet above the ground that was now rising rapidly to meet us. The engine coughed again and the pilot grunted something unintelligible over the intercom. By his actions I gathered we were going to land. Skilfully he brought us in on a small patch of grass beside a low bluff, and whilst the rotors continued to thrash around, he sprang out and began to tinker with the motor. Apparently he was soon satisfied with his efforts for he climbed in again, grinned and gave a thumbs-up sign. We took off and flew up to Mota without incident.

On the bumpy little airfield outside the tin-roofed town that nestled amongst the eucalyptus trees, I saw a twin-engined Otter aeroplane. This was also from the US Army and had carried the fuel for the helicopter up from Addis and thus enabled the search to be carried out.

Time was precious if I wanted another flight before dark, so as soon as the chopper was re-fuelled, we flew down to the gorge again, dropping over the lip of the plateau as if it were the edge of a coral reef, into the abyss beneath. More crocodiles were in evidence but most alarming was the apparent increase in the number of tribesmen gathering about our camp at the bridge. All were well armed and waved their rifles excitedly. Was this the vanguard of the force of three thousand rebels that local chiefs had assured us would attack unless we moved away quickly? I had dismissed this as gross exaggeration and simply thought it to be a threat to get us to leave their area. I'd been sure that they wanted to be rid of the responsibility for us, because whilst we remained in their territory, by tradition we were in their charge. Now I was not so sure and I began to wonder how long forty of us with sporting rifles, shot guns and revolvers could hold out in the exposed bed of the gorge against an attack by so many rebels. Nigel Sale and his party, with one injured man, were still out in the Abaya region, making their way to the bridge. I realised that the problem of searching for Ian was rapidly being overtaken by a far more desperate situation involving the safety of the whole expedition.

The river was running too high for comfort and I did not want to sail on until it had dropped another two feet. We only had enough boats to take ten men and their equipment. Many of the survivors of the white-water team were injured or sick and quite unfit to proceed by river. Ahead of us lay the worst crocodile-infested stretch yet and I wanted John Wilsey to reach the Bascillo River Junction with his relief force before I set out to study the one part of the Blue Nile which was unmapped, unexplored and unknown. It would be a difficult enough stretch of water without interference from the rebels and as we had our last look for Ian, I felt I was sitting on a gunpowder keg with the fuse burning shorter each second.

By the time we landed on the ledge above the camp, my plan was made. Get the walking wounded, sick and other persons up to Mota as quickly as possible. Gavin Pike, a tough young cavalry captain, who had been with me on two previous trips in Ethiopia, would take these men out; I prayed the rebels would let them pass. Nine of our fittest would sail on with me to survey the last stretch and meet John Wilsey at the rendezvous, if he ever got there. I would tell Nigel by radio to make for Mota direct and not come to our camp. All I needed was about four hours to organise this. As I clambered out onto the short grass I noticed two young warriors with their rifles unslung and pointing vaguely in my direction. Trying to appear quite unconcerned, I thanked the sergeant pilot for his help and said just loud enough for him to hear, 'I think we've got trouble here, I'll get your crewman up but keep your engine running.' A precipitous goat track, a foot or so wide, led down the cliff face to the camp. One of the warriors followed me down. I knew his rifle was aimed at the small of my back. Mesfin, our Ethiopian Government liaison officer, came to me and whispered quickly, 'I cannot do anything more with them.' In camp everyone looked worried and watched with drawn faces. The tribesmen were clearly in a truculent mood.

When in doubt, confuse the enemy! 'Good,' I said, 'Thank you, Mesfin, please tell the chief I have been to Mota and I bear important news for all the tribe, but first I must prepare some notes, then I will come and tell them all about it.' Hoping the interpretation of this white lie and the ensuing questions would keep the warriors busy for a few minutes, I seized the confused American crewman. 'You've got problems, Captain,' he said. 'Yes, but with luck you can get out as soon as I start speaking to the tribesmen. Go to the Chief of Police at Mota and get him to come here as fast as possible and sort out these old gentlemen and their people. You are our only hope, so do all you can. Also, please tell my headquarters what is happening.' With that I turned and replacing my beret with my pith helmet, I strolled over to the stone bridge and whilst Mesfin interpreted, gave a long harangue about Ian's death, the search, our scientific work, the medical aid I had brought from Mota for the treatment of all ills and how grateful we were to the tribesmen for looking after us. I threw in the names of Haile Selassie, Churchill and Wingate occasionally for good measure and I was still speaking when the helicopter lifted off the ledge and soared back towards Mota. My audience barely seemed to notice; it was not part of their problem.

To endorse the speech, I announced that there would be a sick parade in ten minutes for the tribesmen. Then, grabbing Ian Macleod's medical kit, I told Corporal Henry to gather together all the spare pills and potions he could find. Together we set up a clinic on the bridge.

The queue of evil-smelling patients stretched fifty yards. They jostled for places and minor punch-ups took place between the warriors to get to the head of the queue. Our meagre medical resources were totally inadequate for anything more than token treatment. Our proper medical officer was himself sick at base and Ian, who had been our best medical orderly, was dead. Treating the tropical sores and eye diseases as best we could, we gave out aspirins for tummy aches and Corporal Henry's remedy for the numerous malingerers was a Horlicks tablet sellotaped to the body over the allegedly painful area. In the case of a particularly unpleasant brave, Henry administered two dozen laxative tablets with a drink of water. He then told the young warrior to run home as fast as possible, lie down and await results! We never saw him again!

As night fell we held a simple memorial service for Ian. Many a tear rolled down a tanned face. We had lost a good friend. I then gave the orders for the next day. Gavin would take out the overland column. Nigel had already been diverted. I would lead the new 'P' group, as it was to be called, down river, to investigate the last unexplored part of the gorge and eventually meet John Wilsey. We would take most of the guns and ammunition from the others. I had a feeling our need might be greater. However, everything depended on the tribesmen letting us go. But I had sent out word to the muleteers of Mota to bring their beasts to the bridge in the morning of the following day.

At darkness the chiefs and most of their followers retired to the top of the gorge and fortunately there was so much preparation to carry out, that our minds were fully occupied until sleep took over.

Once during the night our sentries woke me; a noise had been heard twice on the track above the camp, but the early-warning necklace of stone-filled cans strung across the path had not rattled. Probably a hyena.

The misty dawn was cold and damp and with it the tribesmen returned. Hardly had the sun reached into the gorge when we heard the sound of a helicopter. The Police Chief of Mota, Captain Mulena Alamu, strode into view, smartly dressed in a freshly laundered uniform, peaked cap, shiny boots, black Sam Browne and bearing a .30 carbine and revolver. He walked amongst the chiefs, smiling and greeting them; a diminutive figure, confident and authoritative, just like his Emperor. Crossing the bridge, he spoke with Begemir Province chiefs, who had remained on their own side. Then he made copious notes in a large official book. In no time, this efficient law officer had sorted out the problem with commendable tact and diplomacy.

I had spoken to him through Mesfin and as he left, I followed up the cliff path to the waiting helicopter. Glancing around to make sure he could not be overheard, he said to me in perfect English, 'It is all right for you to continue, but keep your guns handy and a good watch at night.'

'Where did you learn English?' I said in genuine surprise.

'England,' he hissed and climbing into the chopper shouted a good-bye and was gone.

At the bridge we remained under guard. However, following the visit of the gallant captain, we were treated with a new respect and there was no more talk of our leaving nor, for that matter, remaining prisoners.

Miraculously the mules had arrived on time and the overland party was soon shouting farewell as it started up the steep ascent to the high plateau. It did not have an easy journey; ambush parties greeted it throughout the route and at each stop, there was much argument and discussion before it was allowed to pass. The entire province was in a state of turmoil and the rebels were said to be marching on Mota.

Back on the river, we prepared to sail next day. The Beaver made an air drop of supplies at 1515 hours, but many of the items that were free-dropped fell onto rocks and were badly damaged. With foresight, the packers at base camp had placed the whisky inside new socks, so at least we were able to wring out the remains of a few precious drops! Circling above, Alan told me of more tribesmen massing in the mountains around the gorge and said the Beaver had been fired on. We really were in a boiling cauldron and I wondered if our overland party would reach Mota.

However, my first problem was to overcome the fears and anxieties of the team. They had all taken quite a pounding and some seemed apprehensive about the conditions ahead. Reconnaissance by air does not always give a true picture of river conditions and we had been lulled into a false sense of confidence several times. I knew we could easily manage the conditions ahead, but the team needed a lot of persuading. They had not seen the Army reconnaissance boats in rough water and of the six sent from Britain, only two had been found fit for use. Nevertheless, I had no doubt that these craft would manage the conditions I had seen during my air reconnaissance.

It was 21 September. The temperature at 0800 hours was 74°F and during the night we had suffered a moderately heavy rainstorm. We awoke cold and wet on our rocky beds. My knee, injured during the pre-expedition training, was stiff and the pain under my arm pits told me that the poison from infected rope burns on my hands was spreading. Somehow the antibiotics had ceased to work and anyway, we had only a few left.

Our guards were still with us, having spent an equally wretched night wrapped in their voluminous *shammas*. As I dipped the blunt razor into a mess tin of warm water, a white and black fish eagle pitched its yodelling call into the canyon of the Blue Nile. The river hissed and bubbled as it swept on its way. Our sentries, sensing our imminent departure, shuffled nearer like optimistic vultures, hoping for gifts of surplus food or equipment.

Now the team was packing up and was soon ready to move. My helmsman was Sub-Lieutenant Joe Ruston, RN. Joe, a rugged, likeable person, was an engineer as well as being a champion skier. His quick wit and good humour made him an ideal companion under arduous conditions. He and I were to scout ahead in *Semper* and warn the two engineless Redshank inflatables of forthcoming hazards. An ingenious mechanical engineer, John Fletcher, our outboard engine expert, was helming the second reconnaissance boat, *Ubique*, and with him was our crocodile expert, a young zoologist named Colin Chapman. *Ubique* would bring up the tail of the little fleet.

The reconnaissance boats were both equipped with 9½-hp motors and could hold against the current; this enabled them to manoeuvre more easily than the Redshanks. Even so, they were not as strongly constructed. But if anything went wrong, the reconnaissance boats would come to the rescue; or, if we were attacked by crocodiles, they had the heavier weapons necessary for defence. Colin was certain that the crocodiles would not attack, but I remembered he had said there were none north of Tississat and one had strolled into our camp above the falls!

Roger was the white-water expert, so I asked him to brief us all on the tactics. He did this with his usual attention to detail and at 1030 hours we cast off. The river gave us an exciting ride and at times, I judged it prudent to bring the fleet into the bank and rope past a particularly difficult cataract. We shot through most rapids in grand style! Hitting big waves, we were drenched to the skin, but the old reconnaissance boats did remarkably well and we soon became very confident in them.

From the banks antelope stared and birds rose in dismay as we flashed by. The crocodiles were well hidden for we saw none during the first part of the journey. Perhaps the engine noise drove them to shelter in the murky depths.

High on the hills white-robed figures yelled their shrill cries, as they announced us from mountain top to mountain top. At water level the black basalt was so polished that it looked like marble. Making notes in my log I recorded that the river varied in width from around thirty to fifty yards, and in the rapids was moving as fast as nine knots.

The Redshanks paddled on steadily, and it quickly became apparent how useful the powered boats were in escorting, guiding and towing the paddled craft. In the early part of the day we negotiated twelve rough patches and occasionally had to resort to our roping technique.

We were able to inspect a place where Major Cheeseman believed the river had changed course. There was every sign that this happened, but as the water level was sixty feet below the old bed, it must have happened long ago. In fact Cheeseman's original map was correct, but the copies and reproductions showed the river in the earlier course. However, we updated the map and passed on, looking all the time for evidence of minerals and people.

As we journeyed on into the most fantastic vertical-sided gorges, the water was moving like a stream of liquid brown mud, hissing between the cliffs. These sheer walls which rose from the water for some hundred to two hundred feet appeared to be limestone capped with lava. Towards late afternoon we reached some vertical pillars of rock standing in mid-river. This gave me an exact position, as I recognised them from the air reconnaissance. I felt instinctively that if we were to find out what minerals, tribes, animals and archae-ological remains lay in the Northern Gorge, it would be in these sinister canyons, through which I knew no white man had sailed.

Suddenly we caught sight of a roughly built dwelling, perched high on the cliff on the western or Gojjam bank. This was a niche in the rock, closed off by a stone wall. A doorway in the wall had a timber door frame. Was this evidence of a lost tribe? Waving our Ethiopian flag, I signalled the other boats to pull in to the shore. Stumbling along the rock-strewn beach, we tried to find a route up, but then Joe called out, 'Hey, there's a man up there.' On the cliff top a lone figure stood watching us intently. He did not return my greeting, but regarded us in sullen silence. Then, without warning, he became agitated, shouting and waving us away. This I thought unusual as Ethiopians are most punctilious about returning greetings. However, it could be that he lived alone in the dwelling and thought us to be raiders, although I doubt if few bands of robbers would bother to fly the Imperial Ethiopian flag! But tax collectors might! So after a short inspection, we sailed on in our rock trench, our voices echoing unnaturally and for some way we were completely enclosed in the massive slot. The sun only penetrated for a few hours each day and it was cool, almost cold, at water-level.

A sharp bark to our left surprised us and there was an extraordinary sight. Scampering amongst the rocks was a party of hideous old men clad in grey fur coats. Or that was what they looked like! 'Hamadryas baboons,' called out Colin. The boats slowed, cameras clicked, the baboons screamed with rage and one quite deliberately threw a small stone, then we were past them. They really did look human. 'My God,' I thought, 'so those are the mysterious ape men!' It was easy to see how a legend of a lost tribe could be based on a colony of Hamadryas, living in crevices on these remote cliffs. I was still making notes when Joe said, 'Look at those caves, surely they're man-made?'

On our right were two large openings, situated in the rock face about thirty feet above the water. At the same time, a small cove containing a stream and some low trees appeared on the left. According to my navigation it was probably the Tammi River. 'Pull in to the beach!' I yelled. The caves were too interesting to miss and it was a good time to stop anyway.

The camp site was the most pleasant we had found so far. The stream had cut a narrow gorge, which ran back some fifty yards behind the beach. The little river formed a beautiful waterfall as it entered the cleft, spurting out from the terrace above and sending clouds of spray to gather rainbows in the last rays of sunlight. The water in the stream was clear and slightly warm. Lichen, moss and ferns grew out from the cliff in profusion. Beneath the stunted, twisted trees was a plentiful supply of firewood and a clear area in which to erect our *bashas*.

Across the Nile the mouths of the two large caves gaped at us, one semi-circular, the other triangular. The entrances were partly blocked by a well-built wall of rough stones that was certainly man-made. There was no evidence of any inhabitants and as I studied them with my binoculars that evening, I wondered how we could gain access. There was an overhang immediately above the caves and the only possibility seemed to be to ascend from the river bed. It was obviously a job for our rock climbers.

While supper was cooking, Garth and David our 'military zoologists' went on a lizard hunt. John Fletcher repaired the transom on his boat, which had been damaged during the day. Chris and Roger discussed a plan for getting into the caves on the morrow. Richard Snailham filled several more pages of his notebook. Joe Ruston was working on the engines. Alastair, Colin and I cooked up an awful mess of sardines and rice. After supper I strolled up the narrow canyon, behind our camp and there, whilst trying to clean up my festering fingers, I made another discovery. As I was jumping across the stream, something green caught my eye. I stopped and looked back. The bed was littered with bright green rocks. 'Copper,' I said aloud. Sure enough the stream bed contained many lumps of copper oxide, apparently carried over the waterfall at the end of the canyon. Picking out a few specimens I resolved to return next morning to seek the source.

It got dark quickly, but in spite of our exertions, spirits were too high to sleep and we talked for several hours. It had been a good day. After weeks of painfully slow progress, we had covered seventeen miles in five hours and conquered the worst of the rapids below the Portuguese bridge. From now on we should have a relatively easy voyage, although there might be the odd sporting stretch of water to keep us on our toes and of course, there were always the ubiquitous crocodiles!

Our camp seemed safe from interference, as it would be almost impossible to approach it undetected, but there was the usual risk of a crocodile coming up from the river and chewing a boat. With luck we had left the political problem at the bridge well behind us.

I stood guard from 2200 hours until midnight, spending the time writing up my log by the light of a guttering candle. The night was quiet, warm and dry. I had much to write about and ponder. Were the caves in fact entrances to tunnels leading to an extensive subterranean settlement? Did the Hamadryas baboons live there? How could we get in? Once inside—would the baboons attack us? Was the presence of the copper significant? Perhaps the caves were mine shafts. I felt a great surge of excitement sweeping through me—after all these months we seemed on the verge of a great discovery. No other white men had been here which explained the lack of knowledge of the region.

A sudden puff of wind blew out my candle and I was about to relight it when I heard a sound on the beach—so I remained still and listened. The elation of the previous minutes had vanished—there it was again—the crunch of shingle. My fingers eased the long-barrelled Smith and Wesson from its holster as my left hand gripped the flash light. Flicking on the beam I scanned the beach—nothing moved and I relit the candle to continue writing. I was in mid-sentence when I heard the voice. Unmistakably it said in English, 'Be very careful in the morning.' The hair on the back of my neck rose, but I didn't jump up—in fact I was rooted to the spot, listening in case it came again. I wanted it to come again for I was certain it had been my mother's voice. I heard nothing more, but I was wide awake and alert. That warning caused me to review our plans.

My concern now was the crocodiles that lay ahead. On our reconnaissance I had seen some huge monsters, certainly many more than we had seen elsewhere on the river. Our original plan had gone wrong at this stage, for I'd assumed from scientific advice that the crocodiles would either move up the tributaries or downstream when the rains came and turned the upper reaches of the river into foaming cataracts. But they were still here. This was why I'd despatched John Wilsey with three men to come upstream from Shafartak to meet us. However, he'd had a great many difficulties and, although our sky-wave aerials should be able to get the signal out of the gorge, I had not made direct contact with him for several days, probably due to a failure of his radio. But Main Base had managed to pick him up and learned that two of his 40-hp engines had blown up under the terrific strain of forcing the rapids. A third engine, dropped from the Beaver, had disappeared into the Nile when the parachute failed to open. Unfortunately this load also contained the team's rations, so they must now be living at least partly off the land. Our last spare engine was on its way to them by American helicopter. I knew John wouldn't give up and could easily imagine him straining every muscle to get his boat to the Bascillo River junction. 'At least we're not short of food,' I thought. 'Expect John will be glad to see us.'

Base also told me that the assault boat team had reported an alarming increase in the numbers of crocodiles per mile and they strongly advised that we should not proceed past the junction without their alloy boat as an escort. Until we met John, I had a simple plan of defence against the creatures. First we'd try to avoid them, remembering the bite one had taken at an assault boat the previous month. Each boat was to carry a sandbag full of stones for use as a deterrent. Finally, if all else failed, we would open fire with our heaviest weapons and thrash the water with paddles. Colin, who had been working on crocodile surveys in Ethiopia for several years, considered an attack to be most unlikely. Nevertheless I always had the heavy 9.3 mm Mauser rifle ready, just in case. I only hoped that if we did meet an angry 10-metre croc, this would stop it.

I reckoned we needed three days to explore this fascinating area and with luck, John should have reached the Bascillo by then. Healthwise we were not in bad shape. Most people's cuts and lacerations were now healing or at least the infection was not spreading. Our supply of anti-biotics was almost exhausted and, acting as the medic, I found we only had a few tetracyclin tablets left. My own injuries were giving little trouble; the knee only hurt occasionally and I could dispense with the walking-stick. My torn hands were of more concern. The nylon rope that had cut through to the bone during my earlier rescue from the river had led to an infection that sent a jabbing pain to my elbow joints and armpits, but with constant cleansing and dressing, I hoped to keep going for another week. As the moon rose over the gorge I thought again about the voice, and wondered why I should take such care in the morning.

Midnight came and my duty ended. 'All quiet?' asked my relief with a yawn. 'Yes, I think so,' I replied a little uncertainly.

Heavy rain fell while I slept and at dawn the baboons' barking chorus roused us from our damp sleeping-bags. We wolfed the breakfast prepared by the last sentry and then, while the air was still cool and with the canyon in deep shadow, started to explore the caves. Joe lightened *Semper*'s load to the minimum and then, with his engine racing against the current, he took Chris across the river. Festooned with rope and climbing equipment, the mountaineer stood in the swaying boat. Joe brought his craft with throttle wide open against the cliff and as we watched apprehensively from the other side, Chris studied the rock face, then he sprang upward, found hand and toe holds and started climbing at once. Had he slipped he would have plunged into the swirling brown water. In a minute or so he was in the cave and lowered the rope, which Roger, who came across next, helped to secure as a fixed line. Richard was the last to go and soon all three climbers were safely inside the caves. Quickly and with some regret they discovered there was no tunnel and the caves were uninhabited.

'The place is full of pottery and basket work,' yelled Chris. Joe ferried their archaeological finds back to camp, while Roger shot a small bat for the zoologists. It appeared that we had discovered some ancient refuge, probably deserted for many centuries. The floor was deep in bat dung giving off a nauseous smell, but the remains of an old leather rope provided a clue to how the former dwellers had got in. Perhaps in the dry season there was a ledge beneath the caves.

Just before midday the cave party returned and we spread out their discoveries for photography. Gazing down at the potsherds, bones, fire carbon and aged leather rope, I heard a distant whooping cry. This was the usual way that one Amhara shepherd signals to the next, but it was repeated and sounded excited. I couldn't read the strange language, but I had heard our guides use it often enough to realise that the tone had much to do with the message.

'I think we'll have a quick lunch and press on,' I said.

'What, and leave the caves only half explored?' said several of my chums with obvious disappointment.

'Yes,' I said crossly, 'just grab a Mars bar and let's pack up and go.' I had intended to continue the exploration in the afternoon. Quite why I suddenly changed my plan, I'll never know. The tone of the shepherd's cry would not have been sufficient by itself. Something made me uneasy. Perhaps it was the voice of the previous night, but I have felt this once or twice before when danger threatened and there is no doubt that when you are living in the wilds, your wits become very much sharper. But the matter didn't seem all that urgent and I knew it would take us at least thirty minutes to pack up and load boats. However, I simply felt we must move.

I was so taken by the beauty of the waterfall behind the camp, that I decided to take a quick snapshot before we left and record the site of the copper. In the little canyon it was cool and pleasant and I spent a few moments deciding which would be the best angle for a photograph.

The sharp crack of the rifle and the shower of chippings from the rock face made me duck instinctively. I looked up. There, at the top of the bluff, a hunter, silhouetted against the blue sky, stood clutching his rifle and watching me. 'Look out, you idiot, be careful. You nearly hit me,' I shouted in anger and ludicrously, also in English. The man opened the bolt of his rifle to reload and I suddenly realised that it was me he was trying to hit! Instinctively my right hand flew to my holster, but I had taken off my belt a few moments before when going to commune with nature. Now it was lying together with my revolver on my pack in the camp.

My feet hardly touched the ground as I raced back down the gorge, leapt the stream-bed and rushed into the camp. I don't think I've ever run so fast in my life. 'Blashers running?' said the look on the faces of my friends, but before they could speak, I shouted, 'Hurry, we must get out quickly, just grab everything and get into the boats.' Now we moved fast and I had just loaded my pack on to *Semper* when a horn sounded several short, strident notes. A second later a bullet smacked into the shingle a foot away and I looked up to see the cliff top on the far side of the river alive with some thirty armed tribesmen, their white *shammas* billowing in the wind. They were only sixty yards away!

A wild fusillade of shots followed, ricochets whined off the rocks and spurts of water sprang up from the river. Our attackers waved their weapons and screamed blood-curdling war whoops. Up on high ground beyond the cliff top, I could see long lines of white-robed tribesmen coming to join them. Obviously the lone rifleman had given the game away too soon, perhaps my appearance with the camera had surprised him, but what on earth had prompted the attack? This was not the moment for analysis. We all ran for cover under the trees.

13. Blue Nile (Great Abbai). Author in pith helmet with (*l. to r.*) Alastair Newman, Capt. John Wilsey and Lt. Telahoun Mekonnen.

14. Blue Nile. White water. *Photo: Gage Williams*

15. Blue Nile. The Portuguese bridge.

16. Blue Nile. The caves.

17. Blue Nile. The author returning the bandits' fire. *Photo: Chris Bonington*

18. Blue Nile. The island on which the expedition suffered a night-attack.
They escaped downstream (*top right*) in the dark.

19. Blue Nile. The Northern Gorge at sunrise, just after the night-battle with the bandits.

20. Blue Nile. A fifteen-foot crocodile, one of the many which kept the expedition company.

Army training in dealing with hostile civilian crowds brought to mind the words—minimum force. I seized the loud-hailer and dashed out on to the beach. One man seemed to be the leader and addressing him, I boomed out, '*Tanastalin, tanastalin*, we come in peace and are your friends.' To my relief, the firing ceased and Geronimo, as he was instantly nicknamed, bowed low in the customary Ethiopian manner. I realised that they had never heard a loud-hailer before so I hoped to gain time by keeping him talking. After all, they could not reach us. Having completed his bows, the man deliberately raised his rifle and fired at me from the waist. The bullet came uncomfortably close, showering me in pebbles; others followed, plus some sling-shot for good measure. In another attempt at appeasement, I again told Geronimo in my few words of Amharic that we came in peace and offered him a Mars bar! Once again the firing and stone slinging stopped—Geronimo bowed.

'John, for God's sake let's fire back,' yelled Garth.

'No,' I said, 'must try minimum force first, just let me attempt to get them talking.'

'You'll get yourself shot standing out there in your bloody white hat. It's not bullet proof you know,' said another voice. But the rebels, bandits, tribesmen, or whatever they were, were clearly a little confused and as I spoke, they held their fire. Meanwhile the team packed vital kit, but we knew we could not get it all away.

As I spoke, I tried to switch my mind on to track two again. To stay and argue would give us time, but we would be slaughtered once we tried to run the gauntlet on the river. Right, if we did not want to end with squeaky voices, at best we must escape. Perhaps they would stop shooting and we could slip away. I doubted it. Once you've opened fire, the war has escalated and I desperately wanted to cool it down. My heavy rifle was securely packed in *Semper*. Garth's shotgun was in his boat also. David had a .22 rifle at hand, whilst eight of us carried .45 Smith and Wesson revolvers. My own hand gun was a Smith and Wesson .38 special and I knew how to use it. David Bromhead was a marksman and everybody else had received some training. We could put up a pretty good show if only we had more ammo and some cover. But as it was, we were trapped. If need be, we would shoot our way out. At one hundred and eighty feet a good pistol shot will register a fair score on a man-size target. But I did not want to fire. After all, it must be a ghastly mistake unless these people were all simple bandits.

As the tribesmen argued and the loud-hailer impressed them more, I shouted rapid orders to the team. 'We are going out by boat, Redshanks first, keep in under the far cliff for cover. Joe, go upstream and distract them. If they start shooting, zig-zag. John, escort all the Redshanks down river. Joe, pick me up when the rest are clear, we'll regroup half a mile downstream. Colin, you and I will give covering fire, but only on my order.'

I was interrupted by the sudden arrival of several boulders the size of overgrown footballs crashing through the trees. The cliffs behind us were also alive with the enemy. What co-ordination! If only they could shoot straight, we'd be dead. Rocks, sling-shot and bullets rained down as our attackers screamed and yelled. They were not just trying to frighten us and we were certainly surrounded. Already the Bejimir tribesmen behind us were beginning to descend into the gorge. If we wanted to avoid a hand-to-hand fight, we must leave now.

'Listen,' I yelled, using the loud-hailer to overcome the growing noise of the gun fire. 'Get ready.'

'We'll all be killed,' shouted Chris. 'We can't go out there. Call for an air strike, it's suicide.'

David Bromhead explained to him the chances of our getting an air strike.

'I'm bloody well giving orders here,' I said. 'Shut up and do as you're told.' For many it was a baptism of fire and for all of us it was quite frightening.

The rifle fire was now very heavy and it seemed incredible that the inflatables lying in the open had not been hit. 'Right, to the boats,' I cried. Joe was out first, he showed no regard for his own safety and as the storm of shot and stone raged about him, he calmly pushed his craft into deep water, then shouting and shaking his fist, he sped upstream to draw the enemy fire. I watched him for a second and thought, 'In the best traditions of Nelson, I only hope he survives.'

John Fletcher and Colin Chapman were in *Ubique*, and ready to escort the Redshanks on their way downstream. One Redshank was launched and being paddled furiously for the relative safety of the far cliff. The surface of the water was dancing with plumes of spray from the missiles. At any one time six or seven stones could be seen in the air and many struck the boats. 'It will be a miracle if we can come through this,' I thought. The second Redshank was caught up in some reeds by the beach; the crew was struggling desperately to get it into the main stream. I was alone on the beach. Around me lay the scattered remains of our camp. Gripping my .38 Special I looked up to the Bejimir cliff. As I did so, a bullet hit the beach between my legs. The firer stood on a rock slab twenty-five yards away in the Tammi gorge, working the bolt of a short Italian carbine. Raising my revolver, I fired whilst he was re-loading. Slightly to my surprise, he doubled up, dropped his rifle and ran up the cliff path. I probably hit the butt of his weapon and this saved his life, but gave him quite a fright. Behind the slab another man appeared brandishing a curved sword, but as he had no gun, I turned my attention to a group higher up, who carried long-barrelled rifles of an early vintage. One shot drove them to cover and hearing a clang of stone striking metal, I spun round to see a jerry can of fuel standing on the shingle. Nearby lay the precious artefacts collected so laboriously from the caves. But now Joe was planing downstream at top speed, sending pale brown spray up in a fan behind the boat. Weaving in and out of a pattern of missiles, he came on, his revolver clutched at the ready. 'Get aboard,' he yelled. Seizing the can of petrol, I regretfully left the artefacts. Racing across the beach, I was up to my knees in the swirling water before *Semper* reached me. Half falling over the side, I collapsed into the boat. At once, Joe gunned the throttle and we hurtled across the river. The sky above was full of rocks and sling shot. Several lumps, the size of tennis balls, struck the inflatable's tubes and bounced off with a loud 'pong'. Forty yards ahead I could see the Redshanks now coming under aimed fire. Using his engine, John Fletcher was pushing them downstream. 'Fire,' I cried and from *Ubique* came the crash of Colin's .45. I swivelled round and faced the Gojjam bank. Geronimo was there, standing in full view atop a buttress of rock. I saw his rifle kick and a bullet sent a shower of water over me, missing the boat by inches. Joe's tense face was pointed ahead. 'Chris has been hit,' he said in a matter-of-fact way. 'Oh God, what a mess!' I thought.

Geronimo was trying another shot as I took aim. 'Hold us steady, Joe,' I yelled. The Smith and Wesson roared and my bullet struck the rock six feet beneath the white-robed target. His went on towards the Redshanks. In the time it takes to squeeze the trigger, I fired again, the strike was three feet low. Rock chips flew out and downwards towards the swirling current. My last shot came almost at once. Geronimo's head jerked up as he reeled backwards and with his arms outstretched as if seeking support, he fell from sight. I turned to face his followers, but they were now hiding behind the rocks, their rifles silent. Only the odd long-range shot whistled after us and splashed harmlessly into the river. During the battle, Joe had calmly taken Chris's Redshank in tow; now the injured photographer was seated, blood running from a stone wound in his back and trickling down the side of the boat, but he was not badly hurt and already his camera was ready. 'Look left,' he cried. Joe and I, our guns still in our hands, spun round to face the next enemy. 'Click' went Chris's camera. I suppose it may have looked authentic! It was 1210 hours. The whole incident had taken only 10 minutes.

For several miles we towed the Redshanks downriver. The gorge gave way to sloping hillsides, plantations of maize and a few huts. Great square blocks of basalt lay like islands in mid-stream, the results of massive avalanches. When I judged we had gone a safe distance, we halted to reorganise. As I dressed Chris's wound, Joe set up the radio and I scribbled a message for base. 'Sitrep. Attack on camp by forty natives from both banks with rifles, rocks and slings. No serious casualties to us. Fire was returned in self-defence. No enemy casualties. Bonington minor casualty. Do not cause flap over this. Tell base all OK, but much kit lost. Do not release to press.' I hoped that this statement would keep the whole matter at a very low key and that was why I had not mentioned Geronimo or any other enemy casualties. The radio was a Racal squadcall High Frequency fitted with a twelve-foot rod. Such aerials are only designed for short distances. To our utter astonishment, base, almost one hundred miles away, answered our first call, although Mount Choke (13,000 feet) stood between us.

We cruised on throughout the afternoon. Whoops and shouts followed us from the hills. 'Here come the tax collectors,' they probably said. Eventually all was silent, but I knew that dozens of unseen eyes were watching and, sitting with the heavy Mauser on my lap, I scanned the high ground through binoculars.

Now crocodiles were beginning to appear here and there on the banks, but they made no aggressive movement. I estimated we had covered twenty-five miles since the ambush at noon and felt that we had probably outstripped any pursuit. Darkness usually fell at around 1830 hours, so it was as well to stop an hour or so before this. At 1700 we were still some three miles north of the junction, when I saw another canyon ahead. The walls were much wider apart than the previous gorges and I recognised a pinnacle of basalt leaning out from the Gojjam cliff in the far distance. I'd noted this on my air reconnaissance and remembered it marked a short stretch of small rapids and also the start of a longer stretch of vertical cliffs. If we got into any difficulties in those rapids, darkness would probably catch us in that gorge. We drifted on downstream coming upon a long, low, shingle island. A small patch of trees and scrub grew in the centre. There were a few driftwood logs that could be used for defences, firewood looked plentiful, there were no crocs about—as far as I could see. The current was quite fast and even the narrow channel on the right contained deep water. Around the island the river banks were largely devoid of cover and the nearest high ground was at least half a mile back. It seemed a reasonable defensive position and probably the best we should find for miles. 'It will take a determined bunch to attack us here,' I thought.

Crunching ashore on the pebbles, we pulled the boats up on the east shore and established camp under the trees in the centre of the island. In order to get the radio equipment near to the camp, Joe sailed *Semper* into the narrow channel, mooring to a tree.

We were sipping a brew of hot sweet tea that Richard Snailham had cooked up when we spotted three boys swimming diagonally across the river from the Bejimir side. Any bitter feelings we had felt after the ambush had now abated and we waved a friendly greeting to the newcomers, who treated crocodiles and the swift current with such contempt. They came out of the water and stood at the edge of the island, their smooth athletic bodies glistening with water. They looked like any young boys for they were stark naked except for a small silver coptic cross on a string around their necks. These people had probably known Christianity when our ancestors were painted blue, but unlike most natives we met, they seemed timid and hesitant and simply stared at us. Eventually our gestures and offers of small gifts tempted them to come into the camp and once there, they lost all shyness. I doubt if they were older than fourteen. They spoke a dialect none of us understood and even Colin, whose Amharinya was better than most, could not get through to them. They seemed quite amicable and we presented them with aspirins, plastic bags and Mars bars. Like all Ethiopian young men, they displayed considerable curiosity towards our weapons but when they swam home a few minutes later, I felt rather uneasy about this interest. Was it the normal respect for guns, which are a great status symbol in this wild land, or was there more to it? I was still pondering when Joe called me for supper. We had been forced to abandon some of our rations at the Tammi but, although on a reduced scale, the meal was adequate. Luckily there was plenty of rice—a great belly-filler.

As it grew dark I held the usual daily briefing and outlined the plan for our defence and possible withdrawal, should we be attacked that night. We arranged to have two sentries on duty at all times and built a rough *zoriba* or fence around the camp. Colin and I were carrying *ministar* flare launchers which we would keep loaded and close at hand. Each man was given his responsibilities and ammunition was re-allocated.

'It's Sunday and after orders we will have our usual service,' I said. Richard selected a hymn from the Army Prayer Book and just then it began to rain. The congregation, made up of all the members of the group, huddled under my *basha* and we sang, 'Now thank we all our God, with hearts and hands and voices . . .' The words seemed appropriate.

The night was very black and apart from the patter of the rain and the hiss and gurgle of the river, all was silent. I wrote up the log, penned half a letter to Judith and then lay fully dressed on my sleeping-bag. I undid the laces but kept my boots on. Positioning my flashlight nearby, I cleaned and checked my battered old revolver and laid it beneath the pith helmet which served as a pillow. I then oiled the big Mauser and loaded the magazine before placing it in its plastic tube. This I pushed inside the sleeping-bag. The final act was to dress my throbbing suppurating fingers and swallow a paludrine anti-malaria tablet. In the battle at the Tammi I had lost my walking-stick, but my knee was hardly giving any trouble now. It was just after 2200 hours when I blew out the candle and sank into a deep sleep and, as my friends told me, snored like a pig!

In the distance I heard yells and shots. A faraway voice shouted, 'Stand to, stand to,' but it was all a dream. Or so it seemed for a long time which, in fact, could not have exceeded three seconds.

As I came to my hands groped for the *ministar* launcher; the shots and war whoops were very close. Somewhere a hunting-horn was sounding short blasts. Tearing my shirt pocket open, I felt the pen-sized device and rolling out of the *basha*, I thrust it upward and tried to manipulate my swollen fingers to fire it. 'Crack' went the tiny cartridge as the flare curved through the sky lighting up the island and the river. The shingle beach was alive with shiny black bodies advancing on the camp. One figure, carrying a short spear, was only fifteen yards away chasing Roger towards the *zoriba*. My hand was searching for my gun as I saw David, the second sentry, crouched by a tree. He brought up his .45 and its flash and roar came together. In the last light of the dying flare, I saw the leading attacker stop as if he'd hit a glass wall, then sink to his heels and crumple backwards. Another flare rose into the sky almost at once, probably fired by Colin, and in its light I buckled on my belt and drew my revolver. We were all awake now and as I put up another *ministar*, a volley crashed out from the camp. 'They're coming through the trees!' I heard someone shout; 'for heaven's sake, guard the boats,' yelled Chris.

My own area of responsibility was the trees and the narrow channel. I strained my ears to detect any sound from this direction, but in the pitch black between flares I could hear nothing definite. Suddenly a figure came blundering through the scrub. My gun came up and was about to shoot John Fletcher, when I heard him say, 'Joe's down by *Semper*.' It was not until this moment that I realised that the heaviest fire was coming from the river bank on the Gojjam side. The bandits' covering party had been in position there all the time and was now trying to pick us off in the dark. I let go another flare, horizontally this time, at the next rifle flash and to my delight, saw half a dozen white-robed figures scampering away in panic. Meanwhile the raiders were still on the north end of the island and trying to work their way through the scrub. 'I'm firing into the bushes,' I yelled, not wishing to risk the chance of an accident with one of our own men. There was no reply and advancing a few yards, I waited. Low voices muttered about twenty yards ahead. More firing and whoops on my right showed that Roger and his party were busy by the boats. Then I saw a definite movement a few yards ahead, one or probably two men I thought. Someone was calling out in the local tongue on the bank. The figures showed again and I blasted two quick shots, deliberately aiming low in the scrub. With much noise of breaking undergrowth and grunts, the bandits fled through the bush.

'Beach is clear,' came the cry from the right.

'Garth,' I shouted.

'Yeah,' came back the faint Australian accent.

'Take David and recce forward up the island, see if there are any of them still here. We'll switch our fire to the covering party.'

Alastair Newman had joined me and together with *ministar* and revolver we took on the bandits on the mainland. The tactics were simply to watch for a gun flash, put up a flare in its direction and get off a couple of quick shots whilst the target was illuminated. Joe Ruston was already dismantling the headquarters and packing up the radio. 'The aerial's caught in the branches,' he muttered, 'I'll have to climb the bloody tree and sort it out.' As most of the shots from the enemy were passing over our heads through this particular tree, it would be a hazardous undertaking, but the aerial was essential as the radio was of little value without it. He started to climb up the thorny trunk and as he did so, I heard hoots of laughter from the bandits. I'll swear there was a clink of a bottle and I realised that the gentle thudding I'd heard earlier was a ramrod being driven down some ancient musket barrel. To confirm my impressions, there was a bright flash, a roar and a cloud of white smoke jetted out from the trees. A six-inch nail or some similar object crashed through the branches near Joe, who swore loudly. A few minutes later he jumped down. 'Got it,' he gasped. 'See you at the RV,' and, clutching the radio, aerial, pack and machete, he staggered down to *Semper*. Then, continuing to ignore his own safety, he pushed off into the channel and drifted silently downstream between the firing lines. Although there was no moon, the night seemed to be getting lighter as my eyes became accustomed to it. It was possible to distinguish large objects, especially on the water, and the bandits were only twenty yards away from Joe.

The fire fight continued for another fifteen minutes and slowly all of us pulled back to the pre-arranged RV at the far end of the island. Roger had brought the boats down the shore and was joined by Joe in *Semper* from the other side. It was Roger, who as sentry had gone to inspect the boats at 0105 hours, spotted the bandits and challenged them at the water's edge. They had opened fire at once. It was Roger's shouts of 'Stand to' that had woken me as he raced into the camp pursued by a dozen enemy.

Alastair and I pulled back to the defensive position last. There was a low shingle bank, but we were close to our boats and had a completely clear field of fire. Everyone was there. Garth reported the island clear of enemy. Ammunition was quickly redistributed, we had three rounds left for each .45 and although we had more liberal quantities for the other weapons, we were not well off. I checked each man's arc of fire and, coming to Richard, said 'You cover from that bush to . . .'

'John,' he interrupted quietly. 'I feel there is a small point I should raise at this juncture.'

'What on earth is it?' I said tersely.

'I haven't got a gun,' he replied. I found it difficult not to burst out laughing. Richard, as gentle and unassuming as ever, was clutching his penknife. 'Would you like your pith helmet now?' he asked. In the opening stages of the fight I had given it to him to carry to the boats. Guarding it like an Imperial Eagle of Rome, he had carefully concealed it from view throughout the battle. Now he was eager to rid himself of this bulky white target. I took it back and hid it beneath a groundsheet in *Semper*.

It was now 0200 hours and I planned to hold out until just before dawn, then slip away when the light was sufficient for us to see the way through the cataract approximately a mile ahead.

The bandits' shooting was as bad as their tactics and field-craft were good, so I doubted if they would be able to hit us as we moved downriver. I could probably discourage them from following too closely with my rifle. But it meant holding them off for another three and a half hours at least. They were brave men and I suspected some of them were well primed with local alcohol. It is difficult to estimate the numbers involved, particularly as we were fighting at night. However, I believe a reasonable approximation would be forty to fifty of them against ten of us.

There was only occasional firing from the bank and this we returned with the rifle to conserve revolver ammunition. Once I thought I saw a figure swimming the channel between the island and the mainland; if indeed it was a man, my shot must certainly have worried him.

At 0300 hours Richard reported a growing movement on the mainland opposite his post. I listened and could hear a lot of muttering and shuffling amongst the bushes. The bandits were probably massing for another attack, so I put up a flare which revealed nothing. 'If they make another determined attack we shall have to withdraw,' I said. 'Simply not enough ammunition.' No-one questioned the plan, but all wondered how we could negotiate the rapids in the dark. I gave instructions for the withdrawal, and to avoid giving our movement away to any enemy cut-off party, who might be lurking downstream, I said that no engines were to be used except in dire emergency.

The silence was broken by the short, sharp notes of the hunting-horn, just as we had heard earlier. I put up another flare and in its light, I could see a mass of robed figures assembled amongst the trees on the far bank. 'Right, man the boats,' I whispered loudly and, firing several shots at the massed bandits, clambered into *Semper*. 'Life jacket,' said Joe, thrusting one at me as he pushed us into deep water. 'By the way, I think we've been hit somewhere up front, we've got a frightful leak,' he said, and I felt the soft, squashy forward tubes of the boat. As we pulled away from the island, I rummaged about and found one of the foot-pumps. Fortunately, it was easy to connect to the valve and from then on I was able to sit and use one foot to keep the pump going. My hands were free to use the paddle.

We reached the far bank and at once the current forced us against some low trees. 'Push clear quickly,' came Roger's urgent warning, 'or we'll be dragged under the branches.' We had only been on the water for a short time when the whoops and horn blasts announced that the bandits were attacking our evacuated position. 'We've got a good start,' I said to Joe, but he was too worried about his craft to notice the events behind us. 'Keep pumping, we're losing air fast,' he said. To help keep together, each reconnaissance boat took a Redshank in tow and it was in tandem that we reached the cataract. Ahead, in the blackness, we could hear its thunder, but saw nothing. As we raced towards it at some six knots it was an eerie, unnerving experience. The terrifying noise got louder and louder. In daylight it is possible to choose the best route through white water, but now we had no idea whether we were coming upon a small waterfall, a huge rock in mid-river or some shallow rapids that would tear our hulls open, like a knife through butter.

Straining my eyes ahead, all I could see was inky blackness. To our left, *Ubique* and its Redshank were now invisible. The water hit us without warning, hurling us up and over a towering wave; behind us, the Redshank under tow was completely engulfed. A second wave swept over and the rapidly deflating front tubes almost bent double. I lost the foot-pump in the chaos and heard Joe yelling, 'Can't go on like this!' 'OK, let's use the engine to run into the bank,' I screamed back, 'but we'll have to cut the Redshank loose.' 'Can't make it,'' called Joe to the boat behind. 'We're going ashore for repairs.' 'Casting you off, pull in further down, good luck!' was his farewell to our friends. At least they'd have a better chance without us. The tow-line parted and at once they were swallowed up in the darkness and the raging river.

Our outboard started almost immediately and demonstrating his superb seamanship, Joe took the sinking craft astern and out of the main stream. We thumped into a shingle bank and I shot out backwards onto the shore as Joe killed the engine. As I landed, something slightly blacker than the shingle slithered off into the water—I'd almost fallen on a crocodile! For a few moments we sat still with drawn revolvers, trying to hear any enemy, but the noise of the cataract drowned everything. Suddenly from the darkness, two shapes loomed up. It was *Ubique* and her Redshank. They landed ten yards away and we heard their horrific story of a capsize in mid cataract. David and Richard had both gone overboard and were only saved by a miracle. Much kit had been lost including the vital box of rations. We were now soaked to the skin and very cold. 'Where's Chris's boat?' asked Colin. As if to answer him, a light appeared flashing dimly down river. The signal, in morse, read 'O.K.' So they were safe too! Back up river our camp was burning, small showers of sparks cascaded skyward as our enemies vented their wrath on all we'd left behind.

Joe had discovered *Semper*'s trouble, a leaking valve which was easily cured. Somone passed round a handful of boiled sweets and we cracked one or two nervous jokes.

Making a quick reconnaissance, I discovered to my relief that we had landed on a featureless shingle bank, separated from the mainland by a fast-flowing stream. However, we dare not show lights nor speak loudly, as I expected the bandits would not be far away. Thankfully cloud still covered the moon. We worked quietly in the dark to refit the boats and it was about 0415 hours when John Fletcher lost the nut that held on the propeller of his boat's engine. It had slipped from his wet hand into the river. Without this, the propeller could not be secured and therefore the engine was useless. John tried everything his resourceful mind could dream up, but it appeared there was no solution. As a last resort he mixed a paste of Araldite in a tobacco tin and glued the propeller on to the shaft.

'How long will it take to set, John?' I asked.

'About an hour and a half if I can keep it dry,' he replied.

'You reckon that we can sit here in daylight, do you?' I exclaimed.

'No, I realise we must push on, and if necessary I'll lash a plastic bag over the propeller when we go. We'll just have to hope that it will set and paddle meanwhile.' he answered. Fitters like John are worth their weight in gold on expeditions!

It was 0530 hours when the sky began to lighten and I gave the order to cast off once again. We skirted round the tumbling cataract and picked up the missing Redshank and crew downstream. The dawn was fantastic. The growing light revealed an incredible view. Towering cliffs, giant boulders and natural limestone arches were painted shades of brown, pink and yellow. The river was like a mirror, much wider and slower and only a gentle wave or two to disturb the surface. Nevertheless I kept the rifle handy and watched the cliffs. We passed the Bascillo River Junction, but I reckoned John Wilsey must be at the Soita, further south.

Along the banks we could make out the shapes of dormant crocodiles and it was not until the sun began to reach the gorge that they started coming out to inspect us. We watched warily, occasionally hurling a rock to deter them. However, they kept their distance and at 0700 hours Joe managed to raise base on the radio. Once again it was a miracle of communication, for he was only using the twelve-foot rod aerial.

I had just spoken to Nigel, the deputy leader and now base commander, when I saw Joe's mouth open. 'Oh, my God!' he cried and looking up, I saw a leviathan of a crocodile literally galloping with its legs extended. It came towards us at a frightening speed over the shingle. I simply yelled, 'Crocodile attacking!' into the microphone and leapt for my rifle. The giant reptile plunged into the water and came speeding straight at us. A small bow wave was caused by its great head. The huge tail propelled it like a torpedo as I took aim with the Mauser at a point midway between his evil yellow eyes. 'Don't shoot,' shouted Colin. 'He's only curious, he'll stop short.' 'If you're wrong, my friend, I shall kick you off the cloud when we meet in Heaven,' I thought. The huge creature closed to within eight feet of the boat, then without as much as a splash, dived and passed beneath us only to surface on the far side. He then cruised alongside us for about twenty-five yards, giving me a chance to estimate the size, which was even bigger than the boat. At a conservative guess I would have said fifteen feet in length! Suddenly he had disappeared beneath the muddy water again and this time for good. Base was trying desperately to contact us on the radio.

'Sorry for that interruption,' I said and gave them a brief outline of the battle. 'Don't get the authorities all worked up yet,' I said. 'Give me a chance to get well clear before Haile Selassie's jets come thundering in to deal with the bandits.'

'They've got troops standing by to helicopter in and get you out,' said Nigel, who was now in command at Debra Marcos, 'and John Wilsey is twelve miles south of Bascillo junction.'

'Fine, but we need ammunition and food in that order so may we have a drop when we meet John?' I went on. 'Our stocks of rations are almost out up here,' retorted Nigel. 'What has happened to all of yours?' 'Oh, I gave them to the friendly people around here,' I said sarcastically.

We switched off the engine to save fuel and drifted for a while. More crocodiles came swimming out to investigate, but Colin was right, they always stopped short. However, I could see how any inexperienced person would assume they meant business and open fire long before they had got within eight feet of him.

It was 0815 hours as we rounded a bend and saw the dark green assault boat. A great cry of greeting went up and I stumbled ashore to shake John's hand. For several hours the crews swapped stories. Cataracts grew bigger, bandits and aggressive crocodiles multiplied. John himself had a great tale to tell. For seven days he had struggled upstream, his boat leaping rapids like a giant salmon. No-one had ever brought any form of powered craft so far up the Blue Nile before. It was a fine achievement and we were terribly glad to see them.

Having washed, shaved, cleaned our guns and refuelled, we ate a meagre breakfast. Food was very short, but at mid-morning, the Beaver came roaring into the gorge and dropped several bundles to us. They only had one parachute left and that was used for the petrol and ammunition. The rations came in by freedrop and sadly, the pack hit a rock and burst, scattering its contents far and wide. They were all the supplies they had left at base. This consisted of some packets of biscuits, a bag of rice, sardines and cheese plus a four-gallon plastic container of whisky! 'Well, at least we can lay on a cocktail party,' joked the boatman. The whisky container was leaking, so we had liberal gulps before setting off to study the last part of the river.

The remaining time passed quickly. We felt the real pangs of hunger and ate guinea fowl, fish and even a crocodile tail. A new menace hit us: mosquitoes! The dry season was coming and already the trees were turning brown and the river beginning to drop. We had seen little in the way of wildlife—just a few small antelope apart from the ubiquitous crocodile: the noise of our motors had clearly frightened off the rest.

It was 24 September when we sailed from our camp on the Uolaka junction and began the final run to Shafartak. On the radio we heard that quite a reception awaited us and it was hard to realise that we had got through and now, after nearly two months, it was all over.

Sitting in the boat as we made that last day's run, I began to scribble notes for my report to the Emperor. No lost tribe—just some unsociable apes and a large population of reluctant tax-payers.

No radio-active gas or uranium as far as we could tell, but very likely a good deposit of copper. The crocodiles were certainly huge—but nothing above six metres had been seen and there were fewer than expected. Although there'd been massive landslides there were no waterfalls below Tississat and in the wet season, inflatable boats could navigate from the Portuguese Bridge to the Sudan if His Imperial Majesty so desired!

At 1620 hours the Beaver came skimming over the river and we knew we were very close to home. Ten minutes later we ran ashore and the champagne corks flew. A large lady from Texas was amongst those who had come out from Addis Ababa to see us arrive. As we staggered up the beach she turned to her husband and said, 'These guys must be crazy.'

'Hush, dear,' he replied, 'they're British.'

5

Strange Quests
in Papua New Guinea

Their most sophisticated and prized possessions were two steel axe-heads.

'There are still people up there who don't know the outside world,' said Tom, sipping his claret. 'I hope you've got some good Defence Force blokes with you—they don't always greet outsiders with open arms, you know.' I was having dinner with Tom Richards, a prospector, a man of great experience in these parts, who had spent most of his life hacking through the New Guinea bush in search of minerals or Japanese soldiers. Sitting on his verandah in Lae, we discussed the forthcoming reconnaissance by an Operation Drake patrol into the little-known Strickland Gorge—an area often referred to as Papua New Guinea's (or PNG, as it's usually called) last unknown. But PNG is a land of unexplained mysteries that beckons to the curious explorer, with stories of strange animals, fabulous rivers full of gold nuggets, tribes who do not know the outside world, Japanese soldiers still hiding from the Allies and caves deeper than any on earth.

It had all started in 1977 when I'd been visiting the country with a view to locating suitable tasks for the exploration teams of Operation Drake and I'd approached Brigadier Ted Diro, then commander of the PNG Defence Force, for advice. After a careful look at the map on his office wall, he'd planted a finger on the vacant squares around the upper Strickland River and read, 'Relief Data Incomplete.' 'That's a really mysterious area,' he said. 'Few people have been there and we'd love to know more about it—you know, what the river's like, and the people, and the animals and any minerals, too.' I added it to my growing list of tasks for my explorers and went off to the Defence Force library to see if I could find some air photo-

144

graphs—but there was none. 'Haven't got that far yet, sir,' said the Australian captain. 'It's a hell of a place to fly in.' So, clearly, if we were to tackle this little problem, we would have to get our own photos.

The river falls a thousand feet in 75 miles and, for much of this distance, it is enclosed in a deep chasm—the Devil's Race. Low cloud obscures the area for much of the year and thus, even an air reconnaissance was unlikely to reveal what secrets lay beneath the swirling mists and the dark green rain forest. But I felt there must be a series of falls, or perhaps just one big fall on that course. If we were to explore the region and seek the answers to so many questions about the people, minerals and wildlife, we'd need to use that river.

'If you get clear weather,' said a bush pilot I consulted in Port Moresby, 'it's because of high wind funnelling up the gorge—even the Army planes won't take it. You'd need a real power bird to get you through; if you hit that turbulence, you'll smash right into the rock.'

Even if one survived a crash, the chances of being found didn't sound too good, and the likely reaction of the tribes of head hunters (who were still thought to exist in remote regions) and crocodiles to an intrusion was not very inviting.

However, a year later, I was back with a full-scale reconnaissance party, including my old friends, Vince and Barbara Martinelli and the use of a powerful light plane with a first-rate Australian pilot, Noel Frewster. We dropped Vince off at Wau to examine the wartime mountain trails, then Noel, Barbara and I flew up to Wewak on PNG's north coast to try to make a low-level air reconnaissance of the high-altitude valley of the upper Strickland River. We were in luck for, within a day of our arrival, favourable weather was indicated and Noel decided to have a try. Barbara had the still cameras and took the rear seat, whilst I held the Canon 8mm cine in the front and flicked it on to 'slow motion'. The twin-engined Cessna 301, named *Olivetti* after the company who sponsored it in an air race, was an ideal aircraft for the job and we were soon climbing south into the towering peaks.

At twelve thousand feet, we crossed a rocky ridge and winged our way through the crags and peaks of this little-known land. Suddenly, Noel pointed. 'Look, it's clearing,' he shouted. Sure enough, ahead of us the clouds were rolling back to reveal an emerald-green valley surrounded by towering cliffs and dark mountains. Barbara's camera was already in operation as I raised my cine. Noel took the Cessna through the valley one thousand feet above the ground and we got a good view of the river winding its way fairly gently at first and then tumbling over rocky ledges in foaming fury before it plunged into the narrow, vertical-sided gorge. I felt the aircraft bank sharply and looked up to see a wall of rock racing past a couple of hundred feet away. Blasts of wind shook the Cessna as it twisted and turned through the mountain pass. Noel gripped the controls, his face a study of concentration; beads of sweat ran down his cheeks. 'Hold on,' he hissed through the intercom as the nose lifted over a jungle-covered ridge. Our bodies flattened against the seat back as the surge of power took us up, missing the trees by fifty feet. The tumbling brown river had almost disappeared in the dark green foliage which now covered the entire valley bottom and seemed to close over the top of the canyon. Eventually, we emerged from the mountains and saw the endless flat swampland of the lower Strickland ahead. 'That's fine, Noel,' I yelled. 'Can you take us back at low level?' The Australian made a funny face and we reloaded our cameras. The return journey was the most exhilarating flight of my life. Manoeuvring his aircraft like a fighter, Noel hurtled through the great cleft in that dark green wilderness. Barbara and I concentrated on filming, but the gravitational forces on some of the turns were such that my arms felt like lead and I could hardly lift the camera. Cliffs and jungle shot past the wingtips. We saw underground rivers emerging, huge caves, strange trees and then a single rope bridge strung across the river. 'So someone does live down there,' I thought. Even so, there was no other obvious sign of any human habitation. Back at base that night, we celebrated and worked on our reports with enthusiasm because we knew that we now had the vital information which would enable Roger Chapman, the experienced explorer who had acted with such gallantry on the Blue Nile expedition, to tackle another fearsome river exploration task for us, in 1979. His tasks would include mapping the river, reporting on the state of the local people and assessing the crocodile population for the Government.

In the nineteenth century, the famous naturalist Alfred Russel

Wellan described this huge island. 'The northern coast of New Guinea is exposed to the full swell of the Pacific Ocean and is rugged and harbourless. The country is all rocky and mountainous, covered everywhere with dense forest, offering in its swamps and precipices and serrated ridges an almost impassable barrier to the unknown interior; and the people are dangerous savages, in the very lowest stage of barbarism.'

Indeed, it had not changed very much since the first European, Jorge de Meneses, a Portuguese, landed on the north-west coast in 1511. He called it 'Ilhas dos Papuas' after the Malay word 'Papuwah' meaning frizzy haired. Thirty-seven years later, the Spaniard Ortiz Retes, whilst sailing along the north coast in an attempt to reach Mexico, thought the people reminded him of those of the Guinea Coast in West Africa and so he named it 'Nova Guinea'. In 1971, following various annexations by the British, Germans and the post-war Australian administration, the National Identity Bill established the country's name as Papua New Guinea and four years later it became independent, remaining within the British Commonwealth.

PNG is altogether a new nation, emerging rapidly from a background of tribal wars, cannibalism and almost total isolation. Today, it is a land of extraordinary contrast. The major towns which, up until forty years ago, had no outside contact, now have supermarkets and fast-growing western consumerism, whilst the highlands and hitherto unexplored territories remain dominated by primitive and inaccessible tribes. The inhospitable terrain is such that in remote areas many tribesmen have never seen a car, still less a train, but are quite familiar with aeroplanes passing overhead. Strong inter-tribal feuds are still a feature of the more remote areas and people will not mix or marry with neighbouring but hostile villages. A reflection of this geographical and social isolation is that, in a national population of under three million people, there are 700 languages, a quarter of the world's total.

If the nation is young politically, it is also young geologically. The subterranean plate upon which it sits is moving north at the rate of approximately four inches a year, meeting the South Pacific plate coming the other way. This continuous collision has thrown up huge mountains rising to over fifteen thousand feet and a string of volcanoes along the northern coast, known as the 'ring of fire'. Concealed high in the mountain complex are wide fertile valleys and it was here that the majority of the island population lived, cut off from the rest of the developing world for so long. Even today there must be many small tribes who have never met outsiders.

Between forty and two hundred inches of rain deluge the country's rich forests annually. These hold a dazzling profusion of fascinating creatures. The largest moth in the world, *Coscinoscera hercules*, with a wing area of over forty square inches, is found here, as are wallabies, gliding possums, red bandicoots and spiny ant-eaters, for this is the world of the marsupials which rear young in pouches of skin close to their bodies, quite unlike the placental mammals found in the rest of the world outside the Australo-Papuan region. There are seventy species of snake, giant monitor lizards, tortoises and the largest crocodiles in the world, but the finest creatures of all are to be found amongst the 650 bird species which inhabit the island, the famed birds of paradise. Magellan was the first to bring to Europe some of these glorious birds of unimaginable colours and feathered plumes almost a yard long, as gifts for Emperor Charles V. They were believed to originate from some celestial paradise as their legs and feet were removed by early collectors, leading to the misconception that they: '. . . keepe themselves continually in the ayre, without lighting on the earth, for they have neither feet nor wings, but only head and body, and for the most part tayle.'

Their brilliantly coloured plumes of feathers are designed to attract during courtship-displays which are some of the most spectacular in the animal kingdom.

The plants, too, are equally diverse; 12,000 species of flowering plant have so far been recorded in the region and further research is likely to add several thousand more. Vandopsis, with blooms over six feet long, is just one of the 2,500 types of orchid that fill almost every niche. The people use the plants and animals of the forest to decorate themselves for ceremonies and battles. Bird-of-paradise feathers, vegetable dyes of scarlet and yellow, leaves as ear-rings, possum fur and cowrie shells all combine to create a head-dress and costume characteristic of the tribe.

We were about to descend on the least explored of the world's major islands, and the eyes of Andrew Mitchell, our scientific co-ordinator, gleamed with eager anticipation as he described the possibilities of scientific exploration to me.

Writing in his book, *Operation Drake, Voyage of Discovery*, Andrew described the scene at the field HQ, which we set up when Operation Drake arrived in PNG. 'Operation Drake had its head-quarters, or TAC HQ, in a collection of wooden houses that formed the Lae Lodge Hotel. Tents and radio masts were scattered about in the hotel grounds around which men in jungle-green uniforms scurried back and forth carrying stores, mending engines, planning movements, shouting orders and making occasional detours to the swimming pool. On a typical day the Operations Room resembled the Stock Exchange attempting to cope with a collapse of the Western financial system. Eleven different people try to use two telephones to discover why ten Young Explorers [YEs] have not arrived on the flight that morning, where to obtain paint for the ship's hull, spare parts for a vehicle stranded in the mountains, alcohol for botanical specimens and a boat to transport three scientists and a journalist to one of the camps as the local village captain, who had promised his, was now in prison on charges of drunkenness. On the other end, ten YEs try to explain why they missed the flight, three newspapers want to know if any romances blossomed on the ship's Pacific crossing or if we have discovered the longest lizard in the world yet, and a company director offers to sponsor a local Papuan. No one can get through because the lines are permanently engaged. Around the walls impressive flow charts show who is supposed to be where and what they are responsible for, intermingled with press cuttings and photographs depicting the expedition's progress. The Operations Officer, in this case Captain Mike Knox of the Royal Highland Fusiliers, is visibly going grey as he attempts to match the ever growing requirements of the expe-dition's projects in the most inaccessible country in the world with the limited availability of light aircraft, aged Land-Rovers, and the occasional landing craft. Sara Spicer-Few, the Public Relations Officer, encourages sponsors to donate food, office space, medical supplies and motor cars whilst the Quartermaster, Warrant Officer Len Chandler, refuses to let anything out of his store unless it is prayed for and Signals Sergeant Pete Lavers relays copious messages to the other side of the world on his remarkable Plessey Clansman radio.'

As commander of this band, my job was again like that of a conductor of a newly formed orchestra but with quite a number of untried instruments and a shortage of scores!

Andrew described our deployment. 'Out of this seeming chaos a remarkable array of projects began to take place covering the whole of the country. Forty Papua New Guinean Young Explorers had been selected and sponsored to join the expedition, each for a month, and with those from other countries they were sent off on initial jungle acquaintance courses amongst the forests and rivers to the west of Lae where the TAC HQ was based. Experts from the Papua New Guinea Defence Force (PNGDF) Igam Barracks taught them how to cope with snake bites and the rudiments of medical care in the jungle. A three-day march across raging rivers and sticky swamps accustomed them to conditions and working together as a team.

'Following this the young people were deployed amongst the various projects in progress. Roger Chapman prepared for his battle with the Strickland and our other team leaders were soon growing thinner and fitter as they tackled the fearsome mountains. Some youngsters continued their jungle course by searching for wartime aircraft that had crashed in the mountains of the Finisterre Range. Papua New Guinea saw some of the fiercest fighting of the Pacific War. In January 1942 the Japanese occupied New Ireland and set up a garrison of 200,000 men and ships in Rabaul. Later they occupied Lae and much of the north coast, finally advancing on Port Moresby, the capital, across the Owen Stanley mountains along the Kokoda trail. Here the Allies held them aided by their knowledge of the country and the appalling terrain through which the Japanese were attempting to advance. In September 1943 General MacArthur evicted them from Lae and Salamaua where the underground hospitals and gun batteries visited by the YEs now lie overgrown with creepers and vines.'

However, one of the most exciting tasks that we undertook was to seek some of the 325 allied aircraft that were still missing in this awful jungle. What had happened to them? Our aim was simply to

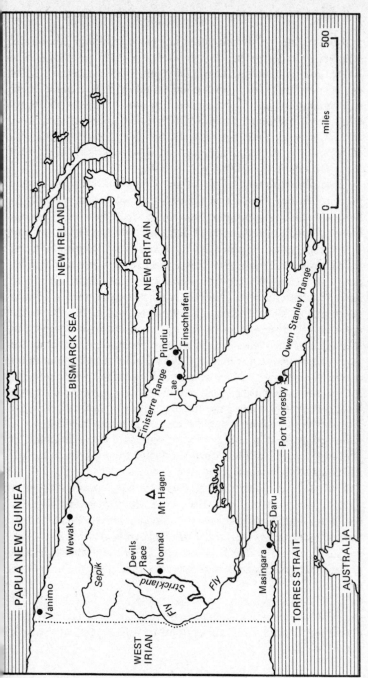

5. Papua New Guinea: Strickland Valley.

find planes, most of which had disappeared without trace, so that relatives could learn what had happened to their loved ones. Robbie Roethenmund, the slim, thoughtful young American, made our first discovery when he led a patrol which found a US DC-3 troop carrier still containing bones and weapons. But one of the most successful quests was carried out by my old friend and second-in-command, Mike Gambier. Built like Tarzan, this tough ex-Royal-Marines Major was just the sort of man we needed to tackle some of the most testing terrain in the world.

The task was to seek a flight of four US fighter bombers that had been lost in 1944 on their way back from a raid, most probably by flying into an ill-mapped mountain top in the Finisterres. However, it was pretty unusual for a complete flight to disappear without trace.

In early August, Bob Salzberg, an American missionary living off the Markham Valley some 65 miles from Lae, had been to see us. He had heard that we were trying to fix up an aircraft search and reckoned that even if we found no crashed remains, we might like to attempt to walk north over the mountains to the sea. 'I'll tell you,' he enthused, 'you will see sights that will take your breath away. You may not find the planes but the walk will compensate for that. See you in September at the mission.' What a character! Without Bob's entrée to his 'parish', Mike would not have known where to begin the search, so after a very dusty and tiring drive down the Markham Valley, the patrol reached the mission, setting up hammocks for the night between various trees and across the bungalow's balcony.

Besides Mike himself, the party consisted of five YEs including Adrian Penney, a recently qualified doctor from Britain, and Seth Elisha, a solidly built shipping clerk from Lae.

That night, the Salzbergs entertained them to supper and spoke of their ten years in rural New Guinea. It was obvious that Bob had found fulfilment amongst his parishioners and also that he had walked over most of this area of the Finisterres to visit them. 'I tell you, it's over 90 per cent mental and 10 per cent physical!' The patrol was to remember his words many times over the next three weeks.

In the past, black magic had been widely used in this area and employed by its practitioners to coerce the tribe's members into obedience through fear. In all primitive societies, fear of the dark and unknown is enhanced by a belief in good and evil spirits, but in PNG they have traditionally also believed in an existence after death, which accounts for their comparatively swift conversion to Christianity.

Some years before, Bob had been instrumental in curtailing the activities of a local black magician who, on being arrested, had paused for a last look round at the door of the police van. He pointed his finger at the missionary and proclaimed in a loud voice for all to hear, 'you will die within a month!' 'Now you've done it,' Mrs Salzberg said when he told her that evening, 'what are you going to do?' 'Nothing,' said Bob, and he didn't. He did get sick, but shrugged it off and continued running his mission. The locals were very impressed as he was the first white man, to their knowledge, to be threatened by a curse and to have survived. Two years later the ex-convict returned, but was no further trouble. Bob's magical powers had been stronger than his and he accepted the position.

Next morning, as the first warming rays of the sun probed into the valley, they left the mission with Bob and drove twelve bumpy miles and 4,500 feet up to the village of Tauta.

During the making of Tauta's inclined grass landing-strip, one enormous rock had defied all efforts to remove it. The villagers piled up wood and burnt it, then doused it with water to cool and crack it. For a week the battle continued then suddenly it split right down the middle and according to the people, a large bird flew out and headed off down the airstrip and away over the deep valley beyond. The elders, unsure anyway of the wisdom of clearing jungle for the introduction of modern technology, sadly shook their heads and muttered '*Massali*' (evil spirits).

The airfield's opening ceremony was attended by a government minister who landed in a three-engined Junkers. These old aircraft had a curious defect in that they performed faultlessly if the pilot took off again within five minutes of arrival or waited over half an hour for the engines to cool. On this occasion, however, the minister was in a hurry and fifteen minutes after arriving, the aircraft taxied for take off, revved up and, gathering speed down the inclined runway, took off. At this point, the carburettors, temporarily starved of fuel through vaporisation caused by the heat of the previous flight, cut the engines and the plane dived into the opposite hillside killing all on board. The elders appeared unmoved and went home knowing that the *Massali* had taken their revenge.

The patrol was lent an empty bungalow overlooking the airstrip and were about to search out a guide when Willie, the motorcycle-riding local patrol officer who bumped his way over the rough tracks, informed them that nobody would move from the area for three days at least, as they had arrived at the start of the PNG independence day celebrations.

From villages all over the region came dancing teams decked out in feathers and grass skirts to compete in the 'sing song' competitions. In far-off Lae, we also saw many teams assembling for the tourist-orientated Morobe show, but here in the mountains, Mike's patrol were the only visitors and were treated to a superb and very natural display. Sleep was hardly possible with the singing, yelling and drumming continuing all day and night and, by the Monday (two days into the celebrations), they had waited long enough and agreed to make a move, independence celebrations or not. So, donning their kit, they set out to find one Paul No No, a guide they'd met with Willie the day before. Paul had agreed to take them to a wrecked aircraft he'd discovered the year before, even though the local tribesmen refused to go near it for fear of evil spirits. Was this one of the planes that had disappeared without trace in 1944? Of course the guide had no idea.

Paul No No lives by hunting and is well known in the central Finisterres, where he may be seen slipping along barefoot in a pair of faded khaki shorts surmounted by a threadbare blue singlet. Slung over his left shoulder is a carrier bag containing, amongst other things, his betelnut, lime powder and mustard beloved by the natives and in his right hand he carries his long jungle knife. He travels light, living off the land as he goes.

Paul reckoned it would take them four days for the round trip. They had, however, decided to save weight by taking rations for only three days, stretching the food to cover four. In the event, they were away seven days and were exhausted and very hungry by the time they returned.

Paul surveyed the patrol's bulging packs, long trousers and hiking boots in amazement, but accepted them with a shrug, and swung off on to the 'road'. Within minutes the steep gradient began to tell and

Mike realised that he was not as fit as he would have wished. '90 per cent mental!' he said to himself and pressed on.

They paused for a rest at the top of the ridge and took in a fantastic view. Below stood a neat, compact village—round which a river curved. On three sides gardens and coffee plantations stretched away to the jungle, while beyond the land rose to the full majesty of a ridge over 10,000 feet high. Toiling up towards us came a family carrying sacks of coffee, arms full of fruit and bundles of bamboo arrows, obviously destined for market via Tauta's road. Paul chatted to them, whilst the patrol sucked in much-needed air and took photographs.

Hardly pausing, Paul led them through the village and its clustered women and children, on towards the mountains. The memory of the hours they struggled up and down these fearsome gradients until camping that evening in a most unsuitable spot (Paul had hoped to reach a hunting-hut before stopping, but they were too exhausted to climb further), is blurred. PNG's topography is not just 'folded' it is positively 'concertina-ed'. Razor-sharp ridges are thousands of feet high and exceedingly steep. Most of the time they would have been using ropes if there had not been trees or roots to hang on to. A two-thousand-foot near-vertical climb to a ridge top, then a descent of a thousand feet, and up again. Seth's legs gave out first. The youngsters divided his kit between them and pushed him on. Mike reckoned he came closer that day to asking someone to carry his rucksack than ever before. However hard they tried, it was impossible to keep up with their guide who skipped up the rocks like a mountain goat following a six-inch-wide path that he called a road. He must have suffered agonies of frustration waiting, but it never showed. They warmed to Paul. That night Seth flopped down and, with much passion burning behind his eyes, declared, 'When I am a minister, I am going to blow all these mountains flat and build roads everywhere!'

It was now obvious that progress was slower than Paul had expected and so the journey would take longer. They tried to eke out their rations. Next morning, they felt stiff, but stronger, and after three hours' climbing gained the top of a razor-back ridge which was followed for several hours. At this altitude, the rocks and trees were festooned with grey moss covering everything and hanging down from the branches in long flowing 'ropes'. Occasionally it was possible to see down through the vegetation, but their view was of the jungle's top shrouded in cloud. Paul congratulated them on reaching this point by offering the information that no patrol officers ever came this way, in fact they were the first outsiders to do so.

By mid-afternoon, the track began a gradual descent along a ridge from the 10,500-foot range they'd crossed and later reached a tiny grass-roofed hunting-hut belonging to Paul's brother-in-law, where they camped. It was from here, the year before, that the brothers-in-law had found the wreck to which they were being taken. But now Paul looked ill and began to shake. He felt very tired and Adrian pronounced he was suffering an attack of malaria. Mike fervently hoped he would recover, for without his expert knowledge, they would undoubtedly get lost. Luckily, by next morning, the worst of the fever had passed, so leaving their packs by the hut, they set off early, behind a slightly slower guide, crossed three spurs, traversed a last slope and suddenly they were there. Like a stricken animal, the plane lay on the slope; ferns, vines and shrubs grew around the wreck. Water dripped from the trees and formed rivulets on the aluminium. The patrol stood in silence, breathing deeply and taking in the strange, unnatural scene.

To begin with, there was little to see except a fuselage. Mike soon realised it wasn't one of the lost fighter bombers, but a P47D US Army Air Force fighter that had ploughed into the mountainside, presumably whilst climbing and banking steeply, probably attempting to avoid the rising ground. The port wing lay alongside the aircraft, the starboard one was buried underground. Of the pilot there was no trace, but the cockpit canopy was partly open and the parachute harness missing, testimony to the man's escape. Flying just above stalling speed with the cockpit open, to obviate the danger of a jammed canopy during landing, was standard practice during the Second World War amongst fighter pilots expecting to crash land. This one had managed a soft landing and they wondered if J. W. Harris, whose name adorned the aircraft's side beneath the cockpit (together with a sexy pin-up and four small rising sun flags, denoting the kills to his credit), had ever got back to civilisation.

It was quite a tight squeeze getting into the cockpit, but once settled in the seat, Mike studied the controls. Amazingly one—the oxygen flow indicator—still worked. The clock had stopped at 12.20 plus 40 seconds (so they knew the time of impact) and the altimeter confirmed their map reading—they were 8,200 feet above sea level.

The ground around the area was littered with hundreds of live cannon shells and debris, but it rather looked as if the pilot had survived the crash and climbed out alive.

Feeling like time-travellers, the patrol looked at the technology of 35 years before spread around that jungle-clad mountainside. It was uncanny to think that no white man had seen the site since 1944 and unnerving to contemplate the pilot's fate. Perhaps he broke his back or legs and crawled so far before death brought welcome oblivion; he could have got lost or, worse still, been eaten. The patrol members shuddered at the thought. 'Well, we may not have solved the mystery of the missing fighter bombers, but we've certainly found the answer to another disappearance,' said Mike.

Next day, they began the return to Tauta early, but by an easier route. Thick cloud enveloped the mountains, making it impossible to see the surroundings. Seth discussed the situation with Paul and said it would be nice to see where they were going. At the next stop, without a word, Paul started collecting dried grass and dead 'spindly' vegetation, piled them up beside the path and lit a fire. It was not a large fire, but gave off a lot of heat. He kept it going with more bushy twigs and from time to time, squatted down, peering into the mist. They could not understand his purpose until, after about ten minutes, someone said, 'the fog's clearing!'

So it was. Amazingly, the cloud was parting as the fire drove a 'wedge' of hot dry air into its mass. However, this was not all, for the clearing process continued and twenty-five minutes after the fire had been lit, they could see down a cleft of clear air to mountain tops twenty or more miles away. To left and right, the white rolling masses obscured all view, but directly downhill, a clear corridor of air was now open. Was this some ancient skill or black magic? There was no obvious explanation.

Satisfied that he had shown them that they were still several thousand feet above the river valley for which he was aiming, Paul extinguished the fire. Within five minutes, the cloud had closed in again and the patrol was once more enveloped in its folds. They resumed their blind journey down the mountain. Years ago, Mike had heard about 'cloud clearing' on mountains, but had never really believed it until now.

Some hours later, they 'met' a local, or rather heard him scuttling up above the path to get away from the strangers. Paul called to him to come down and a brief shouted exchange ensued, but he remained hidden. A little later, they passed an old woman who appeared to be scolding Paul, for she spoke very loudly and roughly. Finally, the explorers struggled up to a collection of huts perched above the river they'd been following and met a man who informed Paul that he was overdue for his next appointment! This was apparently to guide someone else on a hunting trip and necessitated his leaving the patrol to find their own way home.

This news was both odd and very worrying and Bob Salzberg later expressed his amazement at their being left to fend for themselves. It certainly surprised them, for up to the meeting with the old woman, Paul had seemed happy to stay. Now he could not get away fast enough. Mike was concerned about losing the way back and since they were pretty exhausted and with little food left, it was essential to complete the journey without further delay.

By now, it was late in the day. The road led down across a stream and up over a large hill, and since they would have to camp on high ground with little likelihood of finding water, they washed in the stream and carried up sufficient water for the night. The climb was very hard work.

The next morning, Mike awoke with a swollen left leg. His mosquito net was intact and, to his knowledge, nothing had bitten him in the previous twenty-four hours. That day's march was, for him, doubly difficult as the leg continued to swell. By evening, it was hard to bend as the swelling extended from foot to groin and, by the following morning, his leg looked as if it was encased in a pneumatic splint. Adrian could find no cause for the problem. One of my old friend's many attributes is his ability to use alternative medicine, or as it's sometimes known, 'esoteric healing', a great asset on an expedition! So, he 'healed' it and reduced the size, but the enforced exercise exacerbated the swelling, counteracting his efforts to make it better.

Gradually, pieces of a 'nagging' jigsaw began to fit together: Paul's sudden withdrawal from the team after meeting the local tribesman who, it will be remembered, feared to go near the aircraft for fear of the *Massali*—and the locals would have known the patrol had been to the crash site; the subsequent refusal by anyone to lead them to a second wreck lying nearer to Tauta—which they had originally agreed to do; and now, for no obvious reason, Mike's leg swelling up. One way to stop a team is to incapacitate the leader and possibly something was trying hard to do this to them. Was it black magic? Mike resolved to stand out against this influence (if that is what it was) and, by 'healing' his leg and keeping going, disappoint any onlookers and negate further complications.

After their return to Tauta, his leg got better, but he was then assailed by awful nightmares—imagining that a huge spider (and he can't stand the things) was poised behind the 'privvy' door waiting to pounce on his back in the night. This in itself was strange, since Mike is normally completely 'at home' in the dark. However, his fears evaporated as soon as they left Tauta for the Salzbergs' mission, almost as if the malign power felt it need no longer fight them as they had left its area.

Back at TAC HQ, I passed the details to USAF Headquarters in Honolulu. Within a few days came the reply. Yes—the P47 was on the record. It had taken off from Nadzab Airfield on the morning of 29 April 1944. After a short radio message reporting that he was west of Faitah village and testing his guns, nothing more had been heard of the pilot or the plane. However, it wasn't Harris in the cockpit that fateful day, but First Lieutenant Marion C. Lutes of the 312th US Bomber Group. He'd been on a day off and wanted to fly a fighter! The USAF HQ added that Colonel J. W. Harris, USAF (retired) now lived at Austin, Texas, and when passing through America on my way home, I called him up and told our tale. 'Well, I always wondered what the devil happened to my plane,' he said.

We soon exchanged photos of the P47—before and after the crash. Seeing the 'pin up' on the fuselage, James Harris commented, 'Well, she's certainly weathered better than I have in 35 years!' But we never did find the fighter bombers.

The sun had just dipped over the tall palms, as I stood on the verandah of TAC HQ watching the evening migration of the flying foxes. Tom Richards clumped up the steps, and seizing a cold beer that Margot, my PA, was in the act of opening, flopped onto a chair and stretched his short brown muscular legs.

'What do you think that is, John?' he said, passing me a small lump of shiny black rock. I weighed it thoughtfully in my hand; it felt rather light and seemed to be breaking up into fragments.

'No idea, Tom,' I replied.

'Well, I reckon it's coal, not the old brown stuff—this is proper coal.'

'So what?' I remarked.

Tom quickly explained that PNG had no energy-producing fuels and that, even now, a charcoal plant was being considered by the government. If someone could find a coal field, it would be a great boost to the economy.

'Hey,' I called out to Nick Ray, a TA officer with geological training. 'Can you analyse this?' Nick came into the office and eyed the lump suspiciously—but next day, after a trip to the local technical college, he came back smiling. 'It's coal all right—9600 British Thermal Units Calorific value,' was his report. 'Not bad— not bad,' mused Tom, when I told him. 'Well, get on with it, lad—let's find the seam.'

The police had recently arrested a local witch doctor on suspicion of using explosive from old wartime shells to do a spot of illicit fishing. However, close examination of his 'gun powder' showed it to be coal dust, made from lumps or 'plums' he'd found in a river. Now Tom had a sample and, clearly, one way to find the seam was simply to follow the river and its tributaries, but as it rose at 11,000 feet, this didn't sound like a picnic. Nevertheless, Robbie Roethenmund, my young American assistant, set out with his patrol with tremendous enthusiasm and optimism. They flew in to the area of a small hill station named Pindiu and the hunt was on.

The group included two geologists from the University of PNG and among the YEs who took part was a young English girl, Lorna Gibbons, who told of her adventures in a series of letters to her family.

On the second day, as she trudged up a steep, narrow, muddy path, Lorna had her first confrontation with the loathsome leeches that are an almost unavoidable feature of jungle life. 'They were much smaller than I had imagined,' she wrote. 'They were like tiny

21. (*above*) Papua New Guinea. The P47D U.S. Air Force fighter in 1944, its pilot, Col. J. W. Harris, at the controls.

22. (*left*) The symbol on the wreck of the fighter as discovered by Mike Gambier's expedition.

23. Papua New Guinea. The Kagwesi Crossing on the upper Strickland River. Staff Sgt. Dave Weaver, RE, pauses to rest.
Photo: Major J. R. Chapman

24. Papua New Guinea. A wigman from the Highlands in full regalia poses next to Roger Chapman. *Photo: Capt. Jim Masters*

worms, sitting half off the ground, bending this way and that as though they were watching us. We seemed to draw them to us like magnets and every five minutes or so we had to remove them from our boots as they attempted to get inside. For once, no one particularly wanted to stop for rests on the way and so we walked continuously, flicking off the leeches when we saw them.

'Our carriers, however, were barefoot and were immediately attacked. We watched in fascination as they casually pulled them off—obviously used to them. It was at this point that I took a closer look at my own feet only to discover that the leeches had taken a liking to my woolly socks, had crawled through them and were busy feeding! My immediate reaction was, I should think, identical to that of anyone else in this predicament for the first time. "Agh, leeches, where's a lighter, get the salt—do something." A lighter was quickly produced and within seconds I was leech-free. All that was left were a few trickles of blood.'

Lorna was surprised how quickly she and her companions grew accustomed to the attentions of the leeches, casually flicking them away without any fuss. The pace of the march was gruelling. 'Uphill we walked and downhill we walked, never on the flat for very long and continually stumbling over stones and roots. At times it was hard to see which way the track went and occasionally it was so overgrown that there was no track at all. Often we would see huge spiders, bigger than our hands, sitting in their webs by the side of the track, sometimes scurrying away and sometimes sitting there in open defiance.'

That night, the patrol stayed in the village of Hamomeng, where they were allocated a hut in which to sleep. 'In the evening we sat outside on the "village green" eating platefuls of hot taro and sago round a lantern with the villagers,' wrote Lorna. 'Despite the fact that we had two different languages to contend with, everybody ended up in hoots of laughter as both sides described their way of life, which ranged from high-rise building and Concorde to the spirits living in the nearby jungle. When sign language failed, the three members of our group who were from PNG were always happy to translate, adding their own views on the conversation as they did so.'

Two days later, the patrol stayed the night in the village of Kobea, where Lorna had a sore on her foot treated by the local medicine man. She was reluctant at first to entrust herself to his skills and would have preferred to avail herself of the patrol's first-aid kit. But she submitted suspiciously and, when he squeezed a brown liquid from some leaves he had picked up from the jungle and applied to the sore, the pain and throbbing stopped almost immediately. It was an impressive demonstration of the powers of herbal medicine—all that is available to the tribesmen of the forest.

There was more magic to come. 'I awoke in the morning to the sound of drums, which had apparently been playing right through the night. We had been told the previous evening about the spirits of the area and now we were to see a spirit ceremony. It was conducted by the spirit man of the village, who appeared wearing what looked like nappies held up with a beaded belt and adorned with necklaces and a mask which, with its feathers and pointed nosepiece, gave him the appearance of a bird. Brandishing an axe in one hand and a spear in the other, he danced around a wooden bowl filled with a black liquid, chanting all the time. Eventually, he scooped up handfuls of the liquid and threw it up into the air. When he had finished he stood there, chest blown out, looking very pleased with himself. With the aid of our translators, we discovered that the aim of the ceremony had been to send away all the evil spirits in the area since they were believed to be hiding the coal from us.'

By searching along all the stream beds in the most appalling terrain, Robbie's party eventually staggered into a leech-infested gully and there it was—a glistening black coal seam, running with rain water in the failing light. The ten-foot-thick band had been revealed by the erosion of the stream. Somehow, under these conditions, it seemed incongruous to be finding coal. That night, it was a joyous and excited Robbie who radioed the news of his discovery to us at TAC HQ and within twenty-four hours, Tom and I were on the way to inspect the find. Landing at Pindiu, we marched out through the dripping forest. The rain fell in sheets and within seconds we were drenched; however, morale was high and within a few hours, we were at the seam. Tom was overjoyed and to celebrate produced a cold roast duck and a bottle of Australian claret from one of his many packs that a team of buxom Marys had been recruited to carry.

Having dined in the pouring rain, we slogged on mile after mile to try to trace other points in the valley where the seam might emerge.

Tom's victuals for dinner were a side of roast beef with more fine claret. He certainly knew how to live in the field and his carriers even produced a double camp bed!

The next day, villagers led us up a rocky gorge to another seam and from this, Tom was able to estimate that the field contained 45–50 million tons.

The march back to Pindiu was sheer hell—the rain fell in rods, turning the steep track into a torrent. Up and down, up and down we staggered, our clothes sticking to us. No one spoke—the only noise an occasional muttered curse as the walkers flicked aside the more persistent leeches. My legs felt like lead and even the well-fitted belt kit cut into my damp groaning body.

Every few hundred yards, Tom would pause, whip out his geologists' hammer and seizing a piece of rock, tap at it enthusiastically, but after several minutes' close examination, he'd hurl it away and cry, 'Come on, come on then, let's keep moving.' It took me some while to realise that this was Tom's way of winning a pause for breath!

When we stopped, we simply sat in the rain, inhaling deeply. Once, I pulled off my jungle boots and squirted a dose of ammonia and soap solution over my socks. 'Keeps leeches away better than anything I know,' advised Tom, taking a few calories of Scotch from his battered old hip flask. Lorna's boots were already full of blood from wounds where the loathsome worm-like creatures had been torn away from the flesh.

So, we struggled on over hill and valley, river and stream. The rain was unabated and I have never been so thankful as at the moment when, with dusk falling, we hobbled through the clinging cloud into a small village. Robbie—as fit and tough as a young stag—had gone ahead and a welcome fire blazed up to greet us. 'Just the moment for a bottle of Kanga Rouge,' grinned Tom, as we huddled around the flickering logs—then he added his own contribution—a lump of Pindiu coal. 'Bet the buggers have never tried to burn the stuff,' he laughed, pulling the cork from his last bottle of red wine with accomplished ease.

The discovery may turn out to be of immense value to the country and plans to start mining it are under way. It would be nice to think that it was the spirit man at Kobea who made it all possible—and why not? In that extraordinary country such things seem somehow less far-fetched.

Meanwhile, far away in the west of PNG, Roger Chapman was enduring even more unpleasant hardships, as he led his patrol into the gruelling conditions of the infamous Strickland Gorge.

I'd chosen Roger for this daunting task because of his experience, which included the navigation of the treacherous white-water cataracts of the Blue Nile in Ethiopia and the mighty Zaïre in West Africa on previous Scientific Exploration Society expeditions. Our earlier air reconnaissance had revealed many terrifying rapids and reports showed that the water level could rise from three to six metres in hours; also, the strong winds would make resupply by parachute difficult. I'd been told that a group of porters had once been blown off a rope bridge, to be swallowed up in the boiling torrent beneath. Roger proposed to shoot the upper rapids with two Avon Professional inflatables, equipped with alloy rowing frames. Later, he'd meet up with a larger scientific team at the village of Nomad to make a collection of animals and plants and take a census of the crocodile population from the lower Strickland.

The seventy-five-mile stretch of foaming rapids and cataracts came cascading through a cleft in the mountain 2,500 feet deep, and nobody had ever thought of trying to find a way through and exploring the upper Strickland by riding the swirling waters in an inflatable boat. But the precipitous banks made this route far more preferable. Roger's plan was to take a party of eight men through in two inflatables, but first he needed to go and have a close look to make sure that the venture was at least vaguely feasible. The aerial survey was no good by itself; you cannot really judge the severity of a rapid from the two-dimensional view you get from above, and, apart from that, some sections of the river were in deep gorges, permanently obscured by foliage.

His thorough preliminary research showed that only four white patrols had ever before penetrated these wild and inhospitable regions—the first one a mere twenty-five years previously. All four were led by Australian Kiap officers—the equivalent of the British

Colonial District Commissioners—in the days before PNG was granted independence.

The real pioneer was Des Clancy, who, in 1954, went in with three representatives of the Australian Petroleum Company and one hundred and fifty bearers, guides and armed escorts to search for oil shales. They followed the course of the river as closely as possible along the Gorge and eventually carried on through to the lower reaches where it broadens and meanders more sedately for some four hundred and thirty miles before joining up with the Fly River. They never did strike oil, but Clancy came back with some interesting information about what lay hidden under the umbrellas of low cloud that had always frustrated the aerial map-makers.

At one point, a location known as the Kagwesi Crossing, the whole of the mighty river is channelled through a crevice in the granite no more than ten feet wide. It was, he reported, an awe-inspiring sight. Later, he was forced to climb out of the Gorge, because of the impassability of the terrain, but, from a vantage point three thousand feet up above the river he got a distant view of the gap where the water gushed out of the mountain ranges into the plain below. The mist and cloud that rose like steam from the raging torrent caused him to christen the spot the 'Gates of Hell', while the churning white-water rapids beyond it, he named the 'Devil's Race'.

Two years later, another experienced Kiap officer, J. P. Sinclair, set out with one white companion and one hundred and six bearers intending to cross the river at Kagwesi Crossing. But when he arrived there, he was greeted by a sight even more astonishing than that which had taken Clancy's breath away. It was the rainy season and the river had risen more than twenty feet, so that the water level was actually above the narrow fissure—but the line of it was clearly and spectacularly marked by a fantastic mare's tail of spray that was hurled many feet into the air by the tremendous forces created under the surface. So great were these forces, that hefty logs were being thrown up and then bobbled like feather-light table-tennis balls on the crest of the fountaining jets of water.

The two other patrols that ventured into the area between 1968–72 struck out into the interior of the Muller Mountains, with the specific aim of trying to contact the native inhabitants for the purpose of completing a national census. Roger actually managed to track down members of each of these teams and they were able to supply useful briefings about the conditions and people he could expect to meet.

They confirmed that the terrain is as harsh and inhospitable as one is likely to find anywhere in the world. When you are not scrambling and hacking your way up and down almost sheer-sided ridges covered in dense undergrowth, you are having to pick a careful path across the limestone rock, so sharp-edged that the soles of the toughest boots will be shredded after a few miles. Even seemingly open areas, that appear from the air to be smooth carpets of green turf, usually turn out to be covered in kunai grass fifteen feet high, that is so difficult to cut through that a fit man can be reduced to sweat-soaked exhaustion within a matter of yards.

Roger also learned that the interior tribesmen were often extremely primitive and that their reactions to outsiders would be unpredictable. The early patrols had adopted a policy of sending ahead shouters—native guides who would go forward and literally bellow out advance warning of the party's arrival in the area and call in any tribes in the locality for a meeting. Salt and tobacco would then be handed over as a gesture of friendship and, once the ice had been broken, impressive shooting displays with rifles would be laid on to discourage any hostile notions. There had never been any attacks, although one of the census patrols had narrowly avoided an ambush.

It was against this background that Roger led out his ten-strong reconnaissance party, which included an Australian expatriate government lawyer, Bob Woods. There were also four native bearers and two members of the PNG Defence Force, who were to act as liaison officers.

The bearers were recruited from villages around Lake Kopiago, where the base camp for the expedition was sited. Finding suitable men was not too easy. There was a marked reluctance to venture deep into the mountains, partly because of the punishing conditions and partly owing to the risk of straying into enemy territory. However, with the help of the District Officer and a show of hard cash, resistance was finally overcome and four fine, strong-looking individuals were taken on.

They were all from either the Duna or the Huri tribes—otherwise known as the Wigmen on account of the extraordinarily elaborate head-dresses they wear. To see the males strutting around like peacocks on market day, while their womenfolk get on with the business, is quite an experience. It is like watching an exotic Easter Bonnet Parade. Each crowning glory seems more extravagant than the one before—towering structures of hair, feathers, fur and flowers that are often shaped rather like Napoleonic hats. Quills or bamboo are traditionally worn through the nose, but, since the advent of Western influence, ball-point pens are very much in vogue!

It did not take long to discover that the going was every bit as tough as everybody had warned it would be. Within three days— before they had even reached the Strickland River—the party lost the services of the two local soldiers, who had to return to base when their legs gave out under the strain and badly swollen knees threatened to bring them to a complete and painful standstill. Everybody else was suffering, too, as they sweated, slithered and clawed their way through the forest, stumbling under the weight of their fifty-pound packs as their feet caught in the tangle of roots and creepers. Even the bearers, who were to carry food and equipment, found it hard to cope at times as the patrol pressed on at a murderous pace. They were on the march by 0645 every morning, in an effort to make the most of the cool part of the day, and did not call a halt until 1600. They then had just about enough energy left to set up camp and cook a meal before collapsing, exhausted, into their hammocks by 1900. By that time, they were normally so tired that neither the mosquitoes, nor the regular drenching downpours disturbed their slumbers. Each night, I talked to Roger on the remarkable Plessey Clansman radio. He didn't complain, but I knew the going was very hard. I promised to come in with the next RAAF Chinook resupply helicopter, to see how they were doing.

Once they reached the river, it was a matter of following its course as closely as possible, carefully charting every feature and grading each rapid on a scale of one to six, depending on the degree of danger and difficulty it presented. They had already passed the Kagwesi Crossing a few days before—and found it every bit as awesome as Clancy and Sinclair had promised. Now, they were about to enter one of those tantalising and mysterious blanks on the map.

Having camped for the night on a narrow ledge above the river, they awoke to find that the torrential rain that had bucketed down while they slept, had transformed their surroundings. The level of the water had risen so dramatically that they were effectively cut off on their ledge and could neither advance, nor go back the way they had come. There was only one way out—and that was upwards. It meant climbing a hair-raising three thousand feet up the side of the gorge, which was almost sheer in some parts, but there was no other alternative.

It took nearly ten hours to claw their way to the top. They had to move with the utmost caution, hauling themselves up on vines, roots and the most tenuous handholds in the crumbling rock. By the time they eventually made it, they barely had the strength to rig their hammocks and swallow a hurriedly prepared meal of dehydrated food before flaking out.

The next night, Roger's voice was excited. 'We've found some people,' then unusually bad conditions cut him out, but words like 'primitive', 'stone axes', 'no white men' came through and we knew that Roger Chapman had achieved the ultimate goal in many armchair explorers' minds. Quite simply, he'd bumped into a lost or unknown tribe.

That morning, they'd decided to strike inland, away from the gorge, in search of a suitable clearing in which to land the planned resupply helicopter. After cutting through the jungle for about three hours, they picked up an old hunting track and followed that for a further couple of miles until they reached a stream which provided a welcome excuse to stop for a cup of tea. It was as he bent to scoop a billycan of water for the brew, that Roger noticed something he had not expected in such a remote area: the distinctive smell of woodsmoke—from someone else's camp fire.

The patrol immediately crept further along the track until, around a bend, they glimpsed through the trees a small clearing in which stood two, low, rectangular huts, with wisps of blue smoke filtering through the thatched roofs. Then, figures were seen moving about and the sounds of children playing and pigs squealing floated across the forest.

At once, Roger sent ahead two of his Duna bearers—Harirega and Ayape—as an advance party, and when he saw that they received a friendly welcome, he led the rest of the patrol forward into the clearing. As he did so, Ayape directed towards him one of the men with whom he had been conversing in a strange dialect, and when Roger extended his hand, the small bearded man grasped it firmly and held on determinedly, clearly not wanting to let go.

There then followed a bizarre four-way conversation. Roger spoke in English to Bob Woods, Bob translated in Pidgin—the nearest thing to an official language in PNG—so that Harirega could then rephrase the message in Duna for the benefit of Ayape, who was the only one familiar with the dialect spoken by the tribesmen.

In this tortuous way it was established that the village they'd discovered was called Tigaro and that the inhabitants were nomadic Pogaians. There were five families in the group which numbered fifteen altogether. The man who was hanging on to Roger's hand so affectionately was called Kiwanga and the chief, who was away working in the village 'gardens', but was due back at sunset, was named Kemba. When he eventually made an appearance, he confirmed that nobody in his small tribe had ever seen a white man before—a fact which seemed to be rather amusingly borne out by the way in which Roger's white team members were subjected to close scrutiny and the occasional curious prod.

The fascination was mutual. Kemba and his people were clearly untouched by modern civilisation. Their most sophisticated and prized possessions were two steel axe heads, which they had traded with other tribes in the Bulago Valley, where they had been originally introduced by one of the later Kiap patrols. Otherwise, they had only stone tools and implements and their other possessions were made from natural materials. Barbed or notched arrows of razor-sharp split bamboo were used with six-foot-long hardwood bows for the daily cuscus or wallaby hunt. Some arrows had three or four prongs for catching birds or fish. The women appeared in the evening, carrying taro and sweet potatoes or 'Kau Kau' in 'bilums', net baskets hung from their heads. They wore only grass skirts, while the men covered themselves with a loin cloth in the front and over their backsides, a hanging bunch of 'tanket' leaves known evocatively in Pidgin as 'arsegrass'. Most wore thin armbands, also of bark. Kemba, the chief, sported a necklace of large cowrie shells and a half moon shaped 'Kina' shell on his dark chest. They existed on a diet of root crops, grown in their forest 'gardens', augmented with whatever they could hunt down.

Their precious domestic pigs are only slaughtered on very special occasions and are otherwise treated with loving care. The women walked around clutching piglets as if they were their own children and will even suckle them in emergencies. It was a standing joke that the men guarded the pigs more jealously than their wives and children. A tribesman once told me, 'women and children very easy to make—pigs more difficult!'

Friendship was further cemented with gifts of salt and tobacco, and it was agreed that the patrol would spend the night in the village before clearing a landing-site for the helicopter the next morning. The villagers watched spellbound as Sergeant Dave Weaver prepared the powerful Plessey radio and called me up in TAC HQ, three hundred and fifty miles away in Lae. Eventually, they grew bolder and fingered everything of metal, glass or plastic with child-like glee. Cigarette lighters and binoculars were considered quite amazing.

My arrival next day, in a giant RAAF Chinook, brought the Stone Age face to face with the 20th century in the most spectacular fashion. The idea of a simple supply drop was changed because it was decided that the patrol might as well take advantage of the situation and hitch a lift back to the banks of the Strickland. Alas, the stone axes had not cleared the last few feet of tree stumps and landing proved impossible, so we had to remain in the hover as Roger's patrol struggled aboard.

In all honesty, I can say it was one of the most worrying ten minutes of my life, as the huge machine bucked and swayed in the jungle clearing. The 'Lost Tribe' stared in amazement at our monster, which might as well have been a space craft in a city dweller's back yard. Some wept with fear, but were so terrified that they were immobile. Apparently, when they'd seen the first carriers climb onto the open ramp, they thought the great bird was devouring them!

At last, Roger, wild eyed with exertion and through trying to scream orders above the hideous noise, hauled himself up the steps, his arm muscles flexed as he tossed his rucksack through the open door. I handed him a set of earphones and a microphone. 'That's it, then,' he yelled—almost blasting our ears off. 'Speak normally, for

God's sake,' I called and his tense, weatherbeaten face lit up with a grin.

As the Chinook lifted off and rose above the tiny jungle clearing, with a deafening roar from its powerful engines and the hundred m.p.h. downdraught from its twin rotors creating a mini-hurricane that raised a swirling cloud of dust and whipped the surrounding foliage into a frenzy of dancing branches and wildly fluttering leaves, fifteen near-naked brown bodies prostrated themselves on the ground, their hands clamped over their ears, their foreheads pressed to the earth, their eyes not daring to look up. As the scene receded out of focus below them, we peered down anxiously at the prone forms and wondered what must be going through their minds. 'We've given them their income tax forms,' quipped Bob.

Fifty years previously, when aircraft first arrived in PNG, similar encounters had given rise to the cargo cults among the primitive peoples, who understandably concluded that the strange white men who descended from the skies in the bird-like machines packed with wonderful goods must surely be gods. It was fascinating to speculate about the legends that might grow up around the meeting between Chief Kemba's people and Roger Chapman's patrol. The event would surely pass into local folklore as the tribal story-tellers raised their sing-song voices over countless camp fires and spread the news in the traditional way to the remotest corner of the forest.

After some tense manoeuvring, we dropped the patrol at the Bulalo River junction to continue the reconnaissance on to the 'Gates of Hell', but the nearer they got, the tougher the going became, and they began to realise why Clancy had been content to view this fascinating spot from a distance. When they did eventually reach it, they were all in a very sorry state. Dave Weaver's face was puffed and swollen from insect bites and his lips were cracked and bleeding, so that he looked as though he had just taken a hiding from Muhammad Ali; others were covered in cuts, sores and a blistering rash caused by brushing against a leaf with a sting many times more powerful than a normal nettle. Their arms and legs were a mass of festering tropical ulcers, resulting from open sores that refused to heal in the humidity, and Roger had a particularly uncomfortable variety of complaints. A spider had bitten him on the hand, causing his whole arm to swell up; he had a nasty abrasion all down his right shin which just would not heal, and a terrified porter had punched out one of his teeth as Roger dragged the non-swimmer across a torrent. But to cap it all, he had a bad dose of diarrhoea. No wonder he wrote in his diary towards the end of the trip: 'Frankly, all of us will be pleased to see the back of this miserably wet, tangled stretch of river. It is only cups of tea and a sense of humour which keep us going. Our main problem is that we have to cut every inch of the way with machetes. There are no trails on the steep, muddy banks because no-one has ever been here before. And, as I listen to the torrential rain on the waterproof sheet above my hammock, I can well understand why!'

Despite this, he started making plans for the return visit to this mysterious area and his full-scale river-running venture, which took place later, and discovered a great deal about the region. There were no huge waterfalls. It was just one long, terrifying water chute from the mountains to the swamps.

But the news of their discovery had not gone unnoticed by the world's press. 'Explorers Find Stone Age Tribe', shouted one headline. 'The Tribe That Time Forgot', screamed another. News of the encounter between Operation Drake and the Pogaians, who had never before come into contact with white men or the outside world, was given predictably sensational treatment by the press and this, unfortunately, caused us some embarrassment. It was not that the newspapers got the facts wrong—just that they put them together out of context in such a way as to create a highly dramatic and rather misleading impression that did not go down too well with a newly independent local government, that was anxious not to emphasize the primitive side of life in PNG.

Roger's original report of the meeting, which he gave us by radio, was relatively matter-of-fact. He was fascinated, but not unduly surprised, to have come across people who had never seen white men before, in a region where white men rarely venture, and where the more isolated communities are known to have little or no contact with the tribes in the neighbouring valleys, let alone the outside world. Indeed, Bob Woods, who worked with the PNG government, had quite expected to make some 'first contacts'.

But when a visiting reporter picked up the story, he did not hesitate to include all the local colour he could muster, including references to cannibalism, before filing it to London in a form guaranteed to catch the jaundiced eye of any news editor. By the time the sub-editors and headline-writers had finished with it, the final version that reached the world's breakfast tables had been blown up into something only marginally less miraculous than the discovery of Conan Doyle's 'Lost World', complete with real live dinosaurs!

Immediately, all hell broke loose. We were inundated with calls from radio and television stations around the globe, all wanting to follow up the story. A Japanese television company was ready to spend millions of yen on flying a news team out to get exclusive film coverage of the tribe. The big American networks were also keen to get in on the act.

When the story hit the headlines, I was in Port Moresby awaiting the arrival of our Chairman, General Sir John Mogg, and George Baker, the ex-High Commissioner. They could not have arrived at a better moment and the next day were able to placate the Hon. Michael Somare, PNG's Prime Minister. The diplomatic way in which the General and George handled the situation solved the problem and, I felt, greatly enhanced our image. Nevertheless, the PNG government, whom we could not afford to offend, made it clear that they were far from happy with the prehistoric image of their country which, they felt, the story projected. They were particularly upset by suggestions of cannibalism. As far as they are concerned, there is an important distinction to be made between cannibalism and the offence known officially as 'interference with the human body'. This latter involves eating flesh from a body that is already dead—as against going out and killing somebody specifically with a view to eating him—and was once quite common practice in PNG, as it was in several other parts of the world. It is now outlawed, but old customs die hard and cases still occasionally come to light. It is a subject about which the government is understandably sensitive—especially as it was doing its best to encourage a tourist trade!

In view of all this, we had to go out of our way to play down the more sensational aspects of the story. Even so, it remained as one of the highlights of the entire expedition into that mysterious land.

6

The Loch Ness Monster
and Friends

'If that there monster gets into the waterways of England, God only knows what damage it will do!'

The air in the bar was heavy with tobacco smoke and the delightful aroma of malt whisky as we stood in a corner watching the dying sun sinking behind the Island of Rhum.

'Excuse me one moment,' said Adrian through his dense red beard, as a thin man with a ruddy, weather-beaten face touched him on the sleeve. Tim Dinsdale, Corporal Thomas and I continued our conversation whilst Adrian talked intently with the newcomer at the other end of the room. A few moments later, our bearded friend returned and with suitably furtive glances, spoke in a low voice. 'There's been a sighting,' he said, adding quickly, 'this afternoon—near the Chapel.'

I was faintly amused and my new-found friend sensed it. 'I expect you think we've set this up specially for you,' said Tim, but I could tell from his expression that he hadn't and I felt that these people were deadly earnest and quite sincere. Already I knew that the Loch Morar Expedition was a serious attempt to solve one of the world's greatest mysteries and that this group of engineers and scientists were not the sort of people to gamble their meagre hard-won resources on something which they thought was a hoax or a myth.

'This man lives beside the loch not far from here,' said Adrian, a tinge of excitement in his voice. 'Apparently, his wife and her children watched a big hump moving about for several hours this afternoon, and he's agreed to allow us to question them.'

Although the hour was late, it was still daylight in this remote corner of the West Highlands of Scotland and we set off at once for a lonely cottage on the shores of Loch Morar.

The lady who opened the door was clearly worried and nervous, and she welcomed us as if ushering in guests to a funeral. Her children sat or stood in the parlour where a low fire glowed in the hearth. They seemed stunned and overawed, but tea and cake were produced and then expert monster investigator Tim Dinsdale and the current expedition leader, Adrian Shine, began their questioning.

The woman then told us her story, quite firmly and without a trace of emotion. She had been gardening in front of the cottage at about 2 p.m.; it was a fine clear day and the surface of the loch, some 200 yards away, was still. Suddenly, she heard a splash and, imagining it to be wild duck alighting, looked up, but what she saw left her speechless and clutching the hoe for support. About 200 yards out into Loch Morar and therefore around 400 yards from her, was a great dark hump. 'So high it looked,' she said, indicating with her hand a vertical distance of about 3 feet. Then, full of fear, she did what every mother would do—called out to her children. They came running and saw the hump; the girls ran behind the house in terror, but the little boy, a tough lad, whom I guessed to be twelve years old, seized a garden fork and raced to the shore. However, the monster, if that is what it was, took no notice of them.

The amazing part of the story was how for almost three hours the 'thing' submerged, surfaced, and darted hither and thither 'as if it were trying to catch fish,' said the woman. Eventually it had headed off up the loch leaving a big wake.

Tim questioned her with great tact, but with an insistence on detail. She'd lived for fourteen years by the loch and she had never seen anything like this before. The frightened woman knew the difference between salmon leaping, otters playing, ducks landing, floating logs, patches of weed and upturned boats. What she had seen bore no resemblance to any of these. She kept saying, 'It was just like a whale.' 'How do you know what a whale looks like?' asked Tim. 'Because I'm the daughter of a fisherman,' was the instant reply.

Tim made her repeat the story—but her recall was faultless and except for the size of one or two dimensions, her son's description confirmed it in every detail.

Sitting in the old armchair in the corner of that small sitting-room, I had no part in the proceedings, but I was fascinated. When we arrived, the woman had asked us all what we did and made us swear that none of us was from the press. The thought of any publicity was totally abhorrent to her. This I learned later was because of a local superstition that says that Morag, as the Loch Morar monster is known, was the harbinger of death, and this was confirmed by the sinking of HMS *Hood* during World War II, with many West Highland men in her crew. It was said that on that fateful day, Morag had been seen rising from the dark peat-stained waters. Ever since then, its appearance has been regarded as an omen of ill fortune. Although, as far as I know, nothing terrible happened on this occasion.

It was midnight when Tim switched off his tape recorder and we all stood up, thanked the woman and her family for their kindness and patience and strolled out into the twilight. In June, darkness only lasts for an hour or two this far north. The surface of the loch was still, nothing moved, there was not even a ripple.

How on earth could so large a beast inhabit a few square miles of water and remain unknown to science? But I had seen people interrogated in the Army and I knew that liars usually have a motive. I could see no motive for these simple folk to lie and I was quite convinced that they had been describing accurately whatever it was they'd seen.

Many explorers claim that it's curiosity that drives them on—and I feel that this is an important motivating force in my life. Thus, the mystery of the so-called Loch Ness (or for that matter Loch Morar) monster has always intrigued me.

Loch Ness is Scotland's largest lake, 23 miles long and over a mile wide; this vast area of dark, peaty water is surrounded by magnificent scenery. Nowadays, roads run along both sides of the loch and every year hundreds of thousands of tourists pass by on their way through the Great Glen that cuts right across Scotland.

From as early as 600 AD, reports of sightings of a strange creature have been made. Early stories told of a 'Water Horse' that was believed to live in the deep, dark waters.

When, in 1933, a new main road was built along the north shore and many more people gained access to the loch, the reports began to multiply. Since then there have been over 3000 eye-witness accounts. Photographs have been taken, films made and teams of serious scientists have studied this fascinating mystery. There have been many hoaxes, but zoologists who have examined the genuine evidence believe that there is a case to answer and that the animal, if that is what it is, is quite unlike any known living species. With the introduction of sonar and stroboscopic cameras yet more convincing results have been accumulated and today, fewer scientists are cracking jokes about monsters! There are plenty who remember the coelacanth's comparatively recent emergence from extinction.

Not many people realise that there are other lochs in Scotland also said to contain monsters and other bodies of water elsewhere in the world that have similar phenomena.

This was about the sum total of my knowledge when, in 1976, I drove into the little village of Morar that nestles on the west coast of Scotland and looks out towards the bleak mountains of Skye. I had an open mind on the subject, but if I were really truthful, my scepticism was probably greater than my belief.

At Morar I hoped to find an area on which to train my Regiment the following year. Defence funds were scarce and transport was in short supply, but we could go anywhere in Britain, if we could get there by train. Mallaig (near Morar) was about the furthest it was possible to go by rail from our base at Dover. Hitherto I'd believed all the monster sightings were at Loch Ness, but now I discovered that Loch Morar was a more popular spot for serious investigations, although not linked to Loch Ness.

I'd heard that a monster-hunting expedition was in progress there and that they occupied the best camp site on the shore. I decided to make friends and see if we could be helpful to each other.

It was the experience in that lonely lochside cottage that convinced me there was a mystery to explore. The first question I asked myself was why it should prove so difficult to solve.

An important reason is depth. Loch Ness is almost 300 metres deep and Loch Morar is even deeper. If the creature were vertebrate, bones might be dredged up, but the enormous depth and the bisected underwater terrain made this extremely difficult. Attempts had already been made, without success.

All surface-based research is plagued by rough water. Loch Ness is an extensive stretch of water upon which the winds, channelled by the Great Glen, play havoc and can very quickly turn the placid surface into a stormy inland sea swept by squalls. Other Scottish lochs suffer similarly and, as I have since learnt, can upset even the best-equipped expedition.

There is also the question of visibility. Highland rivers carry down their peaty water which reduces underwater vision to a few feet. It's like diving in a cup of strong tea. Light only penetrates for a fathom or two from the surface giving the lochs an eerie, frightening feel that has been known to terrify even experienced divers. Those who have descended into the depths have seen steep rocky walls with huge ravines and overhangs. One early expedition even reported seeing giant eels. It's no place for the faint-hearted as I found when I descended into Loch Morar.

Although the visibility was better than in most other lochs, we soon lost sight of the surface. Only the hiss and rattle of our demand valves broke the stillness. As I switched on my powerful underwater lamp, an endless cloud of tiny particles swept upwards through the beam. Their movement told me I was descending, but I saw no sign of the bottom until a few moments later, when to my horror, my fins touched something dark and slimy. I jerked my feet back, but it was only a boulder on the loch bed! At 23 metres I was still barely a stone's throw from the shore and even with the lamp, could see only a few feet around me in this still, cold, dead blackness. I felt claustrophobia grip me as never before. Clearly, the only way to identify this mysterious creature would be by using highly sophisticated equipment and the latest electronic means, I told myself. Mere man alone was not likely to succeed.

Indeed, Adrian Shine, whom I'd met that eventful evening at Morar, had already reached the same conclusion. Adrian, over six foot, had earlier built himself an immensely strong fibreglass sphere as a submersible observation chamber into which he'd squeezed himself and been lowered into the loch. At 10 metres or so, anchored to the bottom by a net full of large stones, he'd sat in a pre-natal position clutching an 8 mm cine camera, peering expectantly through the armoured glass portholes. Air was pumped down from above and when he wished to return to the surface, he did so somewhat dramatically, by releasing the net and flying upward like a huge ping-pong ball—often leaping clear of the surface.

However, Adrian's approach was quite methodical. Working with scientists and students from the Royal Holloway College and various universities, he set about examining the fauna and flora of Loch Morar to see if there were sufficient food of one sort or another to support several large aquatic creatures. It was assumed that in view of the time that reports had been made there must be a breeding population. He started by making a biological survey and carrying out a bone search using a boat fitted with a glass dome in the hull. Alas, this eventually hit a rock and sank, but not before its task was completed—having surveyed over two hundred miles. Having decided there was enough food, he'd set up apparatus to attempt to film the beast underwater. For his purpose, he'd developed an upward-scanning underwater video camera which proved to be very effective—if only Morag would oblige by swimming over it.

In the meantime, I'd given Adrian some backing with some of my divers from the Junior Leaders Regiment and a few young soldiers with image intensifiers to watch the surface of the loch at night. We did this as a training exercise and there was no doubt that, in spite of the ferocious midges, the young men had a most enjoyable time. I spent several nights lying in the heather scanning the darkened water through the 'night sight'. Victoria, my younger daughter, usually came with me and produced a hip flask at suitable moments to raise my morale. We certainly saw ducks and were amazed at the clarity of vision possible with the equipment, but with the exception of one Junior Leader who swore he'd seen a dark shape on the surface, there was nothing to report.

However, Adrian was not despondent and we all concluded that no one would believe a surface sighting anyway—no matter how good the photographs. I was constantly puzzled by the simple questions—'What sort of creature is it? A huge fish, a mammal or a reptile?'

By now, Sir Peter Scott had studied all the evidence and especially some amazing underwater photos taken in 1972 by an Edgerton strobe-flash camera and recorded simultaneously on sonar. This breakthrough had been achieved in Loch Ness by The Academy of Applied Science from America and after 'computer enhancements', the photographs showed various parts of what appeared to be a large animate object. The most impressive picture was of a huge diamond-shaped fin or flipper. There seemed no question of any hoax, and hoping to gain vital protection for the creature, Sir Peter had given it a Latin name 'Nessiteras rhombopteryx', which meant 'The Ness Monster with the diamond fin'.

Of course, there were still those who scoffed at all this and reckoned all monster hunters were at best harmless nuts or at worst publicists seeking to gain glory and financial reward. However, those that I met did not strike me as being in either category.

You could not meet a more sincere, cautious and dedicated man than Tim Dinsdale. An aero-engineer who has spent over twenty years researching this phenomenon and is now the leading chronicler of this mystery. Neither is Sir Peter Scott, the world-famous naturalist, a person to be easily fooled by some old wives' tale. There were a host of other, less well-known people, including priests, policemen, school teachers, and crofters who had made sworn statements regarding their personal sightings on Lochs Morar and Ness.

Tim Dinsdale had studied one hundred separate eye-witness reports, obtained over twenty-six years, from 1933 to 1958 and in his book, *Loch Ness Monster*, he produced excerpts from this analysis together with his conclusions. This was very much our bible.

Although there are early historical references, by far the majority of sightings were made in the period 1933–34. This may have been due to the lochside road-building project, which cleared trees and vegetation, giving good views to a great many. Local people, who are less inclined to talk of the monster for fear of ridicule, would be the only ones to see it in winter. However, in summer every tourist who passes Loch Ness hopes for a sighting and many think they have seen something. Thus there are more reports in the summer. Tim believes there is evidence to suggest that Nessie may prefer sunshine—or perhaps warmer water. Most appearances do seem to occur during the first few hours after dawn and this might point towards the monster being nocturnal.

Opinions vary as to the general appearance of the creature. Some say the head is horse-like, others that it is the size of a cow's, only flatter; that of a large dog or even a goat. Some describe the neck as long and undulating, others as about five feet in length and one foot thick. Details of the face vary too. Eyes like wide slits or even large and shining. There are reports of stumps, like broken-off horns, on the top of the head. Some folk have gained an overall impression of a reptile. The variations are endless.

Despite these comparisons of head appearances, the question of profile does not seem to cause so much disagreement. Most relate to a reptilian head; some with a pair of horns or ears or even a snout. When considering size, one should remember that scale and distance are difficult to estimate when viewed across water.

A number of viewers have observed white markings on the cheek and throat. The mouth, estimated to be about eighteen inches wide, has been seen to open and close, as though the creature were breathing and even a vapour or 'steam' has been reported coming from the mouth.

However, the most pronounced feature appears to be the vast body, the head being a tiny extension to the neck. Those who have witnessed it at close quarters recount an ugly head, with eyes hardly visible. When eyes have been seen, they have been near the top of the head. Whatever the description, it appears they are not the type of eyes usually associated with any known fish.

The head and neck are of notable zoological concern, displaying equally perplexing qualities. When they appear on the surface of the water, they are usually at an angle of about thirty degrees; if the animal is moving at speed and only a foot or two may be visible. On other occasions the neck may appear vertically to the height of six feet, thick where it joins the massive body, but tapering to the head. A few sightings have referred to a mane, or hair, being observed on the back of the neck.

Sometimes the neck emerges gracefully from the water without the body being visible. The head has been seen to turn quickly and shake furiously, showing signs of sight and awareness of movement and it has been known to dive suddenly at the sound of engines or voices.

Judging from these accounts of angle, movement and height, it must be a very muscular creature. If the numerous viewings are to be considered—and all should be—it is quite unlike any known living species.

The body is described mainly as dark in colour and a series of humps or like the 'whale' that the lady of Morar saw—some reports state that it stands to about 4 feet and is 12 feet in length. These descriptions are all very varied, but the overall impression is of an enormous mass.

Most sightings refer to the humps, but the number varies from one to nineteen and in some cases, have been described as coils. Until further studies are carried out, all that can be done is to try to assess the size and shape of all these projections. They appear to be quite solid and thus could not relate directly to a backbone. The most common opinion is that there are three humps which stand to about 4 feet above the surface, are separated by 6–8 feet of water and cover a length of approximately 30 feet. They are certainly not fins and no known species has such a body shape. Amazing though it may seem, these humps appear to be capable of changing shape. It has been known for the creature to be seen with three humps, swim off and then return a few minutes later with no visible humps at all. Witnesses have reported rounded or triangular humps actually changing shape!

Another source of constant debate is whether or not the animal has fins or paddles. Most people have only noticed the splashing, but a few sightings have reported seeing front flippers. This is an important factor for zoologists. If it can be firmly established that the animal has flippers and not legs, it may help identify the original species to which it belongs. Unfortunately descriptions vary greatly. Some report seeing flippers splashing in the water, others paddles working alternately in a turning movement, others that a paddling movement was seen from the front and the back and again, that the wash was caused by movement under the surface. This mystery will also remain until more research can be carried out, but evidence does point to the existence of flippers and, in all probability, the rear ones are the larger.

Few descriptions exist of a tail, but these are consistent. They tell of a powerful appendage thrashing in the water, with the disturbance being up to 20 feet behind the humps. This is an interesting factor, especially as it could be used in swimming. There has been only one sighting of the tail out of the water and then the estimated length was 6 feet and the overall length of the animal 20 feet.

However, as other estimates have been of a much larger animal, one would expect the tail to be longer.

As mentioned previously, it's jolly difficult to judge distance and size over water, but we know from close-quarter sightings that this is an enormous creature up to forty feet in length, nose to tip of tail.

There have been few variations about the colour of the monster. Most have reported it to be grey or a reddish brown and some reports have indicated olive or darkish green or just dark, but these latter opinions could have been clouded by shadows or light on the water. Some have described the part visible below the water to be lighter than that above. It could be that the animal is able to change colour or that colour varies with age and sex. The former is characteristic of reptiles, but has not actually been observed happening. Again, clear sightings or film are needed before this can be clarified.

There have been differing reports about the texture of the skin, some describing it as tough and rough looking, others as smooth, dark and shiny. All reports agree that it is skin and not scales, but as Tim Dinsdale points out—a rough, wet surface seen in the sun at a distance could appear shiny and therefore smooth, but a smooth surface, whether wet or dry, could never appear rough. Although it could possibly belong to the reptile family, it might just as easily be a mammal or amphibian if the similarity to elephant's hide is adhered to, and one must be left pondering until more evidence emerges.

The effect of a sighting on viewers is generally one of amazement. Some have exclaimed about its size; others about its appearance, likening it to a prehistoric creature. Many have been awestruck by its strangeness or its graceful movement across the loch. The very size of the creature must greatly impress viewers and at close quarters, it is understandable that awe is sometimes turned to fear.

Most witnesses who have seen the animal moving, agree that it does so at great speed—anything up to 35 m.p.h. Accounts tell of it travelling rapidly in a straight line, but zigzagging when moving slowly. It also appears to be fond of basking on the surface. If these reports of great speed are accurate, the animal must be incredibly powerful and streamlined to enable its large size to slip through the water. This would also account for the mass of disturbance and wash that are continually recorded.

Another extraordinary factor remains—the manner in which the monster submerges. It has been seen to dive in the normal way; head, neck then body, but only when suddenly startled. Most accounts tell of it just sinking vertically with little if any water movement. The latter could be achieved by altering its shape.

It has been known to swim around for anything up to ten minutes on the surface and enjoys basking in the sunshine. On a few occasions, it has stayed on the surface for as long as forty minutes.

Tim found that the most common places for Nessie to appear were opposite populated areas. This he considered to be of significance. For if people were fabricating stories about seeing a monster, they would be unlikely to say they had seen it outside their own homes; on the contrary, they would probably claim to have seen it in some remote part of the loch.

He had carefully noted the best conditions of visibility, wind and water for sightings, but he felt it pointless to attempt to analyse the very many reports, which varied from one extreme to the other. On some occasions he found that the creature had been seen within a few yards of an observer, in broad daylight. Conditions at the time had been quite still and the surface a leaden mirror when the monster had come swimming along. At other times it was seen over a mile away, beating its way through the short waves on a windy afternoon when the visibility was closing in. However, regardless of the conditions, those who watched were quite certain that they really had seen a huge living thing and not some ordinary, everyday object, such as a log.

He suggested that this assurance is more understandable, when reading an account of two young people who 'watched the monster at a range of some 3,500 yards and reported they could see it quite clearly at this distance with the naked eye!' He felt, and I agree with him, that 'If this report is true, that animal must be of a size that puts it outside the category of any known freshwater species—and thus it remains a complete enigma; but from out of this analysis it is possible to construct a picture of the beast which gains its shape and form from the words of a hundred different people.'

Although few of these good folk could claim expert zoological knowledge, I too felt that the outline of this picture that Tim Dinsdale's research had produced was probably fairly near the truth.

Meanwhile, the Scientific Exploration Society had given its approval and support to Adrian Shine's expedition, which had now moved to Loch Ness where the Academy of Applied Science continued to operate. Adrian and I discussed the possibility of following the US Navy's example and using dolphins to carry a strobe light and video camera in a quest to locate the monster. However, Dan Osman made some enquiries for us in Miami and it was generally considered that the chemical composition of the peaty waters would harm the dolphin. I later heard that the Academy planned to do something similar. They intended to use a pair of these highly intelligent creatures that had been trained in Florida to home in on Nessie. Alas, one of the dolphins died before it could be brought to Scotland and the idea was shelved.

To support his expedition at Loch Ness, Adrian had built a huge, inflatable, motorised pontoon on which he'd mounted a substantial cabin containing a sophisticated FURUNO sonar, and when I visited him in 1981, he was overjoyed at the success of the 40-foot rig and the Underwater Sonar 'contacts' obtained. These appear as a blip on the screen when the sonar beam bounces back from an object detected underwater, rather like an echo-sounding of a hunted submarine, or radar detecting incoming planes at an airport. Public interest was growing and by now an excellent, truthful 'Loch Ness Monster Exhibition' had been opened at the Drumnadrochit Hotel on the north side of the loch. Ronnie Bremner and Tony Harmsworth, who'd put it together, quickly created a centre to which we gravitated and where evidence could be displayed. Ronnie and Tony were genial hosts and they did much to create a spirit of co-operation between Loch Ness explorers.

By 1981, the attention of the various serious monster-hunters had turned to sonar and underwater video or photography. One particular well-equipped boat was the *New Atlantis* of Caley Cruisers, whose highly efficient director, Jim Hogan, had it fitted out with the latest sonar. Tim Dinsdale was aboard in May that year when a Caley expedition, with one boat trailing a special video camera, set out on a search.

A small team of experts was responsible for the sophisticated equipment and the interpretation of the charts. Work began just off the high, south-west shoreline in ideal weather conditions. Soon the sonar picked up a large, moving object. When Tim went aboard *Highland Admiral* he found that the TV monitor had produced a clear picture of the bottom silt, twigs and other objects over 200 metres below. They continued scanning the bottom surface for nearly an hour, using a 20-watt bulb for illumination. The potential of this method became increasingly obvious.

Adrian was also highly successful with an underwater TV camera, lent to him by Tamtec Ltd, which he lowered to the loch bed and, using a 250-watt light, found some strange 'shrimps' that could not be identified by marine biologists at the British Museum (Natural History). Later, in 1982, he succeeded in trapping three quite large fish, each over half a pound in weight, at a great depth. One was still alive when brought to the surface and as this goes to print, the scientific examination of these creatures is eagerly awaited. He'd also dredged up samples of the sediment in which were found living molluscs and worms.

Adrian Shine's work has shown us that there is a food chain in the deep waters of this mysterious loch—perhaps sufficient to support a much larger beast. However, in spite of the undeniable sonar contacts showing what appear to be large moving objects in the murky depths, the only real way to advance towards the final solution of the mystery is to discover exactly what these contacts are.

During Operation Drake, we'd made use of the Goodyear airship *Europa* for environmental studies in the Mediterranean. Tim Dinsdale was quick to realise the possibilities of this splendid craft for work over the Scottish lochs and, together with Andrew Mitchell and Dr James Buchanan, put up a proposal to run a scientific expedition using the airship in the Great Glen. I discussed it with our good friend Bill Gowen, the Goodyear Public Relations Manager in New York, and Chris Aked of Goodyear UK. The company liked the idea and the 1982 Great Glen Airship Expedition was born. The Scientific Exploration Society and the British Chapter of the Explorers Club threw in their support. Bob Williamson, an artistic explorer, designed a beautiful commemorative philatelic cover and an energetic new recruit to our team, Phyllis Angliss, became 'Philatelic Phyllis' and rushed off to Jersey with British Caledonian Airways to get the last stocks of the Operation Drake airship stamps.

The idea was to sell the covers to fund the expedition and, thanks to the generous help of the *Daily Telegraph*, this is exactly what we did.

By the time *Europa* appeared over Inverness Airport, a whole series of experiments had been organised by James Buchanan and as I was now running the Army Youth Adventure Training Scheme at Fort George, the whole project fitted together extremely well.

The youngsters of the Fort George Volunteers, as our unusual unit was known, were delighted with the idea of a spot of monster hunting from an airship and James had assembled an impressive array of scientists. Many old chums joined in, including Adrian who put his 1907 Humber sailing barge *Phyllis* into the expedition for sonar surveys, Chris Sainsbury who came along to film it and Bob Williamson who produced a 1930 Puss Moth monoplane.

It wasn't all monster spotting, and James's scientific programme was in itself a pretty ambitious undertaking. The weather looked promising on 2 June as *Europa* came obediently to her mast at Dalcross, Inverness. In fact, we were lucky for, apart from twenty-four hours of mist and low cloud, we had unusually good flying conditions. Ian Bustin, a young officer from The Royal Regiment of Wales, was to help co-ordinate the programme and with the minimum of fuss we had a pretty efficient expedition in the field.

Broadly speaking, the programme was to do two flights a day, dividing the time between the scientific research and surveillance over Loch Ness.

Airship flying is the perfect way to travel. The great bulbous creatures are relatively quiet; there's plenty of room in the cabin and not even seat belts to restrict you. Visibility is marvellous and if you want extra air, just open a window. With a top speed of around 50 m.p.h., the *Europa* usually cruises at 30 m.p.h. Although she can climb to 8,500 feet, the pilots prefer to operate under 3,000 feet. As far as range is concerned, *Europa* could cover five hundred miles without landing—but as there's no lavatory aboard, you'd be pretty cross-legged by then!

As part of the scientific studies, the dispersal of sewage from Inverness into the Beauly Firth was studied by Dr Julian Hunter of the Highland River Purification Board, who had red dye poured into the outfall and then, flying in the airship, he photographed its movement on the ebb and flood tide. To us laymen, it seemed to show that it all flowed back to Inverness when the tide turned! 'Good for the salmon,' commented Chris Sainsbury, who was filming the experiment from Bob's Puss Moth.

Aerial photography was also used by the Forestry Commission to assess the wind and storm damage to plantations in the Great Glen.

Other scientists from the Macaulay Institute of Soil Research and Aberdeen University experimented with some very sensitive photographic and video equipment fitted on *Europa*. These experiments were aimed at evaluating space imagery from NASA's Landsat, Seasat and Space Shuttle SIRA programmes. Dr Colin Stone described the airship as an ideal 'stable, slow-moving platform for collecting low-level air information for future space missions, in particular the flights of the space shuttle.'

On Sunday 6 June, we clambered into the eight-seater cabin of the massive craft. I sat up front with Enzo, the pilot, whom I'd flown with on Operation Drake, and we pushed the aerial of the Army radio out through the open window. With this, I could talk to my mobile HQ and also to Adrian on his barge.

Richard Snailham took the cine camera and climbed in next with the scientists and their heat scanner. There was just time to brief the team on their areas of observation before we slipped gently from the mast and, with our engines ticking over, were walked to the take-off position. Then, with an effortless roar, the twin engines pushed us up at a steep angle into the blue sky.

Rising majestically above the airport and heading for Loch Ness, we easily picked out the Kessock Bridge and Inverness football ground as we flew south-west. The engines, sounding like a well-tuned motorcycle, purred away astern. At a steady 30 m.p.h. we approached the pewter water of the loch and moved down to rendezvous with the sonar barge. 'Hello, this is 1,' came Ian Bustin's voice on the radio. 'We have you visual—over.' '9, OK, with you in figures 10 minutes,' I replied.

The familiar sight of Urquhart Castle, the sun lighting up its crumbled ramparts, appeared ahead. Several motor coaches had brought dozens of tourists to swarm over the ruin. 'They've got a bonus today,' said Richard.

The altimeter read 750 feet. 'Can you go lower?' I asked and Enzo took us down until we were level with the castle's ancient tower. You could see a hundred cameras raised as one to catch this remarkable picture.

Adrian's barge was already on station and as we circled, he opened the throttle and began to creep along beneath us. Down in the spacious hold, the scientists and operators scanned the screens as the sonar probed the depths. In the half light, the steady stream of red, yellow and green blips passed by like a slow-moving rainbow. Once, a tremor of excitement went through the crew as a huge blip appeared. 'Side echo,' muttered Adrian, ignoring it and scanning on. All eyes were glued to the sets, just as above in *Europa* we all longed to see a long, dark, leathery neck, or a massive hump emerge dramatically from the surface—but nothing happened and our joint patrol continued. Several times, we dived down to examine unusual shapes in the water—but they were just the result of sediment.

'High wind is bad for us,' said Enzo, as he swung the great silver craft around over Fort Augustus and headed up loch into the freshening breeze. 'We'd better go home.' With engines droning, the airship slid over the rippling waters 500 feet below, but by the time the white-walled cottages of Dores appeared on our port bow, the wind had gone and as we began to climb over the Caledonian Canal, we saw trouble ahead. Beyond the swaying mooring lines that dangled from our nose, was a rising grey wall stretching from the tree tops into the sky—a bank of mist rolling in from the North Sea, brought by the easterly breeze. It looked curious and innocuous, but I could see from Enzo's expression that he was none too happy. Behind me, Richard Snailham looked up from his notes and raised an eyebrow; the scientists peered out into the swirling cotton wool as the mist began to envelope us and the engine note changed as we slowed. Enzo swung the vertical elevator wheel back and the mooring lines swung in to meet us as our bulbous nose rose. The *Europa* was probing forward through the dense banks of fog at a few miles an hour. Our expedition radio was dead—we were too far from control and Inverness Airport was now closed, but we could hear Goodyear's base station as Enzo searched for the landing ground.

It's a weird feeling to fly in mist in an airship—with windows open and the billowing vapour drifting past, I quite expected to hear a fog horn. Suddenly, something was level with us—to my amazement it was a seagull which overtook this monster of the skies and flew on unconcerned. 'I believe we're over the Moray Firth,' said the pilot and we dropped lower until a patch of dark green conifer forest showed briefly below. Even the trees were wreathed in white mist. 'Blimey—it's down to ground level,' muttered someone. Navigating by beacon, we knew that the airfield must be near and so we crawled forward, a few hundred feet above Inverness-shire.

We were almost on the field, when the cloud base lifted a little and we saw the grass-edged runways. Enzo heaved the great wheel forward and our nose dipped towards the red-and-white mooring mast. Already, the ground crew were running forward through the long grass to seize the bow lines and guide us to the coupling. The engines gave one last triumphant roar and died. 'Phew,' said Richard. 'Quite exciting, yes?' said Enzo.

The next day was to be our last and Nessie had coyly refused to be enticed to the surface, or even within sonar range of *Phyllis*.

At 1455 hours on 7 June, I was manning our control radio in bright sunshine at Urquhart Castle, whilst *Europa* made her final sweep up the loch above the sonar barge. It was a warm afternoon. Sally Harris, my PA, had produced a jolly good bottle of cool white wine for lunch and I was feeling that even if we didn't see Nessie, it had been an enjoyable little expedition. Suddenly, I heard Adrian's voice in my headphones. 'Hellow Zero, this is One—Cold Contact. Over.' 'They've got a sonar target,' I yelled to Chris, whose cine camera was in action nearby. Already, a steady stream of bearings were being sent out from the barge to the airship. 'Green 20, range figures 15 zero metres, moving, speed figures one point 5 knots, depth figures 14 metres,' came Signalman John Sinclair's voice. We could hear the higher revs of *Europa*'s engines as she closed rapidly with the barge.

'Red 50, range figures 75 metres, speed figures one point 5, depth figures 18 metres,' came fresh directions. By now, we could see the airship and the barge together about a mile south-west of the Castle. 'Hello 2, this is 1—you're right above the target,' said Adrian, as the huge silver craft hovered 250 feet up, just ahead of the *Phyllis*. Tim Dinsdale was on the edge of his seat, peering down, but he knew from an experiment we'd made with a submerged dustbin lid, that whatever it was the sonar had contacted would have to be within 8 feet of the surface if it were to be visible.

Down in the twilight of the hold, Dave Morgan, a New Zealand Gunner on my staff at Fort George, helped John Sinclair hold the contact in the sonar's beam. 'It was like chasing a bat on a dark night with the narrow ray from a flashlight,' said Dave. For thirty minutes they kept it there, whilst it moved around the barge in a 300-metre-diameter circle and at one time, Adrian got his vessel within 66 metres. The horizontal display showed the target to be between 14 and 18 metres below the surface—then it disappeared out of range just as suddenly as it had come. Tim saw nothing, which at least showed it wasn't a huge bubble of gas, or a decomposing log rising from the loch bed.

We were elated, and Adrian went on to get a total of thirteen major sonar contacts that year. He's still analysing the results as this goes to press, but the expedition taught us a great deal about Nessie-hunting, and we were greatly encouraged by the results. I feel that this is a very complex problem; however, by bringing together leading experts and the latest scientific techniques and equipment, we'd made an important advance. Of course, detailed analysis of the results is essential before any firm conclusions can be reached, but I firmly believe there is a case to answer at Loch Ness and not all those who claim to have seen something strange there can be branded as liars or alcoholics.

After the airship had departed, *The Daily Star* telephoned to ask if we'd like to try a hot-air balloon over the loch. Adrian and I had talked about this as a possible aerial observation post and so I was delighted to give it a try. The newspaper kindly persuaded Greenall Whitley, a well-known brewery company, to lend two balloons and, having first given some of the Fort George Volunteers a tethered lift up in a field behind Urquhart Castle, we set out into the sunrise to cross the loch. There was hardly a breath of wind as our propane gas burners sent their fiery blast into the envelope and it took twenty minutes for us to cover the two miles across the water. To demonstrate the control that was possible, our pilot touched down in mid-loch and we drifted along on the surface of the water for a few minutes before rising up again. However, as we reached the far side, it became apparent that what little breeze there was would take us up into some pretty inhospitable-looking hills and so we returned to the water again to get Adrian to tow us a short distance with Jim Hogan's cruiser *New Atlantis*. Then, coming opposite a convenient clearing, the drag rope was released and we popped up from the loch. However, as we cleared the low fir trees beside the road, we needed a hand on the ground to guide us down. 'Excuse me,' I called to a small tent which shared the clearing with a camper wagon. 'Could you grab our line, please?' The tent flap opened and an attractive, scantily dressed French girl stepped out and looked round to see where the voice had come from. For a moment she saw nothing. In the meantime, a rather older gentleman in loosely tied striped pyjamas had emerged from the camper, rubbing his eyes and then they both saw our balloon and ran to take the dangling rope. At this point, striped pyjamas' wife, in nightie and curlers, appeared, failed to see us, but found her beloved jumping about with a lightly clad blonde. French man then crawled out of the tent and, still on hands and knees, gaped in astonishment at the unbelievable scene. A nasty international incident was only avoided by the necessity for all to pull like mad to get us down safely. However, apart from having a good laugh, we had learned that a hot-air balloon, tethered behind a boat, was a real possibility for aerial observation on a calm day.

Lochs Morar, Ness and Shiel, all of which have reports of 'monsters', were at one time connected to the sea and there have been many reports of sightings of similar-looking creatures in the sea itself. So, it seems reasonable to conclude that if we are dealing with a large unknown aquatic animal, then it's been trapped in these lochs and evolved to adapt to fresh water. Could it be some form of giant mammal, like a seal, or is it an unknown amphibian, such as a huge newt? Sir Peter Scott's idea of a long-necked plesiosaur is controversial, but even this extinct reptile cannot be dismissed. Many people I've met in the Highlands are convinced Nessie and Morag are gigantic eels. Some three-foot elvers have already been discovered in the sea to support this theory. But others talk of an invertebrate—a great worm, or some other boneless animal.

When I asked James Buchanan what he thought, he mentioned the possibility of our target being a giant sturgeon. An eleven-foot specimen was caught in Wales in the 1960s and far bigger specimens are not unknown. They do have a strange long snout for bottom

25. Papua New Guinea. The chief of the 'lost tribe', with Roger Chapman.
Photo: Bill Neumeister

26. Loch Morar at sunset.

27. Loch Ness. The airship 'Europa' and sonar barge 'Phyllis' at work near Urquhart Castle.

28. Ickham Pond. The explosion.

feeding. Is this the monster's neck?

Adrian and Tim are now making plans to continue the search and this winter, whilst they're earning enough to keep going next year, there will be a search for new equipment that can tell what it is at the end of that fascinating rainbow.

However, that is not the only underwater mystery with which I've been involved. As commanding officer of the Junior Leaders Regiment, Royal Engineers, at Dover, I was always looking for interesting projects to exercise our young men's skills. One day, we were asked to help solve a problem that was causing concern at the village of Ickham.

It transpired that Mr Alf Leggett, a man of great character who ran a lovely Norman hall as a home for elderly folk, had a lifelong passion for goldfish. After an exciting spell of wartime service as a Royal Navy officer, he had sought more peaceful pursuits in this sleepy Kentish village and was renowned for his success as a breeder of these attractive fish. But one day when Alf inspected his pond, he noted a sudden and alarming decrease in its population. Next day a further reduction was apparent. The local angling society was consulted.

'Hmmm,' its members said. 'Could be a monster perch, gobbling them up,' and set to with rod and line to catch the cannibal. However, in spite of their valiant efforts, Alf's goldfish continued to disappear. The local policeman was consulted and also the Water Board. Alf, armed with a shotgun, sat in an apple tree, waiting to shoot the swine if it surfaced. But although he fired several times, no writhing monster appeared.

'Might be an eel,' suggested a professor of biochemistry.

'Or a heron,' said a senior police officer. 'Had a nasty case of goldfish nicking in the Midlands once—turned out to be a bloody great heron, ate two hundred a day it did!'

Alf rose early, shotgun in hand, and waited for the predator but none appeared and now only a handful of goldfish remained. Then someone suggested that it was possible that a lady had emptied a tank of tropical fish into the pond when her young son had gone off to boarding school.

'That must be it, then,' said the regulars in the village pub. 'All these mild winters and hot summers we have been having—whatever it is has grown and now it's thriving on Alf's fish.'

Like wildfire the rumour spread through the leafy lanes of East Kent. 'It's the Russians mucking about with the weather that's done it. If that there monster gets into the waterways of England, God only knows what damage it will do.'

News was scarce and the press, smelling a good story, was quickly on to it. Trade at the village pub increased and once their gullets were suitably dampened, locals were quick to recall forgotten tales of dark doings dating back to Chaucer.

Meanwhile, Alf's former naval chums, reading of his difficulties, began to write in from all over the world. My RSM's uncle lived nearby and told Alf, whose last goldfish had now disappeared, that there was only one thing for it—'Call in the Royal Engineers!' The RSM did a reconnaissance and reported that the willow-surrounded pond was set in a beautiful garden next to some glasshouses.

'A few pounds of plastic explosive underwater would certainly kill anything there,' he said, 'but there is no safe place near enough to the pond from which you can see the demolition on firing.'

'We've got an exercise on next week,' I replied. 'We could use one of the Ferrets [a small armoured car], get it close to the water's edge and fire the demolition electrically from inside the turret.'

Thus it was, the following week, that I set out in my staff car to visit the exercise. As we swept through the manor gates I was mildly surprised to notice a large number of cars. The Adjutant met me and led us across the beautifully mown lawns. Rounding a hedge we came face to face with a tall man in a deer-stalker hat clutching a shotgun.

'Mr Leggett, I presume?' I said. But before he could answer, we were surrounded by a horde of press men. In fact it was later reported that more members of Fleet Street had come to watch the attack on 'Jaws' (as it was instantly nicknamed) than had greeted President Carter on his recent arrival in Britain. Alf had risen to the occasion and had provided a splendid lunch with lashings of booze to cheer the newspapermen, and whilst I questioned him about the monster, the Junior Sappers got down to the mucky business of laying the explosive on the pond bed. Spencer Eade, the local Army public relations officer, was smiling gleefully as he strode up and down amongst the assembled press. Having got the approval of the Ministry of Defence for the PR exercise, he had clearly done an amazing job.

'Must have every national paper in the country here, John,' he enthused.

Whilst the charges were laid, the cameramen jockeyed for the best positions to photograph the explosion. In the process, a TV team crowded on to a small footbridge which, much to the joy of their rivals, collapsed, precipitating the luckless crew into the pond.

I was more than conscious of the proximity of the glasshouses and questioned our Staff Sergeant on the quantity of explosive.

'Only a small charge, Colonel,' he said seriously, and I believed him. Finally all was ready. The Junior Leader who was to fire the demolition climbed into the turret of the armoured car, which had now been drawn up behind the hedge, its machine-gun pointing menacingly at the muddy waters. I moved back amongst the press and the empty bottles.

'All clear,' came the shout from the sentries and, as the count-down commenced, the cameras were raised. 'Three, two, one, fire!'

The roar of the explosion was barely deadened by the water. Great spouts cascaded high into the sky, much of it drifting down upon us. The only immediate casualty was a duck that happened to be passing and laid an egg in fright. A subdued cheer went up and champagne corks popped.

I explained that it was unlikely that we should find anything that day, as any monster lurking therein would almost certainly have sunk into the mud. However, the Press was eager for a picture and was delighted when the odd dead minnow was discovered.

'Well, that should have fixed it,' I said, and we strode away across the lawn for a welcome cup of tea in Alf's kitchen. As we did so we came upon a group of old ladies seated on the lawn.

'Good heavens, Alf, I should think they must have been scared out of their wits,' I said.

'No, stone deaf, all of them,' he winked. But as we passed by, one old darling reached out and beckoned.

'Mr Leggett,' she wheezed. 'I think I heard something just then.'

Alf bent down and shouted loudly in her ear. 'Don't worry, dear, it was only an atom bomb they've dropped on London.'

The poor lady looked perturbed. 'Oh dear, does that mean I shan't get my paper in the morning?' she asked.

Spencer was on the telephone, looking worried. As he came away, I said. 'What's up?'

'Oh well, you can't win them all,' he groaned. 'That was my boss on the line. He has just told me not to promote the story after all, but I had to explain that it was too late, we'd done it. Apparently there is a programme on the TV tonight which is critical of defence expenditure and he thinks our story may not give quite the right image.'

He was right. The story that was carried by almost every paper in the country and many overseas, and told and re-told on television and radio, was far from serious, but it did show boy soldiers having the time of their lives and recruits flowed in! At least the explosion had gone off as planned, no damage had been done and Alf Leggett was happy. Some people didn't think it especially funny, but a lot did. One extremely important person later asked me how on earth it was that the Army managed to lay on such splendid publicity and went on to inquire why it was that the Navy couldn't do the same! Giles drew two splendid cartoons for the *Daily Express* and the next term we had the biggest intake ever in the regiment. Whether we solved the mystery and got the monster or not was questionable, but later Alf discovered a huge perch, stunned, in a hole in the bank. It had defied all attempts to bring it out; only when an electric fish-attracting device was actually pushed into its lair did it finally emerge. Amazingly it recovered and now lives quietly in a Kentish reservoir—a rather nice end to a fishy story!

7

Animal Mysteries

'They say it climbs trees, walks upright, kills men and breathes fire.'

One of the most fascinating stories I've read about mysterious animals was told by the American explorer, Charles Miller. In *Cannibal Caravan* (Lee Furman, New York, 1939) he describes an expedition into what is now West Irian in the 1930s and describes an extraordinary creature the natives called a 'row'.

I have been scared many times in my life. Several times I have sampled death. But never in my life was I paralysed with fear. But I was paralysed now. My camera was in my left hand, my gun in my right, but they might as well have been miles away. I couldn't reach them.

How long I froze there, waiting for the reeds to move again, I'll never know. Leona says she saw me tighten up fifteen minutes before she started to crawl toward my side, but I can't depend upon her figures. She saw the thing too, and after that you can't be sure of anything.

Leona reached me on her hands and knees just as the reeds parted and a head rose up like something out of the Lost World or King Kong. Except that those were fantasies, and this monster was real. Leona gave a soft sigh and collapsed on the ground. I thought she had fainted and managed to turn my head to look. She was staring wild-eyed at the earth below her face, clutching at a clump of grass with both hands as though to keep her grip on reality. Her shock was enough to partially restore my own senses. I couldn't stay paralysed with her so much more helpless than me.

'It's all right,' I whispered.

Her gaze remained fixed on the earth. She gave no indication of having heard.

Slowly, as though I were directing each muscle from some

97

distant control tower, I moved my camera into line. As if in obedience to my wishes, the colossal remnant of the age of dinosaurs stalked across the swamp.

Once its tail lashed out of the grass so far behind its head I thought it must be another beast. For one brief second I saw the horny point. I heard it hiss—Roooow—Roooow—Roooow. I licked my dry lips, suddenly aware that I had not started my camera.

The spring was already wound for a hundred feet. I pressed the release. To my ears the whirring gears sounded like a threshing machine. Sweat rolled down my face. Ice cold sweat. The Row seemed to catch the sound for it suddenly stopped, reared up on its hind legs, its small forelegs hanging limp, and shot its snaky neck in our direction. It was a full quarter mile away, it couldn't possibly hear the camera, but I found myself cowering back as though that snapping-turtle shaped beak would lash out and nab me. I gasped with relief when the creature settled back.

Up to that time the only thing I had noticed photographically was the Row. Now I was noticing other things. That the monster was a light brown yellow in colour, almost the identical hue of the reeds through which it was passing. I noticed that it was covered with scales laid on like armour plate, that the plates were uneven, almost as though they were designed for camouflage. I looked at my filter indecisively, then left it on. It was giving me as good a contrast as anything. There was no filter in the world that could separate two matching colours, and if I filtered out the grass I would lose my Row so I left it on. Twice more the Row reared up, giving me a good view of the bony flange around its head and the projecting plates along its backbone. Then with a click my camera ran out just as the Row slithered behind a growth of dwarf eucalyptus.

'It's gone!' The words in a low whisper almost in my ear nearly caused me to jump out of my skin. In that one jump I left the Pleistocene age for the present and lived to tell the tale. For a second I didn't think I was going to do it. Then my heart started beating again.

'Yes,' I finally stated, except that no words came. Leona looked at me curiously.

'You're scared.'

I nodded. 'Let's get out of here,' I finally managed to whisper.

'I can't,' she confessed. 'My legs won't move.'

I found mine wouldn't either, at first. They were as though asleep. Gradually some strength flowed back into our bodies. We managed to wriggle back on our stomachs, about as helpless as a couple of snakes with broken backs. Our guides and our Malays followed, also on their stomachs. I don't know if they were too scared to stand up like we were or if they just wriggled because I was setting the pattern. At any rate, I finally decided we couldn't crawl on our stomachs all the way back to camp so I made an effort to stand.

Not until I got to my feet did I realise I was soaking wet. My shirt, I was relieved to notice, was just as wet as my pants. I like to think it was all sweat.

Once I got to my feet I was all set for heading back. So was Leona. So was everybody else. Behind us there was a Row. According to Wroo, there were a lot more where that one came from. And there weren't any cages between us and them. Against a beast like that, our rifles were about as useful as citronella. No sir, it was time for us to go back.

I'd often thought about this tale, but mysterious animals were very far from my mind as the Cessna winged past the billowing cumulus boiling up over the vast Sepik Swamp in PNG. The endless dark green mat of vegetation, bisected only by the huge meandering river, crept slowly past my window. Watching the brown water I saw only the occasional dugout being paddled by jet-black, near-naked warriors. A few brightly coloured birds flitted around in the tangled growth at the edge of the waterway, but for the most part this enormous morass seemed totally lifeless. 'In Africa or South America,' I said turning to the Papuan officer sitting beside me, 'this area would be teeming with wildlife—does anything large live in these swamps?'

'The biggest mosquitoes in the world's down there,' he said with a broad grin; 'then there's the Puk-Puk—that's crocodile, and pigs.'

We talked about elephants and African big game which my friend had never seen, then he said slowly, 'Local men say there's something called Artrellia—a sort of giant crocodile that climbs trees.'

'Have you ever met anyone who claims to have seen it?' I asked.

'No—but there are men at Green River who might tell you about it,' said the officer, adding, 'But I'm not sure if these people just see them in their dreams.'

It was early afternoon when we landed at the new concrete runway at the little border settlement of Green River. The heavy humid wall of heat hit us as we stepped out and in seconds perspiration was oozing from every pore. The Defence Force Engineers Camp was a short way from the airfield and as we bumped along the dusty corrugated road in a battered Land-Rover, we passed lines and lines of the most primitive people I'd ever seen.

'We employ 'em to work on the road,' said the tanned Australian Sergeant Major who'd come to meet us. We stopped to drop a packet of cigarettes to a PNG NCO in charge of one gang and took the opportunity to stretch our legs. Pot-bellied, muscular women were working with their wide-eyed babies secure on their backs in string bags or 'billoms'; their only clothes, a 'lap-lap' around the waist. The menfolk were even more skimpily dressed—most of them only wearing a penis sheath fashioned from some sort of plant and supported from the neck by a thin black string. As they swung their axes, some of which were of stone, they carefully moved this awkward appendage to one side. I was going to ask the Sergeant Major why they couldn't issue some old PT shorts to the workers— but I guessed that Telefomin trousers, as the sheaths are known, were very much part of local tradition.

Bumping along, I turned to the Australian and said casually, 'Ever heard of an animal called Artrellia?'

He shook his head, 'Nope—what is it, Colonel?'

I told him of my conversation in the plane.

'Well—my guess is that they're talking about a salt water croc that gets stuck up a mangrove tree when the tide goes out,' he smiled and then said, 'But there'll be an old chief at the "Mu-Mu" tonight. According to the boys, he was quite a hunter in his day. Maybe he could tell you something—you speak Pidgin?' As I didn't, a young Papuan Lieutenant wearing a live marsupial like a Davy Crockett hat would give a hand.

The aroma of cooking pork wafted up from the fires as we sat beneath the thatched roof of the mess hut sipping our 'tubes of

Fosters'. It was late when the old warrior arrived—he'd put on all his finery for the occasion and seemed delighted that someone was interested in his exploits—but all he knew about Artrellia was based on one sighting over thirty years before—and that wasn't an especially close encounter. However, of one thing he was certain—it was no 'puk-puk'. So I tried to draw what he described—it wasn't easy, but eventually he seemed satisfied with something which looked vaguely like a dinosaur with a long tail.

'He says it walks upright, climbs trees and breathes fire,' I told my hosts. 'Sounds like a bloody dragon,' laughed the Sergeant Major. 'Better send for St George.' I pushed the sketch in my diary and forgot all about the Artrellia.

It was three years later and the Papua New Guinea phase of Operation Drake was in full swing. Our teams of Young Explorers were combing the country for lost aircraft and minerals, mapping and marking trails and doing a wide variety of challenging tasks. There seemed an endless stream of youngsters to find exciting jobs for, and sitting in my Headquarters at Lae, Michael Knox, my Operations Officer, and I spent our days and nights planning and despatching the expeditions.

Working late one evening, I found myself marooned in my office by a fearsome tropical storm. Lightning crackled and thunder crashed overhead, shaking the wooden chalet uncertainly and beyond the mosquito netting the rain fell in rods, whipping the surface of the nearby pool into a frenzy.

'No point in getting soaked going for the car,' I thought, so I poured a shot of J and B into the green plastic mug and pulled over a large illustrated book on New Guinea wildlife that was sitting in my 'In' tray. Attached to it was a note from Alan Bibby, our resident producer. 'See p.278—what do you think?' it said.

So I leant back in the old canvas chair, took a welcome swig of the Scotch and flipped open the volume. The last paragraphs of the page leapt at me, '. . . dinosaur like . . .a legendary giant lizard . . . said to exist in Western Papua . . .'

Oblivious to the raging storm I read on. It appeared that many years ago a young Papuan warrior staggered breathlessly home to his village in a state of shock after a lone hunting trip and blurted out an amazing story. It was said his grandchildren still recall it vividly and they will repeat it, word for word, to anyone who penetrates far enough up the Binatori River to reach their isolated but idyllic village of Giringarede.

It seems that their grandfather was feeling rather weary after hours on the trail and went to sit down and rest on a fallen tree trunk only for the 'tree' to rear up under him and reveal itself as a dragon! It stood over ten feet tall on its hind legs and had wicked-looking jaws like a crocodile. The old man did not wait to see if it breathed fire at him—he ran for his life and never once looked back to see if the monster was pursuing him.

It all sounded a bit far-fetched, but instantly I recalled the meeting with the old chap at Green River. The book mentioned stories about creatures very similar to those described in travellers' tales that have been coming out of PNG since the end of the last century—and many of them have come from very reliable sources. During the Second World War, Allied and Japanese patrols operating deep in the most remote parts of the jungle reported catching glimpses of what was most often described as a 'tree-climbing crocodile'.

Some scientists and wildlife experts came to the conclusion that what people might have seen was a giant lizard of the type first officially identified in 1978 as Salvador's Monitor—a close relation of the famed Komodo Dragon of Indonesia. A number of very large specimens of this reptile have been caught in PNG over the years. One, seven foot in length, was trapped near the mouth of the Fly River in 1936 by a scientific expedition, while a trader named John Senior—who ran a general store on the Kikori River—has a skin nailed to his wall which, in life, must have measured a good ten feet. On this evidence, there seemed every reason to suppose that somewhere in the most inaccessible recesses of the jungle there might lurk one or two outsize freaks—the equivalent of those 'grandfather' pike and other big fish that anglers sometimes hook from deep, dark pools.

As the rain eased off the door opened and in walked our jovial PNG Government liaison officer—Miss Somere Jogo.

'Hi, Somere—you're just the person I need.'

'Oh! What's gone wrong?' replied our cheerful lady.

'Nothing, nothing—but I need your advice; you live in the Western province don't you?'

'Yes,' she said. 'My village is near Daru.'

'Well then,' I said with a smile, 'what do you know about this mysterious dragon?' I handed her the book. Her smile disappeared, her eyes widened and dropping her voice, she leant forward and said with meaning, 'I know it exists—many of my people have seen it. They say it climbs trees, walks upright, especially at night, kills men, makes a whistling sound and breathes fire.'

I gulped the last of my whisky. This girl was deadly serious. 'Have you ever seen one?' I questioned.

'No, but they are to be found in the bush and swamps near my home. The people are very much afraid of them. An old man was killed by a female a few years ago.'

'What do you call it?' I asked.

'Artrellia—or in English, Dragon,' was the instant reply. The last flickers of lightning were on the Eastern horizon as I walked to my car deep in thought. What a challenge.

Next day, a couple of phone calls to Government scientists confirmed the general belief that there was something worth going after—and that the authorities would welcome an investigation. So Dorian Huber, a Swiss Young Explorer, accompanied by Somere, went off on a reconnaissance and ten days later came back with photographs of a seven-foot lizard and reports of others even bigger. These were not Artrellia, but nevertheless, I decided to mount a search for what would undoubtedly be the longest lizard in the world. We planned to base the expedition at Masingara, Somere's village, and have along Ian Redmond, a tough young zoologist, as our scientist.

Masingara is just up the coast from Daru, in the area between the Fly and the Pahotori River, that is generally considered the most likely haunt for any monster lizard.

Things got off to a suitably dramatic start even before my twenty-strong patrol reached Masingara, when we contrived to get lost in some of the most treacherous waters in the world. The Coral Sea is a wonderfully romantic name for a bit of ocean full of deadly reefs, strong currents and shifting shallows. We never really gave this a second's thought as we set out from Port Moresby, bound for Masingara in the MV *Andewa*. Through some excellent liaison by my WRNS adjutant, the little vessel and her crew had been put fully at our disposal by the government—another example of the incredibly generous help and co-operation given to Operation Drake throughout our stay in Papua New Guinea.

After a not uneventful three-day voyage, we came into Daru, the provincial capital, at midday, and whilst the good ship *Andewa* refuelled, I rushed off to find Somere and meet her uncle, Mr Tatty Olewale, OBE, Premier of the Western Province. We found him at home having lunch, and reading from a gigantic leather-bound Bible, whilst his pet parakeet hopped about on his shoulder. The Premier rose to greet us with the words, 'Colonel, it is the Lord who has brought you to us.' I was inclined to agree. In no time Mr Olewale summoned his brother, the head postman, who was able to tell us a great deal about Artrellia. He confirmed that an elderly man had died in the Daru hospital after being attacked by one which appeared to be a female protecting her nest. The Premier wished us well and presented everyone with a small gift, before sending us off with his niece, Somere, and a wizened old pilot as a river guide.

Next day we anchored off Masingara and marched the half mile inland to Somere's well-ordered home village of traditional stilt-supported bamboo huts. There, I was ushered by her brother, Seyu, towards a hundred-year-old woman, who was the most senior citizen and who was said to know more than anyone about the Artrellia, having seen several in her lifetime.

The white-haired old lady confirmed many of the things we had already heard: that these creatures grew to over fifteen feet in length; that they often stood on their hind legs and so gave the appearance of dragons or, to our minds, mini-dinosaurs; also that they were extremely fierce.

This last point brought much nodding from the village hunters, who made it quite obvious that they treated even the smaller six- or seven-footers—which they said were quite common—with the greatest respect. This came as no surprise, since we had already been told of an incident in another village where a captured Artrellia had smashed its way out of a stout cage and killed a large dog, before escaping back into the forest. Now we learned that the creature's method of hunting was to lie in wait in the trees before dropping onto its victims and tearing them to shreds with its powerful claws. Apart from that, it possessed a very infectious bite as a result of feeding on carrion and this could bring death within a matter of hours. There were plenty of stories of men who had been attacked and killed by the Artrellia.

During the next few days, we split into four patrols and combed the surrounding jungle; everyone we met understood immediately when we explained what we were looking for and claimed that they themselves had seen such creatures. The nearest any of us got to a sighting was when the local dogs that accompanied one patrol put up something that crashed off heavily through the undergrowth without showing itself.

'It's said to move at night—so we'd better try a spot of night hunting,' I said to the slightly dispirited patrols. At dusk, three of us set out, armed to the teeth and carrying an Army Image Intensifier which enhances existing light to such an extent that even that of a few stars will enable a soldier to shoot accurately at a hundred yards using the device as a rifle sight. Moving silently along a deer trail, we found an old megapode nesting mound. These strange birds rarely fly, and build enormous nests in which their eggs are incubated by the heat generated from decaying vegetation. This abandoned mound was over three feet high, overlooking a clearing of short yellow grass and as the last glow died over the Western horizon, we laid out our weapons, switched on the telescopic intensifier and settled down to wait.

We took turns to watch through the 'scope for, after about fifteen minutes, concentration wanders and the eye tires of peering at the ghostly green image.

Mick Boxall, my signaller, heard the noise first and I felt his touch. He pointed to the dark line of trees on our left. Yes—I picked it up too—a gentle swish, swish—something was coming. Suddenly, the grass began to move about twenty yards away. My gaze did not leave the spot, but whatever it was must be moving close to the ground. Then I saw the head—or rather a long neck and a head. What on earth was it? My question was answered at once, for a full grown Wallaby hopped onto the path! I'd never seen one in the wild before and had totally forgotten that they existed in this remote corner of New Guinea.

An hour later, there was more noise—this time coming straight at us. It got closer and closer and yet was invisible. When it was almost on top of us, we seized the shotguns and rifles and prepared for battle. Mick had his flash light ready and feeling our attacker must be right in front, I hissed, 'Now.' To my amazement, the beam revealed the most extraordinary creature—rather like a long-eared giant rat, which was sitting up to beg and looking at us with equal surprise. Before we could do anything it had scooted between my legs and dived off into the trees behind us. 'Bandicoot,' muttered the villager who'd come to help us. However, we'd had enough and I decided there must be easier ways of solving this mystery.

The Sunday before Christmas, I went to matins in the little village church. Singing 'Hark, The Herald Angels Sing' in Pidgin did sound strange, but the sincerity of these simple people was most impressive. Strolling out into the bright sunlight, I paused to talk to the vicar. 'Do you really believe in Artrellia?' I asked. He'd been educated in Australia and I reckoned he would be a sensible vicar.

'I know he exists—I sometimes wish he didn't, 'cos my people think him's a devil, like an evil spirit,' replied the pastor, 'but him just an animal—bad animal sometime.'

'Well, if we caught one would it convince your flock that it was no evil spirit?' I asked.

'Sure,' he nodded his head.

'Then how on earth can we do that?'

'Oh, you fellows won't catch him—you makes too much noise tramping around the bush—you needs good hunters,' he stated firmly and added as an afterthought, 'My choirboys is plenty good hunters.'

'How much to hire your choir?' I asked.

'I needs a new church roof,' smiled the little priest, looking wistfully at the tattered thatch. 'How much will that cost?' I asked.

'Ten dollars,' was his quick reply. However, he suggested that I offer the reward at the village council that evening and in that way I'd get all the hunters helping. Ten dollars (or Kina) would be a month's wage. 'But don't tell dem fellows bout d'reward 'til 7 o'clock,' he cautioned, ''cos I wants to leave at 5—oh yes, and can you let me have some shotgun shells?'

Sure enough, the mere mention of money was followed by a mass exodus into the jungle of every able-bodied man in the village, armed with everything from bows and arrows to an antique blunderbuss.

In the meantime, Somere showed us some interesting snakes that she claimed were caught in a nearby swamp. They were almost jet black, more like eels, and apparently quite blind. Their skin lacked scales, but was covered in a mass of tiny pimples. Ian Redmond had never seen anything quite like these reptiles and Alan Bibby was anxious to film them being caught. 'That is not possible,' said Somere, looking very serious. 'They are only caught by the women at a certain time of year—it is a kind of ritual.'

'Goody, bags I go and catch some,' enthused my jolly Personal Assistant, Margot. 'I'll go too,' echoed Clare, the adjutant.

'Make sure you bring me a pregnant fully grown female,' said Ian, with scientific motives in mind.

So we left the all-female expedition to their task.

On arrival at the swamp, Margot noticed the almost naked village ladies plunging into waist-deep mud covered by a thin layer of grass. The women chopped at the grass with bush knives, peeled back the top layer and feeling around with feet and hands, found a great variety of lung fish, long-necked turtles, lizards and snakes. They hurled their catches to other ladies who waited on the bank. Margot learned that those on the side lines were pregnant and were not allowed in the morass 'because they would drive away the mud-dwelling creatures.' Eventually Margot, reduced to battle order of bra and pants, plunged in, causing much consternation because only pregnant ladies wore bras in Masingara. However, Margot explained, amid much hilarity, that she was not expecting, and the strange ritual continued. Eventually she felt something rather large squirming past her legs, and seized it. Out came a very heavy, fully grown, black, eyeless snake—almost six feet in length and full of eggs. So Ian Redmond got his wish. But Margot then felt another serpent wriggling round her thighs—it felt thinner and much more lively. Thrusting her hand back into the mire she grabbed it—or rather it grabbed her and in fact she was bitten four times by a rather unpleasant diamond-headed snake about three feet long before she got it out. Luckily, it wasn't poisonous.

It was as we steamed back down the Pahotori in *Andewa*, after a trip upriver that had produced no actual sightings but many more confirmations that what we were looking for did indeed exist, that Corporal Mick Boxall got a radio message from Clare reporting that the vicar had managed to shoot a big lizard somewhere deep in the forest and was on his way back to Masingara with it. We returned to the village at full speed and by the time we arrived, a large crowd had already gathered around a strange-looking creature which was lying at their feet roped to a bamboo pole. 'It's alive,' muttered Mike Cable as Ian bent to examine the reptile. Chris Sainsbury's cameras were already clicking as I handed the Ten Kina bill to the vicar, who assured me that this was Artrellia. Its dark green skin was flecked with yellow spots and its square head housed a set of needle-like teeth. The eyes twitched malevolently as it tried to squeeze itself out of the vines binding it to the pole, but the most impressive part of its anatomy were the claws—for at the end of its short thick legs were enormous, black scimitars, quite out of proportion with the rest of its body. The tail was long and thin and twice the length of the body. I noticed the village dogs kept well away from the dying beast with its terrible talons. The mouth and tongue gave a red/yellow effect— 'Fire' said the priest and I saw at once how the legend had been started by the tongue darting in sunlight.

Ian pushed in the hypodermic and Artrellia passed quietly into death. As soon as it was safe to handle, measurements were taken.

It was no dragon, but even so, it was still a pretty fearsome-looking specimen at just over six feet from head to tail. Once Ian had performed his post-mortem, he was able to confirm that it was only a youngster which left plenty of room for speculation about what size an overgrown adult might reach. Meanwhile, a small patrol that had been keeping vigil beside a remote water hole, which we had been told was a favourite haunt of the creatures, came back with reports that they had seen several quite sizeable specimens coming down to drink at night, but had been unable to get near enough to photograph them in the dark.

We did catch a glimpse of one monster with a head like a horse peering at the photographers over a fallen log in the first light of day. Ian made several sightings of pretty impressive adult lizards of lengths up to twelve feet and from our specimen we knew that Artrellia was indeed Salvador's Monitor (Varanus Salvadori)—but no-one had dreamed of the size to which these killers can grow. But the question now is how big do they grow? Perhaps Operation Raleigh will find out in 1986.

Our last night in Masingara, we talked to our Royal Australian Signals station in Melbourne and they gave us an interesting news item. Apparently a pair of 90-foot python had attacked a road-mining bull-dozer in Indonesia and after an hour-long struggle, one had been killed. As the next phase of Operation Drake was now assembling in Indonesia, we were extremely interested, but considered it a very unlikely tale. However, during our pre-Operation Drake reconnaissance in 1978, we had come across a rather macabre, and well-documented, story of an incident in Sulawesi. The *Indonesian Times* had reported that a farmer called Ojobuka from Ongka Malino village at the foot of Mount Tinombala, Central Sulawesi, had been eaten by a 20-foot python. 'The farmer was eaten by the snake at night shortly after he left a meeting with the local military leader. He was still able to shout "I am dying". A woman who lived near his house heard the shout and called his family. Later local people searched and found the snake, which had swallowed him, about half a mile from his house. The snake could not move because of its distended stomach. After they killed the snake and slit its stomach open, they found the corpse of the farmer.'

Monty, the python we used to test the courage of British candidates for Operation Drake, by asking them to weigh him, was 13 feet long. I made a note to increase the accident insurance!

While the thought of coming face to face with a fifteen-foot lizard may be somewhat alarming, I doubt whether it would be quite so disconcerting as a run-in with an angry fifty-foot sperm whale—the most alarming experience I had during the entire expedition.

It happened as I was aboard *Eye of the Wind*, after visiting our underwater team at Finschhafen. A school of some forty whales was sighted, many of them leaping awesomely clear of the water, and we decided to get closer in order to film them. So, using an Avon inflatable, we approached to within thirty yards of the school and, not wanting to disturb them, cut the engine. We got some excellent photos and were heading back to the ship when we saw three whales nearby and decided to get one last close-up. My friend and Army helicopter pilot, Frank Esson, had volunteered to handle the engine. Now he shut it off and we paddled gently towards the leviathans. I was filming with my 8mm Canon which has a zoom lens, when I saw a gigantic tail rise out of the leaden sea, then fall and disappear with a great splash. Then, as I adjusted the zoom, a dorsal fin appeared, coming straight at us. 'Shall I start the engine?' asked Frank calmly. But I was concentrating on filming and, looking through the viewfinder, felt strangely detached from the world around me. The dorsal fin came on. 'Shouldn't I start the engine?' shouted Frank, and, without waiting for an answer, he did. It was just as well because by now the bull whale's massive head was right beneath us and beginning to rise. The 'dorsal fin' was still fifty feet away. It was the fluke of its tail! Luckily the engine fired first time and we shot away, pursued for a short distance by the huge creature, its cavernous jaws and rows of molars rising in a ghastly scissor-like movement behind us.

It was a close shave. A second more and we would have been lifted out of the water and probably smashed to death by his tail. We were very happy to find ourselves back aboard *Eye of the Wind*, where the crew had enjoyed a grandstand view of the drama.

I hardly expected to be faced with a mystery at the 1976 Explorers Club Annual Dinner in New York. My friend, Vince Martinelli, had telephoned me from New York a few weeks earlier. He sounded excited. 'John, there's a guy over here with a live humanoid, says it comes from Zaïre.'

'Have you seen it?' I said.

'Yeah! It's about four foot tall, one hundred and fifty pounds, kind of hairy body, but with a more or less human face. It's pretty bald and the skin on the head is yellow, and what's more, it walks upright all the time! Did you see anything like that in Zaïre?'

'Certainly,' I replied. 'If he's got two stars on his shoulder I know just who it is, although I thought he was back with his Regiment.'

'But John,' Vince insisted, 'I'm serious. Some people claim it's a living Yeti and they say it comes from Zaïre.'

Apparently a chromosome analysis of the creature had indicated that it was genetically abnormal. For some reason that I couldn't understand the beast had not then been fully examined by a qualified scientific team. Vince told me that the owners would be happy for me to inspect 'Oliver', as it was known, because of my travels in his alleged homeland. 'I'm no anthropologist,' I protested, but in the end agreed to meet the humanoid. Thus, equipped with a scientific brief when I boarded the Pan Am 747 for New York a few days later, I was all set for the confrontation.

As our US Army friends had turned up in uniform the previous year, I had been asked to attend the 1976 Dinner in full Royal Engineers Mess kit. At least there would be one Red Coat around in the Bicentennial year!

As I dressed for the Dinner, Vince phoned. 'John,' he groaned, 'I'm in a fix, that damned humanoid is fighting mad and they can't get it into its cage to put it on the light aircraft that's bringing it to New York.' Apparently it had attacked its keeper and everyone else it could lay hands on. It looked as if the evening would be a flop—or a terrible disaster!

However, by the time we got into the Hors d'oeuvres room at the Waldorf, we learned that 'Oliver', still in a frightful rage, had been boxed and was on his way. Vince, who was in charge of the 'humanoid's' appearance, was still anxious as we sampled the dishes of peacock, llama, rattlesnake, dried fish lips, wild boar and something called Houma-Houma-Nuka-Nuka-Waka-Walla, which tasted like chicken.

We were seated and well into the main course when 'Oliver' arrived. I was told that I might view the creature privately provided that I accepted full responsibility for its actions. After several false starts, I was permitted to go backstage and meet the keeper, a large South African attired in a ring-master's green uniform. 'Now, you know the risk you're running,' he said, reaching for the bolts on the sturdy box.

The uniformed deputies who stood nearby eased their hands down onto their Smith and Wessons. As the last bolt was drawn, the door swung open and out popped the most extraordinary creature I've ever seen. 'Oliver' was certainly ape-like and as he hopped up on a chair, he seemed to be grinning, although I fancied this was an expression of fear. Remembering my scientific briefing, I asked if I might touch the beast. The keeper seized the length of chain that was attached to Oliver's neck and led him slowly towards me. He walked upright with an uncertain, shuffling gait and stretched out his great black hand. I took it in mine and immediately felt the full power of his long fingers. Oliver studied me and I studied him. His eyes caught my miniature medals and for a moment I thought he would grab them, but instead he simply played with my hand and made a catlike mewing sound, moving his lips as if he was trying to imitate human speech.

From the neck down he looked just like a tall, rather thin, chimpanzee with a patchy coat of hair. The hands and feet were certainly very ape-like, although I noticed that the knuckles were free of callouses. However, the head and face were most unusual. The skin was fair; a pale yellow colour, with very little hair. Indeed, the creature had a bald rather small head. His face looked like a very old man with a bad attack of jaundice. The mouth seemed much smaller and the jaws far less prominent than a chimp's. This feature tended to give it a human expression and I bent forward for a closer look. Oliver 'grinned' and I saw that he was toothless. 'What happened to his teeth?' I asked. 'Oh! He got pyorrhoea so I had to pull them out,' replied the keeper. Perhaps this accounted for the flatness of the face.

Moving slowly, I eased my hand up until my fingers reached the hairy arm pit, then, withdrawing my hand, I smelt it. Oliver had little or no body odour. As he was alleged to have been in a rage that evening, I found this hard to understand. When he shuffled away with his strange upright walk, I pursed my lips and made several high-pitched squeaks. There was no reaction and I wondered if this might indicate a loss of high-tone hearing, possibly attributable to old age.

The Dinner was ending and shortly Oliver must appear before the thousand or so members, so I had to ask my questions quickly. 'Whereabouts in Zaïre did he come from?'

'Oh! On the Zaïre river somewhere near Sierra Leone,' replied the South African.

I tried to conceal my incredulity and went on to enquire who had done the blood tests. A hospital that meant nothing to me was named and then the keeper said he really must leave me. So, from the wings of the Waldorf-Astoria ballroom stage, I watched 'Oliver' do his act. Led by his chain, he walked upright the whole time, his expression changed rarely, apart from the occasional 'grin', which I attributed to nervousness. He certainly gave a most convincing performance as a 'humanoid', but it was my feeling that he was probably an old, well-trained chimpanzee, possibly a mutant, who may have had some treatment to his face. I felt rather sorry for this extraordinary creature.

The TV and Radio pounced on me as I returned to Vince and Barbara Martinelli at the table. 'What do you think, could it be the Yeti, did you see anything like that in Africa?' came the questions. I explained I was no expert and admitted that I had not met anything like it before; but I rather doubted that it was the Yeti.

My only other personal experience of the Yeti mystery was in Nepal on a river-running expedition. With me was my chum the American surgeon, Dan Osman. He's a particularly interesting man and with his quiet, commonsense approach to life and medicine, was just the sort of man needed as an expedition doctor. Relaxing around the fire at night we found ourselves discussing all the usual legends of exploration, the Bermuda Triangle, Fawcett's disappearance, Atlantis, the Loch Ness Monster and, of course, the Yeti. I've always been interested in the stories of the Yeti, ever since I first met Odette Tchernine, one of the leading authorities on the subject. (Her book, *The Yeti*, was published in 1970 by Neville Spearman.)

'Have you seen those people up by the airstrip?' inquired Dan.

'What people?'

'Well, there's some guys with mighty odd toes,' explained the surgeon, telling us how he'd seen a group of locals with big toes that pointed inwards, in severe cases almost at right-angles. Another of our group said he'd try to photograph them when he next went to the strip and we talked of other things.

As the expedition drew to a close, an extraordinary event took place. On the banks of a stream I saw a most unusual set of footprints. They were rather like a monkey's with very big toes. They struck me as being very similar to the photographs I had seen of supposed Yeti tracks. However, in this case the cause was no hairy ape-like creature, but a smiling holy man with a pompom hairdo and deformed feet! In fact, just as Dan had said, his toes stuck out at angles and the feet were wider than usual. Apparently such mutations are fairly common in Nepal and, like those of the Yeti, the feet are described by local people as pointing backwards; however, it is in fact the big toe that points sideways. I felt that this deformity might well be a possible cause of many of the tales of Yeti tracks—there are plenty of gurus and Nepalese quite capable of walking around barefoot in the snow at high altitudes. Indeed, Sir Edmund Hillary shows a most interesting picture of a similar pair of feet in his book, *Nothing Venture, Nothing Win* (Hodder & Stoughton, 1974).

But since then, I've done more research and now I tend to believe that there may be another answer to this mystery. More scientists are now admitting, albeit privately, that there may be something in the strange stories that crop up in many remote areas of the world. But that little problem will need a very special expedition.

Almost every country has a legendary and mythical animal and the oceans are a great source of tales of mysterious appearances. They're great tourist attractions and it would be rather a shame if all the mysteries were solved.

Of course, many will scoff at such legends, but just occasionally a coelacanth turns up and then the sceptics take a back seat for a few years.

8

Volcano Puzzles

Heavy shuffling footsteps, a strange flapping noise, and some terrifyingly loud huffing and puffing.

The tiny Caribbean island of St Vincent is rarely in the news. When it is, the reason is usually La Soufrière, its active volcano that rises 3,500 feet above the jungle to dominate the northern part of the island. It is one of the chain of volcanoes that run through the Lesser Antilles and is noted for particularly violent eruptions.

The quiet life of the people of St Vincent was shattered by a sudden rumble early on the morning of 7 May 1902, and within minutes clouds of red-hot rock and gas were showered out of the mountain. Then came the all-consuming lava flowing so rapidly that their escape route was blocked.

The molten tongues of flaming rock flowed into the rivers instantly bringing the water to the boil and cooking alive luckless natives trying to cross lower down. Over 1,500 died.

The next day a hundred miles away on Martinique, Mount Pélée erupted with equal violence, destroying St Pierre and killing all but a couple of the 30,000 inhabitants.

Then in 1971 a strange lava island had appeared in La Soufrière's Crater lake, the water reached boiling point and the population beat a hasty retreat. But then all went quiet and it seemed as if the monster had gone back to sleep. My friend George Baker had been Her Majesty's representative on St Vincent, and when in 1978 I was seeking tasks for Operation Drake's Young Explorers (YEs) he pointed out that mysterious movements were going on inside the crater. No one was sure what they foretold. Although the volcano appeared to be fairly stable, there had been recent changes in the temperature and colour of the lake which indicated the possibility of further disturbances, and the lava island had grown a little bigger.

Operation Drake's purpose in going into the crater was to be threefold. The main aim was to undertake the first proper thermometric study of the lake for five years, and this was to be carried out in conjunction with the Seismic Research Unit of the University of the West Indies. In addition, the fact that the lake had been effectively sterilised when it boiled in 1971 was of tremendous interest to our biologist, for whom it provided a rare opportunity to get an insight into how aquatic life re-establishes itself from scratch. Finally, the recolonisation of the lava island by flora and fauna was equally interesting, and this was to be examined by the YEs on behalf of our scientists. So it was that Operation Drake's flagship *Eye of the Wind* dropped anchor at Kingstown, capital of St Vincent.

Clambering the 3,500 feet up to the outer rim was no easy task, especially when weighed down by scientific equipment and the Avon inflatable boat which was needed to ferry people across the lake to the island and for use in sampling the water temperatures. The boat was actually lugged most of the way by four YEs carefully selected for the job because of their sturdiness and uncomplaining natures. They included two Gurkha soldiers who, never having sailed previously on anything other than the Kowloon Ferry, were positively delighted to be on terra firma.

After an exhausting climb up the steep jungle-clad slopes they finally reached the rim; and despite the cloud, they were presented with a staggering view. The huge crater was spread out before them with the lake at the bottom and the island covering half its area. This was not the small sandbank I'd predicted but a mass of dull grey rock stretching up to a height of a hundred feet and from the middle they could see smoke, steam and fumes rising gently upwards. There was an air of mystery about the place. 'It's quite unreal, still and spooky,' wrote one of the team in his diary.

Clouds were actually swirling around inside the crater below the level of the rim, and this added to the breathtaking effect; later, when all the cloud and mist cleared, there were equally dramatic views across the island and down to the brilliant blue waters of the Caribbean.

The next task was to get the boat down the almost sheer 1,000-foot inner walls of the crater to the water's edge. This was achieved in just forty-five minutes by the simple expedient of inflating it and skimming it over the top of the boulders and vegetation.

When they reached the shore of the island they were surprised to find the composition was not as it appeared from the edge of the lake. It had looked as though it was made of dust and ash, but on reaching it they found that it consisted of large pieces of rock.

Later, one of the youngsters, Peter Shea from London, told me, 'To start with, we had to climb a very steep slope, 50 to 60 degrees in some places, and this was not easy, due to the looseness of the rocks which kept cascading down in miniature avalanches on top of the people climbing behind you. Even before we finished climbing, we noticed that all the rocks were covered with a dusty green moss, despite the already strong smell of sulphur. We reached the top of our climb and saw before us a long gully stretching up the vent hole of the island. The walking became easier now and, much to our surprise, the vegetation became more abundant. Ferns, grasses, moss and small brush-type plants were observed. We drew close to the vent hole and still the vegetation was present, despite the thickening fumes and steam and the noticeable change in the air temperature. Warm steam could be seen and felt coming up between the gaps in the rocks. We rose up again about seven metres and found ourselves looking down on the very centre of the crater. It was an exciting moment for all of us and, as we gazed down, very definite sulphur deposits could be seen over an area of about ten square metres, along with strongly smelling clouds of sulphur fumes and steam. The rocks were very hot to touch and the warm wet steam could be felt on our skin. We stayed for a few minutes and then made our way back gathering samples of all the plants we could see.'

Meanwhile, the water temperatures recorded were far higher than expected and reached 47°C (117°F). This caused some anxiety since it seemed to show that an eruption could be more imminent than had been generally anticipated. So they staggered back up to the rim and camped for the night, but not before they'd found some wildlife—a rather tired, warm frog who seemed relieved to be captured, or possibly liberated from the inhospitable lava. How on earth it had got there remained a mystery.

It is not often that one spends Christmas Eve taking the temperature of a live volcano. This point was not lost on the YEs, most of whom dwelt on it in their diaries, and the contrast between the familiar connotation of the date and the very unfamiliar environment in which they now found themselves helped to heighten the sense of adventure.

Christmas morning was one they'd never forget, as they looked down at the beautiful blue-green lake and that sinister smoking island. They were the last people ever to see that sight. There was no longer a mystery about the strange grey island in the crater—it was the start of an eruption and the warning was given. Only a few months later at midnight on Good Friday, 1979 a shuddering roar shook St Vincent. In Kingstown church bells pealed and in the Panama Canal port of Colon, plans were made to evacuate people to high ground for fear of a tidal wave following a gigantic eruption.

La Soufrière had suddenly exploded and sent a mushroom cloud of grey smoke billowing nearly five miles high, while cinders were showered over a forty-square-mile area. One witness described it as being like an atomic blast, while another talked of a sound like rolling thunder and a ball of orange fire. The forests on the crater slopes were reduced to blackened stumps, while the banana and coconut plantations were covered in a film of ash that resembled dirty snow. The fallout was so bad fourteen miles away in the capital that the inhabitants wore surgical masks and handkerchiefs over their faces. This time nobody was killed and perhaps that was partly because of the warning which had been made possible by Operation Drake's observations. For those YEs who had gazed into the very mouth of the volcano, it was a sobering thought to imagine what would have happened to them had they been there just a few weeks later. Had they known what was to come so soon after their visit, undoubtedly they would have hurried down the slopes of that mysterious volcano a little more anxiously.

Operation Drake was to have several more brushes with volcanoes, but one of the most exciting was in Kenya.

When, in 1980, I first heard about the mysterious 'Lost World' of the Masai tribesmen that was supposed to exist less than thirty miles from Nairobi, I dismissed the idea with a cynical chuckle. I felt sure that somebody was trying to pull my leg. Either way, I was not about to make myself and Operation Drake look silly by announcing a dramatic attempt to conquer the last remaining piece of unexplored territory in East Africa when the location was actually to be found within an easy Sunday afternoon drive of the Kenyan capital.

'I don't want to end up as a laughing-stock,' I explained to Gordon Davies of the Wildlife Planning Unit, when he asked me why I had decided not to take on the Mount Susua Volcano project. 'The people who suggested it were clearly using the word "unexplored" in its loosest sense—I've been told since that the area is a popular picnic spot!'

Gordon smiled and nodded knowingly. 'That's the outer crater of the volcano—anybody can get up there,' he said. 'But there's an inner crater that's far more inaccessible and in the middle of that there is a crater island plateau that has quite definitely never been explored. I ought to know—I led the last expedition that tried it, and although we reached the top of the plateau we were forced to turn back by the incredibly hard going and the lack of water. There was no way we could have gone any further. All other attempts have failed for the same reason. You'll need to build up stocks of water on the plateau or find some secret source if you're to explore it. Why don't you go and have a look for yourself—then you'll see the problem. It will be very useful to us if you can do it.' Gordon went on to tell me of strange lava caves that led outwards from the inner crater. It all sounded intriguing and rather a curiosity. 'If no-one's been there, goodness knows what we might find,' I thought, as I drove back to Nairobi.

Back at TAC HQ we organised an immediate reconnaissance and, sure enough, as soon as I set eyes on the place, I understood exactly why it had remained so effectively cut off. It was a volcano within a volcano, but it was possible to get four-wheel-drive vehicles up inside the outer crater. However, a rocky and at times almost sheer-sided gorge, one thousand feet across at its narrowest point and about seven hundred and fifty feet deep, separated the central uplifted raft of land from the rim of the inner crater like a gigantic dry moat of a huge castle. To get down into it and up the other side would require mountaineering techniques. On top of that, the terrain was murderous—jumbled rocks and boulders the size of houses, with treacherous crevasses in between, wicked thorn bushes that tear you to shreds if you are not careful and spear cactus with

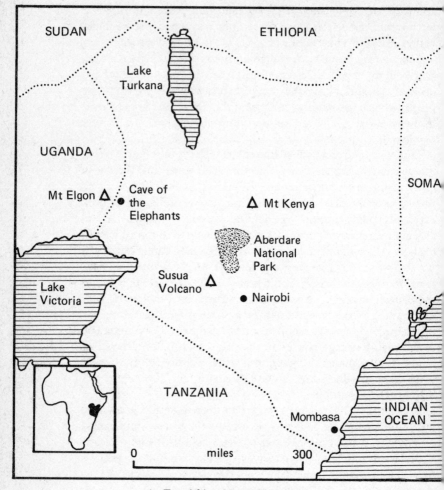

6. East Africa: Mount Elgon area.

sharp, poison-bearing spikes, just like bayonets. And not a drop of surface water anywhere. A strange fact struck me—the central plateau and its surrounding moat was a mass of dark green vegetation, in stark contrast with the surrounding area, which was covered with thin yellow grass. Yet apart from the steam vents, the place was bone dry—or was it? Was there some huge underground reservoir? Could this untrodden land hide some unknown species? An air reconnaissance had revealed a strange conical feature on the southern side of the plateau. It towered above the moat and on the summit were rocks, appearing unusually regular, which gave it the appearance of being man-made. We nick-named it the 'Temple' and planned to examine it. I wondered, could it be an ancient centre of ritual worship?

Our reconnaissance party had quite a hectic two days examining this formidable region. Whereas I had ignored Susua originally because I thought it was likely to be too easy, I now began to worry that it might prove too difficult, given the limited time and resources available to us. From the point of view of logistics alone, it promised to be a nightmare. It was necessary to establish some kind of supply line across the gorge and the only feasible method of doing this was to rig up an aerial ropeway of tensioned steel cable on which a cable car could be suspended. But even if we could find a steel cable long enough for the job, there was still the considerable problem of how to get it up there when there was at least a mile of boulder-strewn lava field between the point which Land-Rovers could reach and the edge of the crater. A one-thousand-foot steel cable, wound on a drum, would weigh nearly a ton and it would be impossible to carry or roll it over such rugged ground. Apart from that, I wondered how we were going to keep the advance party supplied with water once they started hacking their way across the plateau. In the kind of conditions and temperatures they would be encountering each man would require at least one gallon per day, maybe more, and there was no chance of their carrying sufficient quantities with them as they went.

However, after an air reconnaissance with the Chairman of Operation Drake (Kenya), John Sutton, we decided to go ahead. If it seemed like Mission Impossible—well, really tough challenges were just what we were supposed to be looking for. Also, we had had one or two strokes of luck that helped to reduce the odds against us. For a start, we had found a company who said they were able to provide a cable of the right length. What was more, our friends in the Kenya Army could provide the explosives necessary to blast a path through the lava field along which we could roll the cable drum to the crater's edge, and to dig anchorages for the ropeway. Amongst our stores were six cargo parachutes which could be used for water drops on the plateau from the Beaver aircraft which had been flown out to join us from Britain by veteran Army Air Corps pilots Colonel Mike Badger and Major Mike Sommerton-Rayner—the Biggles Outfit as they were affectionately dubbed.

As the preparations went ahead, including the setting up of a base camp, excitement and enthusiasm mounted. Gordon Davies briefed us on the questions he wanted answered. His department needed information on fauna, flora, water sources, the caves, tracks and indeed everything that they needed to know to turn Susua into a unique wilderness reserve.

'There're a great many puzzles to be unravelled—it should keep your Young Explorers going for weeks,' he laughed. In the meantime, John Sutton had invited his committee and many local sponsors to visit us, and one of the Young Explorers, Julia Barnley, working with the boys from John's safari company, organised the most splendid camp I've enjoyed on any expedition.

We decided to tackle the problem on two fronts; to start with there was to be the direct assault onto the central plateau across the moat. Later, we'd explore the extensive lava tubes, a cave system close to the surface on the eastern side of the inner crater. I'd seen these strange long passages on the reconnaissance and wondered if they led right up to the centre of the volcano. But first we attacked the formidable moat.

There was a slight hiccup in our plans when the company supplying the cable suddenly confessed that they had made a mistake and that the longest section they had was actually only seven hundred and fifty feet. This seemed like a major setback, until we discovered that Kenya Railways could splice steel cables, whereupon we bought the seven-hundred-and-fifty-foot length and another of five hundred feet and had them joined. Splicing steel cable is a delicate and precise art, especially when the join has to be good enough to stand being put under high tension, and if it is not done exactly right, you can be in trouble. Kenya Railways did a marvellous job, but even so they were not prepared to guarantee it for more than one and a half tons of strain. This was less than we required ideally and meant that we had to modify our ideas a little and we obviously dared not allow personnel to ride across in the cable car.

John Leach, a rugged and highly experienced Warrant Officer in the Royal Engineers, took charge of the aerial ropeway project and dynamited a path through the lava field, but it still took a full ten-hour day of heaving, sweating and straining by the entire twenty-strong work force to manhandle the heavy cable drum up to the edge of the crater. At the end of it all, people hardly had the strength left to tear the ring-pulls off their beer cans!

To make anchorages for either end of the ropeway, we blasted two narrow trenches, eight feet long and five feet deep, one each side of the gorge. In them we buried the trunks of cedar trees, wrapped in corrugated iron, to act as anchors for the cable which had to be dragged by hand down into the moat and across to the other side before being tensioned.

A team of the toughest YEs available helped John Leach with this exhausting and potentially dangerous task. They had to climb down into the moat and up onto the central plateau with the explosives strapped to their backpacks.

'Basically I had to try and forget what was behind me as I hacked away at the vicious spear cactus that assaults one from every angle like giant hypodermic needles, and manoeuvred across multiple lava fissures,' wrote Bradbury Williams from Norwich. 'Under the careful direction of the Sapper, we laid the explosives in the lava plateau, fixed detonators and fuse wire, and waited anxiously two hundred yards away for the dramatic event. I wasn't disappointed by the spectacle of flying boulders closely followed by a loud "Bang!"

'It took seven hours the following day to haul the steel rope across the gorge. I led the advance party of six YEs, heaving the massive wire to the anchorage we'd made on the edge of the inner raft. Communicating with a small Tannoy, we controlled the exercise which was like a giant tug-of-war and had to be halted every few minutes while we changed hands and caught our breath.'

It was when the cable got snagged on rocks at the bottom of the gorge as it was being tensioned, that Graham George, a muscular Zimbabwean, and Scotsman Steve Ballantyne had a narrow squeak. 'I climbed down from one side, checking the cable as I went, and Graham met me in the middle of the gorge where the cable was jammed in the rocks,' recalled Steve. 'Some of the tension was released and we struggled and heaved to free it. Eventually, it broke free and shot into the air under tension, knocking me for six and catapulting Graham. It was very lucky that he managed to hold on to the cable as it bounced him around ten to fifteen feet above the massive lava rocks. Hell knows where he would have landed if he had let go! It is funny to think of it now, but it was pretty hairy at the time.'

Even the girls were pressed into service as carriers to get the explosives and stores across the moat. On one occasion, Barbara Martinelli, who'd given up her holiday to rejoin Operation Drake, almost didn't go home when a football-sized boulder broke away from the top of the gorge and came crashing down the near-vertical slope. I heard a scream of 'Look out' and flattened myself against the face. Several small chippings struck my shoulders and then with a crunch, crunch, crunch, this fifty-pound lump shot past a few inches from my face. To my horror, I saw it heading straight for Barbara, who was clinging to the fixed rope a hundred feet beneath me—but in an especially exposed spot. It was a miracle that it missed her.

Once the cable had been rigged and the first water cans and equipment were sent over on the little trolley suspended from it, the exploration of the plateau began.

Through the long hot days, the team now toiled to hack a way forward across the plateau. The going was far worse than we'd imagined or, indeed, had realised from our air reconnaissance. Huge chunks of rock lay scattered across the broken ground. They were covered in a sharp barnacle-like lichen that slashed fingers and knees. It was just like climbing rocks beside a sea shore—without the sea.

In between the giant boulders, the deep ravines caused more hardship and everywhere, thorn trees and spear cactus threatened to catch the unwary. Once or twice, snakes were seen, including the much-feared death adder, one of East Africa's most deadly serpents.

'Don't think much of this place—it's just like I imagine hell to be,'

29. Papua New Guinea. The Artrellia (Salvador's Monitor). This six-footer is only a baby.

30. Papua New Guinea. Sperm whale charging the author's Avon inflatable from which this picture was taken. *Eye of the Wind* in the background.
Photo: Robyn Horley

31. Kenya. Mount Susua volcanic crater and plateau. The white 'temple' feature is on the right. The aerial ropeway was erected at 10 o'clock on the photograph.

32. Mount Elgon. Elephants caught by flash-camera in the underground caves.

commented my Devon driver and signaller, Corporal Richardson, who compared everything with his native Exmoor.

Indeed, at times it was very like an inferno. We were over 6,000 feet above the sea and at night the temperature plummeted to frost level. At dawn we stood outside our tents sipping scalding tea and shivering, watching the steam vents on the plateau puffing their vapour into the clear air. It looked rather like a thousand fires as the clouds of condensing steam rose above the dark raft. Then, as the sun came up, the dry yellow grassland of the outer crater began to shimmer with heat and sweat pumped from our pores to stream down our bodies. Only the graceful movement of the giraffe to their feeding ground and the bobbing flight of small herds of gazelle reminded us that this was Africa.

Our scientists spent the next two weeks carrying out a thorough survey of the flora and fauna on what zoologist Ian Redmond described as 'a unique ecological island'. Leaving the comfort of our base camp, the teams picked their way through the lava field, down into the moat and up onto the waterless plateau into a completely different world. The one fear that bothered me was that of a casualty on the plateau. 'How on earth can we get an injured man back to base?' I thought. Thus, when Gordon Davis's son, Ben, went down with violent stomach pains and diarrhoea, I ordered up the strongest medicine we could get. The plateau was no place for an epidemic of 'the runs'.

In the outer crater, there were scattered Masai villages where Barbara and my wife, Judith, did their best to help with some first aid and medicine for the children. 'See if you can find out what they know about the plateau,' I asked. However, the reply was always the same—the Masai, skilled and courageous hunters that they were, would not go onto that land of spirits. We still wondered about the 'Temple' and each day brought our cutting teams nearer to it.

Back in our base camp, Julia Barnley and John Sutton's boys continued to look after us in real Kenya safari style. Even Judith, who'd been on many expeditions with me, admitted this was pretty good by any standard. Apart from the HQ element, Julia also catered for the team whose task was to explore the cave system.

The lava caves and subterranean passages had been created when the volcano erupted. The red-hot lava had spilled over and run down the mountainside. As the outside surface of this molten tide cooled and solidified, the inner core continued to flow, thereby creating hollow underground tubes that opened at intervals into large caverns. The network of passages, ranging in diameter from thirty feet to eighteen inches, was estimated to extend to over five miles. They were once used as a hide-out by Mau Mau terrorists, but now there are plans to turn them into a tourist attraction, and it was with this in mind that some of the YEs helped cave experts John Arkle and Jim Simon to survey and map the tunnel system.

John, an ex-soldier who ran the United Touring Company in Mombasa, had one hair-raising experience when he and Jim penetrated far into the network. They had just wriggled their way through a long section of tunnel that was only eighteen inches high when they burst through into a large chamber. A shaft of sunlight was pouring through a small hole in the roof creating a pool of warmth on the floor of the cave in which was lying, fast asleep, an enormous fifteen-foot python. The two men tiptoed past and continued on their way up the next section of tunnel which turned out to be a dead end, and when they came back, the snake was nowhere to be seen. There was only one way it could have gone—and that was down the eighteen-inch-high passage along which they had no option but to crawl. Their hearts were in their mouths as they inched forward, expecting to see at any moment the shadowy outline of the huge reptile rear up out of the gloom into the light cast by their lamps. In fact, they never did catch up with it, but John admits that the prospect of coming face to face with it in such nightmarishly claustrophobic circumstances still makes his flesh crawl whenever he thinks about it.

In the time available we only had the opportunity to explore a few miles of the system. It's a strange place, full of unnatural shapes of solidified lava, some of these twisted like great ropes, others forming platforms at the sides of the passages and giving the tunnels an appearance of an underground railway station. Stalactites of lava hang from the roof and musical notes can be rung by striking the strange formations.

In one cavern, the skeleton of a bull rhino had been discovered. A gaping hole in the roof told the tale of its end and reminded us not to drive our Land-Rover carelessly through the bush above the passages.

226

On another occasion, we discovered fresh leopard prints in the dust—going in, and we decided to go out! The question of where the caves lead will not be solved for many a moon, but they are certainly most extensive.

Meanwhile, on the plateau the battle continued and flying low in the Beaver I saw something very odd. As Mike Badger swung the powerful plane over the cedar trees, we came to a big clearing. We were looking for suitable parachute dropping zones and as I glanced down, I saw an extraordinary animal. It was rather like an antelope, with a flash of white above the tail. My immediate reaction was to say 'water buck'—but such a creature would hardly be likely to be living on a waterless plateau. Whatever, it was a biggish animal and it would need water. Later we were to discover other large mammals on the raft.

One group of YEs, led by an Air Training Corps Instructor, Trevor Moss, had an uncomfortable encounter with a pack of baboons.

'We had scaled the moat and had just started to follow the main path across the plateau,' he reported. 'Within close proximity we could hear the barking of olive baboons and it was not long before we came face to face with a group of approximately forty of these animals sitting on and around the track. Initially they showed no fear of us, probably because we were the first humans they had ever seen. They appeared inquisitive, and our yelling and shouting did nothing to make them move off the path. Suddenly they seemed to feel threatened and two large males rushed at us with teeth bared. We had machetes, but no guns and the odds of getting away without injury were slim. Luckily, the two animals stopped short, and we decided not to push our chances and retreated back several hundred yards hoping that they would move along in their own time. But it was an hour before we felt it was safe to continue. In fact many of the female baboons acted in a strangely carnal manner towards us. Perhaps they thought we were rather attractive apes.'

A Kenyan YE, Justin Bell, had an alarming experience when he was moving back at last light to one of the temporary camps set up along the route across the plateau. Hearing a soft sound close by, he turned to find a fully grown leopard following him. Justin didn't panic, although admitted he was scared stiff. 'It seemed to have no fear of me—obviously it wasn't hungry,' he said afterwards. 'Why do the animals act like this?' I asked myself. 'It's obvious they have not yet learned to fear man—perhaps because they've never seen him before.'

Hopes that the fiction of Conan Doyle's *Lost World* might come true with the discovery of weird and wonderful creatures, marooned there since pre-historic times, were not fulfilled. But the fact that there was a considerable amount of wildlife up on the plateau was a puzzle in itself since no source of fresh water could be found. The only water came from the steam vents, clearly visible at dawn, but later in the day, as the temperature rose, they were barely to be seen. However, early one morning as I rested atop a large boulder near one of the vents, my eye caught a movement below. A rock hyrax, a small rabbit-like creature with short ears, emerged from a crevice and crept up to a stone on the edge of the vent. Its nose twitching in the sulphur fumes, it began to lick up the condensed moisture. Later that day, I saw several dragon flies—insects normally associated with water. So smaller creatures could survive on the liquid coming from the vents. But what about the large animals?

Thus, while the survey path was cut across the plateau, I began to seek for a pool or water hole, which I guessed must be somewhere amongst the jumbled rock. However, Susua did not intend to give up her secrets easily and after several abortive searches, I returned to base camp, battered, bruised and full of thorns. The mystery of the water remains to be solved.

For me, the most odd thing about the place was its distinctly eerie atmosphere. I am not normally worried about being by myself in remote areas, but whenever I was walking alone on the plateau I always had the feeling of being watched, and that is something I have never experienced anywhere else in the world. Several of the team told me that they had felt the same thing. I think it had something to do with the terrain, the huge rocks and boulders behind which it was easy to imagine all sorts of things lying in wait, and the many unexplained noises. It was quite common to hear a sudden crashing in the undergrowth without being able to see anything. The strangest noise of all was the ghostly whistling that was most notice-able at dusk and about which we had been warned. The acacia trees play host to a particular type of ant which nests in ball-like growths on the branches. These are full of holes made by the ants and when the wind blows through them it creates the whistling.

Now our exploration team were finding it desperately hard work to carry forward water from the head of the aerial ropeway. Using plastic sheets, we managed to collect a few pints of the precious liquid from the steam vents, but this was not nearly enough. This steam was coming from deep within the volcano, for there was no water near the surface. However, by now, the base camp staff, plus all the girls and any visitors we could pressgang, had levelled a 650-yard airstrip in the outer crater and from here, the Beaver was able to fly parachute loads of water to Graham George's team on the plateau.

With the YEs to help him, Ian Redmond had been able to make several transects across the plateau, noting the variety of animals and plants to be found. The results were particularly interesting as the inner area of Susua has been effectively cut off from outside influences since it was created. The Wildlife Department was keen to see if Susua could be developed as a wilderness area for climbers and trekkers, so diversifying Kenya's attractions. With the information we gained, appropriate plans could be made.

The Susua project turned out to be a tremendous success all round—one of the toughest and most adventurous assignments of Operation Drake, but it almost ended in disaster when a wildlife expert flew up from Nairobi to see us in his private plane. He signalled his arrival by doing a few low-level circuits of the gorge. It was then that I realised with a chilling feeling that he was totally unaware of the steel cable that was stretched across it! If he hit that, it would slice through the aircraft like a giant cheese-cutter. I waited on tenterhooks, unable to see what was going on from where I stood in the base camp, but following his progress by the engine sound and tensing myself, ready for the rending crash, each time he came round to the area of the cable. Miraculously he managed to avoid the hazard and landed safely and seemed utterly unconcerned when told about the deathtrap he so easily could have flown into. Far from being chastened, his attitude was so cavalier that, when the time came to leave, he decided to buzz the camp. People threw themselves to the ground as he swooped in low, mowing through all our radio aerials and then chopping the top branches of a nearby tree with his tailplane. We could not believe our eyes. Inches lower and he would have been brought down by the tree. As it was, we were anxious that he might have damaged his undercarriage severely, but were unable to contact his base to warn them to expect a possible emergency landing because our aerials had been destroyed. After our signallers had joined up all the broken bits of copper wire, we still could not get through to Nairobi—but, using the amazing Plessey PRC 320, we did manage to raise the Signals Centre at Blandford in England! We asked them to put an urgent call through to John Sutton in Nairobi, but our fears proved to be unfounded. The would-be Red Baron clearly led a charmed life—his plane had suffered no serious damage and he was able to land normally. However, he was very apologetic when he learned what had happened and kindly paid for the damage to our aerials.

After several weeks' back-breaking toil, these tough young people had blazed an eight-foot-wide trail for two miles from one side of the plateau to the other and up to its highest point at 6,850 feet. There the Kenyan flag was ceremonially raised by a tall young Kenyan, Charles Langat, to the accompaniment of a thunderflash salute. Whilst at the summit, we moved forward to investigate the 'Temple'. Sadly it was a natural feature! Just a huge steam vent bare of trees and topped by unusually regular rocks. Although, who knows, it might easily have been used for Masai initiation rites. It then took three and a half hours to scramble back along the path that had been cleared—an indication of just how thick and impenetrable the virgin terrain had been.

Whilst we were still hard at work at Susua, Gordon Davies of the Wildlife Planning Unit prepared another task for us to tackle. He'd heard of a huge cave at Mount Elgon, an extinct volcano near the Ugandan border, which was housing a herd of elephants. Eager to investigate, Gordon and his team visited Kitium, as the cavern was known. They were alerted to the presence of the elephants as soon as they arrived by fresh droppings near the entrance, and sure enough, as they advanced warily into the darkness, they heard rumblings coming from behind a pile of rocks at the back of the cavern. They quickly decided to find a hiding-place among the boulders below the path at the mouth so that they could watch developments.

There were some anxious moments when a large bull elephant suddenly appeared round a bend in the track outside, clearly intending to join the rest of the herd, and then, scenting danger, came to a halt. He backed off and returned to the top of the cliff, apparently waiting for the human intruders to move. Meanwhile, those inside had begun to leave, but had also sensed the presence of observers. They paused for a moment and then, gaining confidence, moved forward to within a few feet of the hidden watchers.

'We had a very close-up view indeed,' Gordon told me. 'There were between fifteen and twenty in the group and all of them appeared to be females. Some had very young calves. While they were obviously aware of our close situation they showed no sign of aggression and merely confined their activities to sniffing with raised trunks and a little ear-flapping. At a sign from the group matriarch, the party then moved out of the cave in single file, squeezing their bodies between the narrow confines of the wall and various rocks so that the friction made a rasping noise. Youngsters were given the odd nudge to help them on their way. As they went down the narrow defile, clouds of dust filled the air, lending even further to the unusual atmosphere. As they passed the concealed watchers, their great trunks swung down amongst the rocks, sniffing and seeking the humans, but they passed on. But what made the elephants come to this cave? Gordon wanted us to help in a full-scale investigation. This was a mystery I couldn't put out of my mind.

Researching into the history of the area, we discovered that sixty years before, a farmer called Renshaw Mitford-Barbeton had entered Kitium Cave, and got a very nasty shock. Having edged cautiously through the wide, low letterbox-shaped entrance, he then penetrated right to the back of the 250-yard-deep cavern, crawling over fallen boulders, inching past narrow crevasses and skirting dark pools into which water dripped with echoing plops. It was as he prepared to make his way back out again that he suddenly realised with a start that he had company. He heard them long before he saw them—heavy, shuffling footsteps, a strange flapping noise, and some terrifyingly loud huffing and puffing. There was also a sound that seemed to him like the rumbling of giant stomachs. His mind boggled. Whoever or whatever they were, they had him trapped in the dead-end cave. He strained his eyes into the darkness beyond the range of his lamp and then gasped in amazement as he eventually managed to make out a group of huge shadowy forms in the gloom. It was a herd of elephants.

Mr Mitford-Barbeton escaped unhurt when, after an hour that must have seemed to him like an eternity, the elephants left and allowed him to scramble to safety. However, we were to discover that his confrontation was no chance meeting, since the herds regularly visited the cave; they had beaten a well-worn path to the entrance. But the reason why they should want to go out of their way to squeeze themselves into this one particularly inaccessible cavern had remained a mystery for many years—an even greater mystery than the legendary Elephants' Graveyard. Part of the problem was that it was impossible to see what they were doing in the darkness, and lights would scare them off and possibly start a stampede.

When Gordon Davies took John Sutton and me plus several wildlife experts to Mount Elgon, we checked first very carefully to see that the cave was uninhabited, and posted an armed game guard at the entrance.

Following the beams of our head torches, we were soon deep underground when an appalling stench hit us—it was the unmistakable smell of decaying flesh, and on peering into a crevasse, we saw the cause. There, ten feet down, lay the carcass of a baby elephant which had stumbled to its death in the darkness. We pressed on, our lamps startling thousands of fruit bats that were hanging from the roof, so much so that they showered us with their droppings! Finally, we came to the pools, surrounded by recent elephant manure, and then we looked up and saw what attracted the great beasts.

All over the walls and roof were tusk marks—they were mining salt.

'What an incredible story,' said John. 'Salt-mining elephants—it must be unique.' But it wasn't only elephants, for at much lower levels and in small side tunnels, were the marks of wild pig, antelope and giant forest hog.

Analysis of the minerals showed that it contained mirabilite, which has a mild purgative effect and probably helps the beasts' digestion. Clearly we were dealing with highly intelligent animals.

Gordon felt that tourist viewing facilities could be provided by cutting a path up to the entrance and constructing an observation platform. I offered a team of Young Explorers to do this and carry out a survey of the cave itself and hopefully to find out more about the frequency and duration of the elephants' visits.

In fact, the YEs who maintained a round-the-clock vigil outside the cave during the project never had quite such a clear, daylight viewing as Gordon's team, but what they missed in terms of spectacle they more than made up for by way of the drama that surrounded their sightings.

They took it in turns to man the hide for four-hour shifts, accompanied by an armed National Park ranger. Charles Langat took the first night shift and met with almost immediate success. A group of elephants entered the cave, but they seemed to know that he was watching them and they did not stay long. Trevor Moss's brother, Barry, was in a state of tense expectation, therefore, when he arrived to take over the 4.00–8.00 a.m. shift. The camp was over a mile away and after driving in a Land-Rover to the foot of Mount Elgon there was a walk of several hundred yards up the ill-defined path to the cave entrance.

'In the complete darkness this was an incredible and rather frightening experience,' wrote Barry in his report. 'There were known to be numerous wild animals in the area, including buffalo, giant forest hog, and leopard, and one had a sense of acute awareness of the least little noise. We had only just started clearing the path at this stage and it was quite easy to lose it, especially at night. The ranger led on cautiously through the thick vegetation and undergrowth, his rifle loaded and cocked—ready for action. I followed close behind him with my flashlight picking out large trees which we might be able to hide behind or climb in the event of attack by buffalo or elephant. I felt that the blood in my veins had been transformed to adrenaline. It was like walking down a narrow, darkened alley in the middle of gangland, expecting an ambush from every doorway and corner.

'We reached the hide fifteen minutes later and settled in as quietly as possible. The sky was clear and the moon and stars lit up the entrance with an adequate amount of light to see anything coming in or out of the subterranean hall. As dawn approached the only sound to be heard was of fruit bats returning to their roosts, at first in ones and twos, and then in hundreds, fluttering and squealing inches above our heads.'

The next evening more than made up for this slight anti-climax. Barry, Charles Langat and his accompanying ranger went up to Mount Elgon ready to start their stint, but there was no sign of the previous shift who should have been at the bottom of the path for a lift back to camp. After waiting half an hour, Barry and Charles decided that they both ought to go up and check that everything was all right. The ranger was not so keen since he was unarmed—his colleague who was already up there had the gun. 'It wasn't an easy job persuading him that he should come with us,' wrote Barry. 'But eventually he agreed and we set off into the darkness. We slowly picked our way through the dense undergrowth as quietly as possible, stopping and listening at every rustle and sound. Our only weapon was my drawn machete. As we approached the top of the path we heard a loud scream and much trumpeting followed by crashing trees as a herd of elephants came charging down the valley. We froze in our tracks, trying to pinpoint their position and whether they were heading towards us. I looked at my machete, realised that it would be totally ineffective against the charging animals and started looking round for a large tree. There weren't any to be seen and, besides, trees would be no obstacles to maddened elephants. I had seen them push over full-grown trees quite effortlessly. I then thought about running, but the path was too steep and the mass of tangled undergrowth was nearly impenetrable so all we could do was go to ground.

'At last we heard the crashing and trumpeting heading into the distance and we realised that the elephants had changed direction and gone down the other side of the valley. When we reached the cave entrance we found that the two girls who had been sharing the previous watch were in almost as much of a panic as the elephants. They explained that they had been delayed because they did not want to leave while the elephants were there. Then the sound of our approach had spooked the herd which immediately stampeded.'

For Barry the excitement still was not over. A couple of nights later when he went on the 8.00 p.m. shift he was met at the bottom of the path by two girl YEs with the news that there were three elephants in the cave and more hanging around outside. He went up with extra care and tiptoed to the hide.

'For the first half-hour or so I heard absolutely nothing and then, all of a sudden, a terrifying roar came from the back of the cave followed by a sickening thud. I learned later that the thud was the sound of their tusks chipping the salt from the walls, while the roar was the sound of a stomach rumbling! I could also hear a distant whooshing as the jumbos hosed water from the rock pools into their mouths. For a while all went quiet again and my eyes and ears strained into the still darkness. Then I thought I heard an elephant approaching our position, heavy footsteps like some giant mechanical monster making its way towards us. I cowered back until I could retreat no further. Was there really something there or had my imagination been carried away? The sounds then stopped and I never did find out whether I was dreaming or not. But I felt somewhat stunned by the whole experience.'

Considering how few people have ever actually witnessed this strange elephantine ritual, Barry and his fellow YEs were obviously fortunate to have been on the spot at exactly the right time.

There was one thing about the cave of the elephants that still mystifies me—whenever I visited it, I'd noted with an engineer's interest that the roof appeared to be supported by a single pillar—about twenty feet thick, but made of the same mineral salt as the walls. There were tusk marks on it—but very old ones. No fresh mining—very strange, and it posed a question. Do the elephants, who after all are great engineers, know they must maintain this vital roof support or is it pure chance? In Kenya's Aberdare National Park two bulls had been seen to push a young elephant over a ditch and through an electric fence in an effort to get at appetising crops on the far side. The use of Indian elephants for a variety of logging and construction tasks is well known, so perhaps it isn't pure chance. Whatever, the elephants' underground quest for the health-giving minerals is one of the most extraordinary phenomena in the animal world.

9

Ghostly Encounters

========

'Have you seen Freddie yet, Rector?'
'Freddie?'
'Yes, my dear, Freddie—an awfully nice ghost.'

Those curious enough to investigate the unexplained are bound to come across the supernatural. Not that I have ever really seen a ghost, nor for that matter the Loch Ness monster, the Yeti, nor Big Foot. I do know some pretty sensible and honest folk who think they have, though, and until proved otherwise, I'm prepared to believe they have seen something and there will one day be a rational explanation for these mysteries. In the meantime, I keep an open mind and even indulge in a spot of seeking from time to time— simply because I'm curious and everyone loves a mystery.

However, I was not looking for anything other than a good night's sleep when I drove up to the Scientific Exploration Society base in Wiltshire, at midnight. The white-walled Tudor farm was bathed in pale moonlight, the shrubs and trees of the garden casting strange shadows on the concrete patio. As the big Volvo's engine died, I stepped out into the chill English night air. 'Brrr,' I shivered as I hoisted my grip from the back of the car and strode over to the kitchen door. 'Keys in the letter box,' I remembered Jim Masters' instructions. 'We'll be back in the morning.' My old friends Jim and Joan were wardens of the base and returning from a visit to Belize where some of my sappers were stationed. I'd just flown in to RAF Brize Norton from Washington. Next day, I'd motor home to Yorkshire, but with some snow over much of Northern England, I didn't fancy a long night drive after my eight-hour flight across the Atlantic.

The door swung open and warm air spilled out to greet me. The

236

neon light flickered on revealing a note, a newspaper and a bottle of J & B on the scrubbed kitchen table. 'Welcome John,' read the message, 'help yourself. Please use the bedroom at the top of the stairs. See you tomorrow. Cheers, Jim.' Pouring a good measure of man's best friend, I flicked open the *Daily Telegraph* and started to catch up on the news. My heavy diver's watch read 7.30 p.m. (New York time) and having just caught up five hours, I was not the least bit tired. The glass of Scotch was getting low when I heard the coughing—it was right above me. 'How odd,' I thought, looking at the oak-beamed ceiling—then remembered. 'Heavens, it must be Michael—and I've woken him up.' Michael, Jim's teenage son, slept in the room above the kitchen, and although his parents were out, I guessed Michael had come home early, used his own key and gone to bed. So I put away the J & B and tiptoed up to my bedroom where the long hours of travel quickly had their effect.

Waking up with the sun, I stretched, yawned, climbed reluctantly out of bed and tottered off to the bathroom to shave, bathe and note with satisfaction the good tan my short visit to Central America had produced.

The internal walls in the farm were barely partitions and with the creeky, irregular wooden floors, every noise was audible all over the house. I could hear Michael dressing in his room and later, as I lay and wallowed in the steaming bath, I saw his shadow cross the frosted glass door, followed by the 'clump, clump, clump' as he descended the narrow wooden stairs. As I dried myself, he returned and as he passed the door, I called out, 'Morning, Michael,' but there was no reply. Once dressed, I went down to phone Judith and announce my safe return. Michael was still moving about in his room.

Suddenly, there was the sound of a key in the lock and in walked Jim and Joan. 'Sleep well?' they inquired.

'Yes—super, and bless you for the J&B, you know my taste.' We chatted for a moment and then, as Joan put on the coffee, I said, 'I'm sorry I disturbed Michael last night.'

Joan looked at me in a strange way. 'Michael?' she asked.

'Yes,' said I, 'upstairs.'

Joan's brows narrowed. 'John,' she said very slowly, 'Michael has not been here for six weeks—he's away at college.'

'Then who on earth's upstairs?' I said, 'because he's still there.'

Joan turned down the coffee and led quickly to Michael's room. The door was closed, the bed was not even made up—there was just a plain mattress on the springs. I felt rather cold and the hair on the back of my neck lifted. We checked the entire house from top to bottom. All doors and windows were locked from inside. Other than the one in my possession, Jim had the only other key. I must have been alone. 'Leave the coffee—you'd better have something stronger,' said Jim, 'We've got a story you'd better hear.'

The tale they told was all the more amazing because of the personalities involved. Jim and Joan are two of the most practical, down-to-earth people I've ever met. To hear them talking of the mysterious events that had been going on at the farm for the past year left me feeling uncomfortable. It was like finding a life-long teetotaller stoned out of his mind!

For some time the family had experienced strange noises, movements and finally seen a silver-haired lady in Michael's bedroom. Jim, a stolid West Country man, is not the sort to make a fuss and it had taken my own experience to get them to tell all.

One of their most dramatic sightings had occurred quite recently. Jim had been alone in his workshop in the farm with the door open, when he became aware of a cold feeling. He turned around and there in the open door stood a man—medium height, ruddy complexion, fifty-ish, dressed rather like a farmer. As Jim gasped in astonishment, his visitor wore an inquisitive smile, as if to say 'What are you doing here?' Then he was gone—quite literally gone into thin air. Jim, as an ex-parachute engineer and used to rapid action, reacted at once. Dashing out of the room, he checked the doors and windows. All were locked from inside—there was nobody else in the house.

There was no more to tell. However, the farm belongs to a friend of mine, so I told him of the events. He knew of no previous history of haunting, no accounts of terrible deeds, no tales of unrequited love, but he promised to ask around. Several months later, I called in on him. 'Oh, by the way, John,' he said, 'You remember the silver-haired lady—well I've found out something.'

'Go on, tell me more.'

'Well, there was a lady who fits that description; her husband was employed on the farm some years ago—and she died in that bedroom. But from natural causes—no murder or anything. But,' he went on, 'you'll remember the man who Jim saw—well that seems to be her husband; the funny thing is—he's still alive and lives about ten miles away!' I had another whisky and went off to tell Jim and Joan.

We still use the farm and some wardens have experienced strange events. Others, even those owning dogs, have come across nothing unusual, but it's still unexplained and all the more intriguing because it's at the Headquarters of an organisation dedicated to solving mysteries.

So I've never really *seen* a ghost—but I've certainly had some strange experiences which I can't explain.

In 1962, two young boys died mysteriously in an old German Army storage tunnel on my home island of Jersey. Apparently, they had crawled in through a hole in the long-sealed entrance to see if they could find any interesting souvenirs amongst the piles of rotting and rusting equipment.

The *Jersey Evening Post* of 28 May reported the incident: 'One of the most shocking tragedies recorded in Jersey for some consider-able time occurred in a German storage tunnel in St. Peter's Valley yesterday afternoon when two Victoria College boys, sixteen-year-old Richard John Phillips and Richard C. Pratchett, aged 15, lost their lives after being overcome by a concentration of cyanide and methane gases, the cyanide escaping from canisters left behind by the Germans and the methane being set up by dampness and the decomposition of undergrowth in the tunnel.' Eventually it tran-spired that the boys had been overcome by carbon monoxide produced by the smouldering remains of some old pit props set afire in the tunnel by a party of youngsters who'd visited the underground passages the previous day. The victims died as they struggled to reach the open air through a narrow crawl-way dug beneath the concrete plug that had sealed the tunnel. However, would-be rescuers were struck down by some mysterious vapours wafting from the entrance and rumours of wartime cyanide gas were soon circulating. As these rumours spread, holidaymakers cancelled bookings and hoteliers screamed for action.

The local government—The States of Jersey—quickly called

upon the Ministry of Defence to investigate. There were few Jerseymen in the Royal Engineers and it appeared I was the only one below the rank of Colonel. Thus I found myself with an unusual and exciting job in August, 1962: our task was to examine all the old German underground works on the island and, equipped with the original maps, a small team of soldiers sailed from Weymouth on a British Rail ferry loaded with apprehensive tourists.

As we had expected, the German map had been drawn with Teutonic thoroughness and, guided by an islander, Tony Titterington (whom, as a boy, I had spent hours following down some of these very tunnels), we set to work. Tony and I had long been intrigued by the mysterious shafts that were rumoured to contain everything from Nazi treasure to Luger pistols still in their original packing.

Several of the tunnels were as large as a London tube station and, lined with ferro-concrete, looked very similar. However, others had bare granite walls, dripping with water and often blocked by roof falls. There were stories of Russian prisoners of war being cemented into the walls when they died at work. Locals who had lived there in the war told grim tales of fleets of ambulances rushing to and from the entrances following collapses deep inside. There was no doubt that men had died within and some of the piles of jagged rock that we found blocking our exploration had almost certainly entombed workers and soldiers alike. However, many of the tunnels had been completed and were now filled with untidy heaps of military equipment—helmets, anti-tank guns, bazookas, machine guns. Everything lay scattered by the hands of generations of small boys who had crawled in seeking souvenirs. There were more lethal items—the occasional shell and drums of flame-thrower fluid. Working our way forward over the debris, we surveyed, checked roof falls, examined equipment and searched for any unknown passages that might conceal especially dangerous items.

'Cor—I feel just like a bloody mole,' said my cockney Sergeant, as he stripped off his emergency oxygen-breathing-apparatus, miner's helmet and lamp and sat on a rock at the entrance of one long shaft after six hours underground.

'Funny smell in the place ain't there, sir?'

'Yes,' I admitted, pulling a crumpled packet of filter tips from my pocket. 'I'm not sure what it is—it smells familiar, but I can't place it.'

'Well, it didn't show up on the test papers,' said Tony, who'd joined us. One of the soldiers had found something. 'Do you think it's this stuff that's smelling?' he asked, handing me a grey rock-like lump. One sniff confirmed that it was. 'There's barrels and barrels of it in one of the side tunnels,' he remarked. We passed the lumps around and eventually tossed one away. No one really noticed it land with a soft plop in a pool of rainwater. I was just lighting my cigarette. 'Hey, look at that!' said Tony. To our amazement, the puddle was bubbling and boiling, giving off a pungent vapour—I flicked the lighted match at it. 'Pop,' went the gas, igniting with a bright orange flash. 'My God!' said the Sergeant, still holding one of the lumps. It was calcium carbide and the tunnel was full of highly inflammable acetylene gas. We stubbed out our fags and moved away from the entrance rather speedily.

We soon discovered the Germans had used this for emergency lighting and in case any other little nasties turned up, I decided to get some expert local advice.

A number of Jersey quarrymen had been forced to work for the Germans. Virtually enslaved, they were given a little potato soup and black bread at dawn each day, then marched in gangs under armed guard into the growing labyrinths. There, with prisoners of war, imported French workers and anyone else the Hun could press into service, they laboured in the darkness with pick and shovel until well after dusk. Many of those who had survived the ordeal were now dead, but those who still lived would never forget the years in this underground hell, the terror of the roof falls, the screams of the injured and the endless passages down which they shuffled, half starved and cold, knowing that if they as much as paused a jackboot would come crashing out of the darkness to drive them on.

'You know, you could smell a German in there and you learned to step out when you passed him,' said my visitor. Charlie, a small, round, red-faced man, was from the quarries at Grosnez.

'How long did you work in there, Charlie?' I asked.

'Best part of two years—then they moved me to St. Catharine's,' he said in his lilting Jersey-French accent. Charlie and several friends had come to advise us on a particularly difficult tunnel—

where a massive rock fall had blocked our progress. Scrambling together over the fallen granite and rotting pit props, we reached a dead end. 'Reckon they gave up here,' grunted my knowledgeable guide. 'I can't say exactly what happened 'cos I was working in the main passage when this lot came in—but I'll never forget the rumble when she went—then the dust and the yelling.' The pale yellow beam of my miner's lamp lit the serious faces of the grim-looking men.

The next day, I was already in the tunnel when the two quarry-men—Charlie and his mate—groped their way towards me. 'I've found a small air-shaft that we may be able to squeeze through and get behind the rock fall,' I told them. So it was, with much grunting, we heaved ourselves forward on our stomachs inch by inch through the narrow passage. 'Not the place to suffer from claustrophobia,' I thought as I moved aside a fallen pit prop and wormed my way into the shattered passage behind the rock fall. The wood, sodden and rotten, broke away in my hand and I cast a furtive glance at the unsupported roof. The tunnel was littered with debris; an empty bottle, a broken spade, a rusty drilling rod, then our lamps shone down the passage and there was another rock fall. Tree roots hung down from the roof like giant fingers. 'Must be pretty near the surface,' said Charlie and I nodded, looking round. The other quarryman stood watching with us and said nothing, but nodded in agreement. He was slightly shorter than Charlie and I guessed a little older, but I was hardly in the mood for conversation and we only exchanged a few words. Having inspected the chamber into which we'd crawled, I said, 'Well, that's it—let's get out of here.' So we wriggled back through the air shaft into the main tunnel and I led the way to the entrance. Just as the refreshing blast of fresh air hit us, I remembered my maps that I'd put down before entering the narrow crawl-way. 'Blast!' I swore. 'Go on, Charlie—I'll just nip back for my millboard.' A few minutes later, when I emerged, the soldier at the door, whose job it was to check everyone in and out of the tunnel, ticked me off on his list.

'Everyone out then?' I asked. 'Yes, sir,' he replied, swinging back the metal grid over the entrance.

'Oh! Which way did Charlie and his mate go?' I asked, thinking I should buy them a beer. 'Charlie's gone off on his bike,' said the sentry, 'but I didn't see no mate.'

'You must have,' I remarked tetchily. 'You know, the chap who came in with him.'

'Charlie went in alone, sir, and no other civilians have been in this afternoon.' The hair stood on the back of my neck. Yet I knew there'd been a second man. Hell, I'd spoken to him!

'Are you sure?' I questioned. 'Quite sure, sir,' replied the soldier pushing his notebook towards me to emphasise the point.

Five minutes later I found Charlie downing a pint of Mary Ann in the pub. 'Where are your chums today, Charlie?' I said, trying not to seem concerned. 'Couldn't get away from work,' he muttered, wiping the froth from his cracked lips. 'Like a drink?'

'Yes,' I said, 'I would very much.' In fact, I had several!

My father and mother, also pretty down-to-earth people, held me spell-bound with their own tales of the unexplained. They had a marvellous life of adventure and excitement as Parson/Army Chaplain and wife all around the world.

In the 1930s they took up a living in Shropshire. Father was the new vicar and together with their three Alsatians, they had moved into a spacious old rectory standing in its own grounds set in one of the most beautiful areas of England. One summer's evening, Bish had a bad cold and my mother decided to sleep in a spare room looking out over the front of the house. Storm, her favourite Alsatian, curled up on the floor beside the bed and Gwen slept soundly for several hours until she awoke very slowly, aware of a pressure on the bed. Putting out a hand, she felt the coat of her dog, and she was wide awake in seconds. There was something wrong— the great black dog had her forepaws on the bed and, with her face contorted in a terrifying grimace, she stared out of the window above the bed. 'Quietly, quietly,' comforted Gwen, but, snarling wolf-like, the dog showed no inclination to be comforted—plainly she was frightened stiff.

Gwen looked out of the window, saw nothing unusual and opened the bedroom door. In a flash, the Alsatian, its hackles raised, fangs bared, was out onto the landing, flying down the stairs and into the kitchen where the other dogs were already stirring. All hell broke loose—they barked and howled in an eerie way such as my mother had never heard before. 'Shut up, shut up you silly idiots!' she shouted and, seizing a Maori war club studded with human teeth from the umbrella stand, she drew the bolt and flung open the back door. Moving as one animal, the three dogs catapulted into the garden and chased round and round the rectory for some ten minutes before returning, satisfied that they had seen the intruder off. Even so, they did not settle, but paced uneasily about the kitchen, whining and casting furtive glances at the back door. Gwen went back to bed and slept until dawn.

The next day, she told my father of the incident. 'Poachers,' he grunted, reading his newspaper, 'that's what it'll be—after the pheasants, I expect.' So Gwen checked the rearing pens at the bottom of the garden, but all was well.

It was about two o'clock the next morning when Mother awoke, instantly aware of Storm's paws and hearing her low growl. Even her mistress felt a little shiver down her spine. Bright moonlight streamed in through the window and the garden was bathed in an almost blue light. By now the dog was on the bed, hackles bristling, her fearsome eyes staring through the panes into the garden. Her lip rose slightly, as she made a rasping snarl, her whole body quivered. But now my mother was more curious than afraid. 'What is it?' she said softly, gazing along the bitch's long nose. The dog whimpered in reply and then Gwen saw the figure. 'He must have been so close to the house that I missed him,' she thought, as she watched the figure of a tall bare-headed man, wearing a pale raincoat or something similar. His back was to the house as he walked away towards the pheasant pens. 'So that's your game, is it?' Gwen thought. The figure crossed the lawn and disappeared into the trees.

Quick as lightning, dog and mistress bounded down the stairs— no lights, just a torch she had handy. It caught the green eyes of her pets, already milling about by the door to the garden. Sliding the bolt as quietly as possible, she loosed the terrible trio into the night. A blast of cold air caught her as the dogs sprang through the doorway, instantly giving tongue in a hideous cacophony.

Next morning, Bish had recovered from his cold and came down to breakfast. Gwen woke late and found him reading the mail. 'Hello, darling,' he grinned. 'If I stay in bed much longer your ruddy dogs will deafen the neighbourhood. What on earth were they up to last night?'

My mother told her tale, with pride, while Storm enjoyed the praise. 'Walked across the lawn towards the pens, you say?' queried my father.

'Yes, I saw him quite clearly,' replied Gwen.

'Well you must have been at the gin,' laughed Bish. 'You mean to say he walked straight through the tennis court!'

Gwen put down her teacup feeling rather odd. She walked over to the window and, gazing at the high wire fence surrounding the grass court, said very deliberately, 'Yes, I do—that's exactly what he did.' A lengthy discussion on the habits of ghosts and Shropshire poachers followed, liberally scattered with references to canine perception, but it was inconclusive. However, an old lady, who had lived in the rectory as a child, was coming to tea on Sunday afternoon and they agreed that she might know something. 'No prompting, mind you,' cautioned Bish.

On Sunday, as the crumpets were passed, my parents listened to the tales of the lady's childhood—but it was not until the teapot was almost empty that their visitor inquired, 'Have you seen Freddie yet, Rector?'

'Freddie?' asked mother, raising her eyebrows.

'Yes, my dear, Freddie—an awfully nice ghost. We often saw him, but I've no idea who or what he was,' replied the silver-haired lady.

But Gwen's Alsatians never did get used to him.

Bish was always rather sceptical about the supernatural, but, like my mother, he adored animals, especially dogs. He, too, had his favourite Alsatian, Peggy, a strongly built sable-coated bitch, whose party trick was to pick me up by my nappies when, as a baby, I tipped myself out of the pram. Apparently, she would then carry me, bawling my head off, into the house by the seat of my pants.

In 1944, father was a chaplain with the 53rd Welsh Division in France. As the Allies pressed forward from the beaches of Normandy, a large part of the German Army eventually became trapped in a 'pocket' at Falaise. With their backs to a river and orders from Hitler to hold on regardless, they were surrounded on three sides by the invading armies and systematically destroyed as the pocket closed in. The fighting was bitter and confused, opposing units became inextricably intermingled and casualties were heavy on both sides. One infantry company, having attacked the German defences and forced a wedge into the line, was itself pinned down between two minefields and unable to move. The men dug in and fought for their lives. By late afternoon on the second day of their struggle they had suffered many dead and wounded. As a chaplain, Bish decided to try to get through to them with an armoured ambulance carrier and some stretcher bearers to bring the wounded out. Shells and mortar bombs were still falling in the shattered apple orchards as the carrier wound its way towards the isolated soldiers. However, they got through and the stretcher bearers set about the task of collecting the wounded, while Bish gave the last rites to those who would not make the hazardous journey back.

Suddenly, there was a metallic bang and they saw a plume of black smoke drifting up from the carrier. 'He's hit a mine,' yelled the medic and, indeed, that was what had happened just as the driver reversed to make the return trip. Suddenly, all hell broke loose as the Germans counter-attacked, and within minutes it became clear that an enemy unit had seized a farm to the rear of the British position, thus cutting off their retreat. 'There's only one way out, Padre,' said the Company Sergeant Major. 'Through the minefield on our south side.' Bish eyed the deceptively innocent grass, waving in the evening breeze. The same wind fluttered the little triangular yellow flags with their black skull and crossbones that marked the perimeter of the German minefield. 'I wonder if there's a safe lane through it,' he thought and, crawling forward with one of the stretcher bearers, peered through the splinter-slashed remains of a low hedge. Suddenly, a slight movement caught their eyes. To the left, about a hundred yards away, stood the chimney breast of a ruined cottage. It was little more than a pile of masonry, but coming out of the ruin was a beautiful Alsatian, its pale coat a perfect camouflage amongst the grey stones. But as it reached the grass, it stood out, almost white in the fading light and then, to their astonishment, the dog trotted confidently into the minefield and crossed the meadow. As it reached the tree-line on the far side, the Alsatian turned, pricked her ears and looked back towards Bish. I say 'her' because by now my father was quite convinced that this was his long-dead Peggy, the likeness was uncanny. He gave a low whistle in just the way he'd always called her and to his joy the bitch bounded back across the minefield. 'Quick, get the wounded,' he hissed to the stretcher bearer.

'We can't go through there, Padre,' said the NCO. 'It's bloody well mined.'

'Yes we can,' said Bish. 'I know we can—and if we don't, half those poor devils will die.'

So it was that with darkness falling in the warm summer evening, the party set out through the knee-high grass, fearing that every step would be their last. Crouching low, they hardly noticed the weight of their load as they staggered along, eyes probing ahead for some tell-tale sign of earth disturbance. The ominous little pennants swayed in the near-still air. The sounds of battle had died with the day, but no birds called in this field of death. Bish led, urging 'Peggy' forward and when she stopped and looked back, ears pricked, mouth part-open, pink tongue slightly out, he urged her on. 'Good dog, seek, seek it,' he kept saying. The stretcher bearers may have thought him mad, but they followed, knowing the lives of the wounded depended on their getting through. It was only a couple of hundred yards to the tree-line that marked the far side of the minefield, but it seemed like a mile.

They were only fifty yards from the trees when 'Peggy' stopped abruptly and sank down in the grass, her ears flattened. 'Down!' yelled Bish and a split second later came the whoosh of a shell which passed low over the meadow and burst with a splintering crash in the orchard beyond, from which the smoke of the burning carrier still drifted. Twice they saw the dreaded horns of 'S' mines protruding from the soft soil—one touch would be enough to send this killing machine bounding into the air with a deceptively gentle pop, to explode at head-height, hurling steel ball-bearings over a hundred-yard circle, decapitating anyone standing nearby. Then they were there, past the markers, instinctively putting down the stretchers, slapping each other on the back. 'Keep going,' hissed the chaplain, 'I'll catch you up.' So saying, he ran after their saviour, who was now bounding away towards an old barn. At the empty double doorway, the dog paused and looked at the panting padre. The light had almost gone, but he saw his 'Peggy' cock her head on one side as she had done so many times in Herefordshire fields, then she dashed inside the solid wooden building. Bish reached the door—it was pitch black inside, the smell of hay and manure wafted out. 'Peggy,' he called. 'Come here, girl.' There was no movement within and he delved into his first-aid bag for the little German Army dynamo torch he had picked up a week before. Squeezing the trigger repeatedly, he flashed the light about, probing the dark corners of the barn. It was quite empty and there were no other doors or exits of any sort. 'Peggy' had gone just as she had come. Bish felt a tear run down his grimy cheek and he paused just long enough to thank St Francis of Assisi for saving the lives of the wounded that summer's evening. When the war was over, he returned to his parish in Herefordshire and held a service for the animals on St. Francis Day. I remembered these services well, because I always took my guinea pigs and they usually escaped, causing absolute chaos.

Bish's churches were always places of character and fun. He loved young people and his services were anything but dull. However, when we moved back to Shropshire in the fifties, he had four churches to look after and one in particular had something odd about it. It wasn't especially remote or sinister, in fact, it was quite an attractive Norman construction, well equipped with a wide nave leading up under a fine screen to the chancel, flanked by stalls for the vicar and choir. I can't say it was particularly frightening, but it did give me a strange feeling.

Late one autumn afternoon, with the thin sunlight slanting through the copper beeches, father came in to the garage where I was muttering a few rather un-Christian oaths as I struggled to get a difficult 10mm spark plug out of the bowels of my AC Greyhound. 'The police have been on the line, John,' he said.

'Oh, Lord,' I thought. 'Knew the radar trap on the A49 would get me sooner or later.'

'They've caught someone who may have been trying to steal something from the Priory church,' he went on. 'They're holding him at the church and want me to go down. Will you come along?' I gave the wretched spark plug one last wrench, taking the skin off my knuckles to no good effect, so, wiping the grease from my hands, we got into Bish's car.

The church stood alone amongst almost leafless trees surrounded by the cemetery. A small police utility was at the gate. In the porch was our local bobby, the churchwarden and an ashen-faced middle-aged man in a cheap blue suit. Blue-suit was smoking, his hands shaking slightly.

'Afternoon, Vicar,' said the churchwarden and the policeman together. 'Sorry to call you out, sir,' added the officer. 'This gentle-man was seen running out of the church with a bag of things and we picked him up in the field by the river—he's a bit shook up and we'd like you to have a look round to see if anything's missing.'

'Is that the bag?' asked Bish. The constable nodded as my father picked up the soiled brown canvas grip and, dumping it on the bench, peered in. After a moment, he said to the man, 'So you're a brass rubber?'

'Yes, sir,' said Blue-suit. 'I'm sorry I didn't ask permission, but I didn't think that a new vicar had been appointed.'

'Well,' said Bish, 'I'm the priest in charge—there is no vicar at the moment, but you should still ask—but tell me, why were you running out of the church?'

The man looked utterly dejected and, gazing at his shoes, said in a trembling voice, 'There's something evil in there—I've been in lots of old churches, but I've never met something so evil in all my life.'

The policeman frowned, 'He told me that when we found him, vicar.'

We went into the church—all seemed in order; some of the brass rubber's tools lay by the tomb he'd been working on. 'Were you working when you had this feeling?' questioned Bish.

'No, I was looking at the screen—just standing at the steps there,' said the frightened fellow, from the church door, for nothing would induce him to come in. Father walked slowly up the nave and stopped by the chancel steps. I followed a little uneasily. Now Bish was looking to his right at the vicar's pew—the usual seat of the minister during a service. His stare was fixed on that pew. Suddenly, I shivered. The little church had suddenly grown very cold—my father was saying the Lord's Prayer in a low, but very firm, voice. All the time he stood upright gazing at the pew which lay in deepening shadow as the daylight began to die. After a few minutes, I realised that the tension and apprehension was easing and, as if to emphasise this, the setting sun sent long fingers through the west windows which gave the old church a more friendly appearance. Bish walked slowly up to the altar rail, knelt and prayed for a few moments before standing, bowing and returning to where I stood in the nave. 'Do you feel the difference?' he asked. I certainly did and he added, 'It was coming from the vicar's pew—there must be some reason, but I don't know what.'

Back in the porch, we bade farewell to the brass rubber and his posse; there were no charges. When I was next at home on leave, Bish glanced up from his breakfast and said, 'Oh, by the way, John—you'll be interested to know that it's said the vicar of the Priory church, a hundred years or so ago, was hanged for murder. That was his pew that gave us that strange experience.'

But that was twenty years ago. Now I'm commanding the Army's Youth Adventure Training Scheme at Fort George in Scotland, and as I sit in the massive 200-year-old fortress on the shore of the Moray Firth, I've forgotten about all those ghostly encounters. Well . . . almost.

I often write in the quiet of the early morning, before the hordes of unemployed young people from all over Britain are up, yelling, chanting and making a din fit to waken the dead. It was around six this morning when I heard the folk who live in the flat above us walking around, in fact I've often heard them at this time. Later, I remarked to Judith, 'Our neighbours get up pretty early—do you know who they are?' 'No,' she yawned, 'I've been meaning to ask you.'

The immaculately dressed RSM Macintosh of the Gordons was outside Fortress Headquarters, pace stick under arm, saluting, as I walked in. 'Morning, RSM,' I said. 'By the way, who lives in the flat above me?'

He gave me a strange look, 'Above you, sir—why, those are the National Monuments offices. No-one lives there.'

'Oh, well,' I retorted, 'then the cleaners come in pretty early.' With a swirl of his kilt, the Sergeant Major marched off purposefully to inquire into who had disturbed the Colonel's rest. I was on the battlements watching a group of Liverpool teenagers abseiling down the walls, when I felt soldiers stiffening around me—the RSM was approaching. Waiting until we were alone, he said in a quiet tone,

'There's no-one living above you, sir, and the cleaners do their work in the afternoon.' Then he added, referring to the legendary ghost of Fort George, 'Perhaps it's the headless piper.'

'Well, at least it's not the legless one,' I replied. 'Makes too much damn noise!'

Ah well, perhaps one day scientific exploration may enable us to understand even the supernatural. Who knows?—it may be one of our Young Explorers with an inquiring mind and a lot of determination who'll unravel the mystery.